Their Memories, Our Treasure:

Conversations with African-American Women of Wisdom

VOLUMES III-IV

Edited by
Gloria Wade-Gayles
Founding Director
The SIS Oral History Project

Mykisha Arnold
Program Coordinator

Spelman's Independent Scholars

Bernice Appiah-Pinkrah
Crystal Bennett
Noni Bourne
Ebony Carter
Ayo Cummings
Chanel Cunningham
Cindye Evans
Alexa Harris

Kira Lynch

Qrescent Mason
Danielle Phillips
Siobhan Robinson
Kerstin Roper
Niah Shearer
Katherine Strunk-Fobbs
Jody Washington
Kyja Wilborn

The SIS Oral History Project
in the Center for Leadership and Civic Engagement
Spelman College
350 Spelman Lane, SW
Atlanta, Georgia 30314

Editors: Gloria Wade Gayles, Mykisha Arnold and Young Scholars in SIS

Cover and Layout Design by Tiona McClodden

Photography by Tommy Burns

This book was made possible by support from the Andrew Vinings Johnson Foundation, AARP
of Atlanta, and the Dogwood City Chapter of the Links, Incorporated

ISBN 09748565-1-7

THE SIS INTERGENERATIONAL COMMUNITY

WOMEN OF WISDOM
2003-2004

Mrs. Julia Bond
Mrs. Faye Bush
Mrs. Jennie Drake
Mrs. Anna English

Miss Annie Jewell Moore

Mrs. Ruth Scott Simmons
Miss Marguerite Simon
Mrs. Nell Simms
Mrs. Laura Lynem Rates

YOUNG SCHOLARS
2003-2004

Crystal Bennett
Noni Bourne
Qrescent Mason
Danielle Phillips

Niah Shearer

Katherine Strunk-Fobbs
Kira Lynch
Jody Washington
Bernice Appiah-Pinkrah

WOMEN OF WISDOM
2004-2005

Mrs. Georgia W. Allen
Mrs. Leila Barfield
Dr. June Dobbs Butts
Mrs. Cornelia Bailey
Mrs. Ann Cooper
Mrs. Mary Stephens Dansby

Mrs. Elizabeth DeGraffenreid
Mrs. Elizabeth Gross

Mrs. Lillie Harris
Dr. Carrie Johnson
Dr. Zelma Payne
Mrs. Emanuella Spencer
Mrs. Ernestine Vick
Mrs. Ella Mae Yates

YOUNG SCHOLARS
2004-2005

Bernice Appiah-Pinkrah
Ayo Cummings
Chanel Cunningham
Cindye Evans
Alexa A. Harris

Ebony Carter

Qrescent Mason
Siobhan Robinson
Kerstin Roper
Jody Washington
Kyja Wilborn

CONTENTS

PART ONE
Stories of Wisdom

PART TWO
Tributes and Gratitude: 2003-2005

THE PRIVILEGE

Virginia Davis Floyd

Our world is anxiously waiting for a new generation of leaders who understand that in order to create a meaningful future, we must explore and celebrate the past. Spelman's Independent Scholars (SIS) produces this new generation. It is an innovative experience that dares redefine what learning means. For three years, I have had the privilege of working with the SIS project and traveling with students and their mentor, Gloria Wade Gayles, to various research sites. In 2003, I traveled with them to Sapelo Island, Georgia, an historic community rich in Gullah culture. Dr. Shirley Toland, then English faculty at Spelman, also accompanied SIS on this trip. In that same year, I traveled with SIS to Newtown, Georgia, where African Americans struggle against environmental racism. Three SIS students joined me in the spring of 2003 on an eight-day trip to Benin and Togo. In the spring of 2005, as Visiting Scholar of Traditional Knowledge, I served as mentor to fifteen SIS students on another global venture. During our nine days away from the States, we traveled to the Republic of Senegal and to Ghana, spending most of them in Accra. When I was with the students, I could see the making of new generation of leaders we so desperately need.

I have not had the privilege of journeying with them to the living rooms and kitchen tables here in Atlanta where they bond with Women of Wisdom. No one has. This is a journey the students make on their own. In these intergenerational conversations, students learn about sustaining values that translate into family and community, faith and education, resistance and achievement. What women in other lands and cultures have to tell us about these values find echo in the stories of women here in the American South. In the SIS experience, students understand that, throughout our collective existence, we have maintained our culture, history, and indigenous knowledge systems through the telling and retelling of stories that cross oceans, cultures, languages, and time; stories that weave a rich tapestry of wisdom. In each students in SIS developed a deeper appreciation for the journey of sameness and for the transformative power of stories.

They are committed to sharing with others the gifts they have received through/ in SIS. That is why they produced the volume you are about to read. It contains their most treasured gift, the wisdom of African American women of the South who served as their mentors. <u>Their Memories, Our Treasure</u> celebrates the richness of intergenerational learning and intergenerational friendships. The stories included in this volume build a bridge between the past and the present, between young and old, between traditional and modern, between emerging leaders and mature warriors. It speaks to the students' commitment to the responsibility all of us have: to give voice to those who came before us so that we can pave the way to a brighter reality than they realized.

When they complete their year's journey in SIS, students say, "Our lives are forever changed." Mentoring students in SIS and traveling with them to various places changed my life. Reading this volume will change your lives. It is, indeed, the "sacred text" of Spelman's Independent Scholars.

Dr. Virginia Davis Floyd (M.D./M.P.H.) served as SIS Visiting Scholar in Traditional Knowledge, 2004-2005. A graduate of Spelman, Dr. Floyd is Executive Director of Prometra-USA.

THE GLOBAL EXPERIENCE

Kerstin Roper

Instead of Jamaica, the destination for students in SIS, during the spring semester of 2004-2005, was Accra, Ghana. We gathered in the Leadership Center for a departing ceremony and, to the rhythm of drums played by Ghanain students at Clark Atlanta University, we walked from the Center to the back gate of Spelman College, where we bade farewell to our SIS mentor, Dr. Wade-Gayles, who remain "home" to work on the SIS volume. On the flight from New York to London, I wrote this story in my SIS journal. *Many generations ago, two sisters walked together one morning, talking and laughing. At the end of the day, only one returned home. The other was taken over vast, churning waters to a strange land. There she was taught a strange language and branded with a new identity. There she toiled and fought to hold on to what she remembered of home, teaching her children about their real home through stories, songs and memories.* Like my sisters in SIS, I was a daughter of the sister who was stolen and brought to these shores centuries ago. Centuries later, I was crossing those same vast waters with thirteen of my sisters in SIS. The timing of our visit could not have been more symbolic. Ghana was celebrating Independence Day.

Every place we visited had meaning for us, but two will always remain in my memory. One was a village, established by Prometra International. It was one of many villages in Africa with which Dr. Floyd has an affiliation as President of Prometra-USA. No seminar I had attended or documentary I had watched could have prepared me for what I saw and heard in this village. When we stepped from the bus onto the earth, I saw lanky boys chasing a ball across the street while women chatted with one another on a nearby porch. I walked past an older man who was napping in a chair; he opened one eye and curled his lips into a smile. I made a mental note to talk with the women especially about the challenging of embracing their infected neighbors. I could not have known they would join us in the meeting room. They were living with AIDS and because of traditional methods sanctioned and used by Prometra, they were living, not dying. I will always remember the confidence with which one of the women I had seen sitting on the porch spoke about living with AIDS.

The other was our visit to the Slave Castle at the edge of Cape Coast. We crouched in the castle, we tried standing, and we walked blindly, in silence, through its terrifying chambers, imaging how our ancestors felt and knowing now with certainty that what we consider to be challenges in our individual lives are but mirages. I will never forget the sound of our hushed whispers bouncing off the walls we could not see, but which imprisoned us. Finally, we reached the heavy doors and at the bottom of a short incline, we could see the shoreline disappearing under fluffy sea foam. "This is the Point of No Return". Squinting in the sunlight, I could not help but wonder what the men women and children thought after being held in a sarcophagus for so long only to behold a floating prison. All of us in SIS remained silent as we traveled to our next place of discovery, learning, and transformation.

I say "transformation" because the trip to Ghana changed all of us. Moreover, it added new layers of significance to our work in SIS as collectors of stories. We had read the quote Dr. Gayles included in our SIS Workbook—"The world is made of stories, not of atoms"—but it now had new meaning for us. Every place we visited was made of stories. If only we could hear the stories of the women, men and children who were shackled in the castle we visited as tourists. If only! I returned to Spelman with renewed determination to collect the stories my mentors were sharing with me and, as well, to collect the stories of people in my family. We have no way of knowing who will want to know how we lived in the early years of the twenty first century, what we thought, what we struggled against, what we lived for, what we remembered of the past, and what we hoped for the future. Through my work in SIS, I was going to do my part, no matter how small, to leave them stories that will answer their questions.

THE GIFT

Qrescent Mason

As I hold the carefully wrapped gift in my hands, I recall details of events that occurred prior to the making of the gift. I remember a mentor's statement (she wondered if I were listening) that I had filed for safe keeping in my memory. I recall the process of procuring the gift, the many places I visited seemingly without result, and the nights I could not sleep, so focused I was on receiving such a gift. I express my elation at finally having the gift in my hands, and I thank my mentor for enriching my life. I accept the gift with the hope that it will add light to her life and with the promise that it will continue to enrich my own. For years to come, I will open the gift, again and again, my gratitude deepening with each reading. The gift to which I refer is the book you are holding in your hands: Volumes III-IV of <u>Their Memories, Our Treasure: Conversations With African American Women of Wisdom</u>. It represents two years of an innovative learning experienced called Spelman's Independent Scholars (SIS).

The SIS experience preserves one of the most long-standing traditions in African American culture: the oral tradition. It provides women undergraduates at Spelman and at Clark-Atlanta University the opportunity to bond with and learn from older African American women of the South. For those in our nation who say there is a generational divide in African American culture that prevents elders and young people from realizing their importance to each other, Young Scholars and Women of Wisdom in SIS respond, imploringly, "Do not believe this. Please know that we yearn to speak to each other so that we can learn from each other." It is our goal to insure that we do not forget our history and the people who carry that history in their memories. Achieving this goal takes commitment, hard work, dedication, and time. It takes vision; it requires a how-to approach to the experience.

Before we meet our mentors, we complete a number of assignments that open the lens of age. Our faculty mentor asks us to think the ways in which we are privileged by our youth.

With each assignment, we recognized that just as other groups whom we critique somnambulate in their privilege, so do we as Young Scholars in ours. We are asked to recount prior bonding experiences with older women. To some of us, this is an easy task; to others, it is a challenge. The questions that guide us in our work are obvious ones: What does it mean to bond with an older woman? What stereotypes about age should we challenge? Where do we **see** older African American women and how are they presented to us in mass media? What impact do these images have on our responses to and relationships with older women? When the interviews begin, each of us has new questions: Will my mentor like me? Will I disrespect her by privileging my time over hers? Will we be able to maintain the bond we form? Even worse, what if no bond is formed at all? The existence of this book is evidence that the bonding was genuine. To a one, as indicated in our tributes, we became attached to our mentors. The stories we heard in at least four interviews, lasting in duration from one hour to three (and in some cases, four) resonated uncannily with the questions we were each facing in our own lives. More than hope, bonding with our mentors gave us a chance to view our lives from an expanded perspective and, as a result, we have a deeper understanding of principles that are real and worth fighting for.

This volume is a gift to others, but it was first and always will be a gift to students in SIS. For the gift, we will be eternally grateful to the Women of Wisdom for stories that transformed our lives. This is the second volume of the SIS project. There will be a third, a fourth . . . We are inspired by our faculty mentor's belief that SIS will continue "in perpetuity." Our work, then, was only a small drop in a vast ocean of Black women's stories that will influence the education our grandchildren, great grandchildren and the yet unborn of our lineage will receive at schools in the Atlanta University Center and at schools elsewhere in this nation and around the globe.

AN EDITORIAL STATEMENT

Gloria Wade Gayles

What I come through in life, if I go in meself, I could make a book.

from <u>Bullwhip Days</u>

Since its inception in 2000, the goal of Spelman's Independent Scholars (SIS) has been to "make a book" in which African American women of the South journey to sites of memories where rich stories reside. The women would make the journey at the request of younger women who desire a learning experience that goes beyond the pages of course texts and outside the physical confines of college classrooms. This volume celebrates the journey twenty-two older women took at the request of eighteen undergraduate women during the academic years, 2003-2004 and 2004-2005. The students, appropriately called Young Scholars, came from different disciplines, among them biology, computer science, economics, English, history, philosophy/religion, political science, and psychology, but they had in common a passion for intellectual stretching and a reverence for elders. The older women with whom they bonded, appropriately called Women of Wisdom, came from different walks of life, but they had in common an unshakeable belief in the students' promise for inspired and meaningful leadership. This volume gives us an opportunity to take the journey students and mentor took together.

It is the second volume produced by the SIS Oral History Project, and it differs in one significant way from the first volume, unveiled in February of 2004. In that volume, we hear the voices of students and the voices of mentors as they engage in intergenerational conversation. In this volume, however, we hear only the voices of mentors. They are speaking in narratives created from interviews students conducted during the years this volume covers. We made this editorial decision in order to increase the font size of the print, but, more importantly, to focus on the women whose stories made this book possible. It is our hope to produce a volume biennially, making each one an improvement over the previous one.

There are twenty-two women narrators in this volume. Four women are in their sixties; five in their seventies; seven in their eighties; and six in their nineties. There is one centenarian among them, Mrs. Ann Cooper, who is one hundred and four years of age. The women were born in different states and cities across the nation: Alabama (Montgomery and Talladega); Georgia (Atlanta, Henry County, Franklin County, and Sapelo Island); Florida (Daytona Beach); Louisiana (New Orleans and Tinus); Pennsylvania (Philadelphia); South Carolina (Anderson); Tennessee (Bradley County, Chattanooga and Nashville); and Texas (Beaumont). Eleven women were born at home, four by doctors and seven by midwives, three of whom were the women's maternal grandmothers. The women were born into families ranging in size from one child to thirteen children. Two of the women had no siblings, and six were the youngest in their families. Fourteen of the women lost younger siblings to illnesses, such as typhoid, whooping cough, and pneumonia.

In that their life stories date as far back as the first decade of the twentieth century, the occupations of their parents were, understandably, varied. Their fathers were blacksmiths, well diggers, barbers, chefs, cabinetmakers, molders, preachers, railroad wagmen, printers, Pullman car porters, postal workers, sharecroppers, or farmers on their own land. Their mothers were seamstresses, laundresses, cooks, maids, teachers, missionaries, pressers, farmers, and mothers. As Miss Marguerite Simon puts it so well, "My mother was a mother." The work of motherhood is a recurring memory in all of the stories. Twenty women married; two remained single. All of the married women are mothers. Two are adoptive mothers. One woman has nineteen grandchildren, and another has twenty-three great grandchildren and three great-great grandchildren.

Before retirement, the women were teachers, play directors, college professors, nurse's assistants, domestic workers, seamstresses, nutrionists, community activists, entrepreneurs, college professors, entrepreneurs, directors of public libraries, griots of a distinctive culture, and vice mayors of major cities. They worked in hospitals, poultry factories, science labs, churches, colleges, public schools, the YWCA, and in newspapers founded by family members. They founded organizations, and they established businesses. They are sharp, fiercely independent, very political, sometimes angry, always embracing, and, when we least it expect them to be, quite humorous. Most of them are actively involved in work that will make a difference in the world to which the students will go as leaders. No monolithic woman emerges from the group. They are diverse in economic background, complexion, rhetorical style, political affiliations, religious/spiritual beliefs, and dreams, but they tell a similar story about family, community, faith, integrity, struggle, and education—Gibraltar beliefs passed down through the generations in their individual families and then to students through SIS intergenerational conversations, and now to you through the narratives in this volume.

In our presentation of the women, we could have underscored the degrees they have earned and the awards they have received; the committees on which they have served; the programs, or buildings, their work made possible; and the many times they have been recognized as a "first," significantly. You will read their achievements, and struggles, in their individual narratives. We chose, instead, to present each woman to you with a visual image under which we write her name, birthplace, occupation, and a quote from her narrative about her birth family. This editorial decision reflects a belief fundamental to SIS: the mentors represent a community of remarkable women, none among them deserving greater applause for achievements than her sisters, each one giving to SIS a gift uniquely hers: her life's story. After hearing just one story, just one story, students became ambassadors, so to speak, for intergenerational connections. They shared SIS with their peers. It is their hope that none of our mothers, grandmothers and great grandmothers will have reason to say, when asked for their remarkable stories: "Truth is, I never thought I'd see the day when people would be interested in hearing what two old Negro women have to say" (Having Our Say). As Qrescent Mason writes in "The Gift," the women and students scream in one voice, together, against an intergenerational divide. They know they need each other. Clearly, the students need the wisdom of the elders because, after hearing one story, just one story, they began to believe they would indeed become the leaders their mentors predicted they would become. The students bear witness to being transformed. In a sense, then, the making of this volume of older African American women's narratives might very well be about the making of future African American women leaders.

PART ONE:
Stories Of Wisdom
2003-2005

Mrs. Georgia W. Allen
Mrs. Cornelia Bailey
Mrs. Leila Barfield
Mrs. Julia Bond
Mrs. Faye Bush
Dr. June Dobbs Butts
Mrs. Ann Cooper
Mrs. Mary Eloise Stephens Dansby
Mrs. Elizabeth DeGraffenreid
Mrs. Jennie Drake
Mrs. Anna English
Mrs. Elizabeth Gross
Mrs. Lillie Harris
Dr. Carrie Johnson
Miss Annie Jewell Moore
Dr. Zelma Payne
Mrs. Laura Lynem Rates
Mrs. Ruth Scott Simmons
Mrs. Nell Simms
Miss Marquerite Simon
Mrs. Emanuella Spencer
Mrs. Ernestine Vick
Mrs. Ella Mae Yates

MRS. GEORGIA W. ALLEN

Beaumont, Texas

Teacher and Drama Director

Eventually, the master helped my grandfather buy a farm because they were afraid he would start dating White girls as the master's other two boys were doing. So, my grandfather was established on this farm, and he was doing very well independently. He looked around for somebody to marry. On the next farm from him, a man called "Uncle Dice Jackson" lived with his family, and he had sons and daughters. My grandfather married one of the girls, and they had nine children, of whom my mother was the youngest.

Mrs. Georgia W. Allen

I was born May 12, 1919, in Beaumont, Texas, and my given name at birth was Georgia Mae Williams. I hate the name. I just really do. Kids made fun of it, you know, and when you're a kid, the fun making doesn't appeal to you. So, that's why I decided that I would never make fun of people about anything because I know how much that hurts. "Mae" is a name that African-American people use a lot. My mother's name was Lillie Mae, but she changed it to Lillian and I don't blame her. I never had any nicknames that anybody told me about. There might have been some interesting names people had for me behind my back, but I didn't know about a nickname.

My great-grandmother on my mother's side (my grandfather's mother) was a slave who had a son by the master. We never knew what happened to her, and I can't call the man she had a child by my great-grandfather. I would assume that when my grandfather came out of diapers, they sold my great-grandmother and so I know little about her. I don't even know how many masters she had. I do know that her child, my grandfather, looked exactly like the master, and I think that is why he wasn't sold. When the master moved from Mississippi to Texas, he took my grandfather with him. That would have been in the late nineteen hundreds. Eventually, the master helped my grandfather buy a farm because they were afraid he would start dating White girls as the master's other two boys were doing. The boys had the same father, but different mothers. So, my grandfather was established on this farm, and he was doing very well independently. He looked around for somebody to marry. On the next farm from him, a man called "Uncle Dice Jackson" lived with his family, and he had sons and daughters. My grandfather married one of the girls, and they had nine children, of whom my mother was the youngest. The children were from very light to not looking white to very dark. My mother married a man who was dark brown, and that's how I got my color. Her name was Lillie Mae Burkley before she married my father. His name was Jeffrey Williams.

My maternal grandmother died when my mother was a baby, and her sister, Aunt Anna, just loved her. She and Uncle Wesley had their own children, but they loved my mother. They bought a farm down the road from where Grandpa lived, and that's where my mother spent a lot of time. When she was a baby, Grandpa would put one of the boys on a horse to ride him down the road with my mother to Aunt Anna's house, and my mother would stay there for weeks or months and longer. When the crops were in, one of the boys would go to Aunt Anna's house to bring my mother home. But one time, Aunt Anna just would not let my mother go. She just cried and cried. So Grandpa got on the horse himself and rode down the road to Aunt Anna and Uncle Wesley's farm to get my mother. Aunt Anna cried, "I just can't let her go," and Grandpa said, "You gonna have to let her go. I'm gonna let you keep her a few more days and you get her little things together and you send her." A few days later, he sent one of the boys on a horse down to Aunt Anna's to bring my mother home. There was great love among all of them. Anna was the one who had fourteen children. You think that's much? One of her daughters, Mattie, had fifteen! I remember when I was out there visiting one time, I said, "Matt, what were you doing? Trying to outdo your mother?" She laughed and said, "No, I wasn't really trying to outdo Mama. It just happened that way!" Mattie's husband had died, but, fortunately, they had built a house on Aunt Anna's farm. So, Aunt Anna and her daughter Mattie and her family had all those thirty children there on the farm!

I have been to Grandpa's farm several times. One year, I went there with my husband. I took my daughter there when she was a baby. That was the summer my husband went to work on a tobacco farm in Connecticut. My cousin "Buddy" picked me up at the train station and took me out to the country, but I couldn't stand it. I couldn't stand it. It was too quiet, it was too lonely, and it was too dark! Grandpa was long since dead, but Uncle Ulysses—we called him "Uncle Lish"--was living there and Aunt Cynthia was living there, too. One day, I said, "Buddy, what is it that you're doing at the factory?" That was the mattress factory. He said, "Bailing mattresses." And I said, "Could I do it?" He said, "You?" And I said, "Yeah. Can women do it?" He said, "Yeah, women do a lot of it. You really wanna do it?" And I said, "Yeah, I need to make some money. I spent all the money that I brought with me, and I'm getting bored around here all day." So, I want you to know he got me a job. That was in 1943. Some of the women thought that I was Buddy's girlfriend, but he was my cousin. How could he be my boyfriend? They didn't quite believe what he had told them, and they couldn't believe I was a teacher. "No teacher gonna be out here working on bailing mattresses in a factory. She a lie, honey. She a lie!" I just let it alone because I didn't care how I made the money as long as it was honest, you know?

Maybe I need to just start at the very beginning. The three of us - my mother, my father, and I - were all born in Texas. I was born in Beaumont, which is on the Gulf of Mexico. My mother was a maid and one of the best. Back then, my mother had to be a maid because she could not get an education. My grandfather, realizing that was all she could do, sent her to the Capitol to a school called "Eliza Dee Industrial Home for Young Ladies," where girls were taught to be good servants. My mother was an excellent maid, and she was a fabulous cook. She was absolutely great at what she did. She was given to understand, like Grandpa back home, that whatever you do to make a living, you should be proud of. You do it well, and she did. As old folks say, "She wouldn't take tea for the fever."

I can't remember where my father was born, and I don't have any idea who taught him cabinetry, but I know that before I was born, he was a cabinet maker. The man he worked for knew how good he was, and so he would send my father to different places, and my daddy would go happily. The man knew if he sent him to West Hell, my daddy would go. My mother was alone with me, as a baby, a lot because my father was gone a lot. He was in and out. We moved to his mother's house in Fort Worth, and he was still on the go. Going, going, going. He couldn't work today and come home at night because he was maybe in another state. So, my mother was home alone with me in the swamp, and she would say, "I'm tired of sweeping the snakes away from the door in the morning! I'm tired of doing this!" So, my mother decided to travel with him. We moved from Beaumont to Fort Worth, where my grandmother lived. To make the story short, we lived in eight cities in four years. I can't quite remember them in sequence, but I know they were Fort Worth, El Paso, Kansas City, Chicago, Detroit, St. Paul,

Mrs. Georgia W. Allen

Milwaukee. That's only six. I've left out two, but Milwaukee was the last. All the neighbors wherever we lived said what a loving trio we were. "What wonderful people."

We left my daddy once and went home to Texas to Grandpa's farm. My daddy knew where we were. So, he came and found us. And of course, we fell on each other's necks because we just all adored one another, and we went back on the road. My mom would say, "Jeff, we've got to stop. Jeff, we've got to stop." She realized that we were moving further and further north and I needed to go to school soon. Finally, Mom made a serious move. She put me in St. Benedict the Moor Catholic Boarding School in Milwaukee, and she got a job as a live-in maid. My father came looking for us. Bless his heart. Every time I think of his coming looking for us, I just feel like crying. I can imagine how the poor man felt when he came home and found us gone and there were strangers living where we had been living. We sold and bought, sold and bought, bought and sold furniture so much that my mother didn't have any problem at all moving. We'd sell it and just leave.

I was in the boarding school for a month or two while she searched the map for a place where he would not come looking for us because she knew what would happen if he found us. We would get back together again. We adored him, and he adored us. She found Cleveland on the map and didn't know a soul there. So, he wouldn't come looking for us there. He would only go to some place where he thought we would go, and he didn't have the slightest notion that we would ever go to this big old place. We boarded a train for Cleveland and arrived in the city about midnight with a couple of trunks and some luggage and no idea of where to go. I was a little whiney kid, hanging on, you know, moaning and groaning. My mother asked some people where she could find a nice hotel, and we ended up in one of the worst slums in Cleveland. She asked the wrong people, but it was midnight and we had to settle down there. I was six at the time.

Eventually, my mother got a room with a family named the Turners. They were what was called "sanctified and holy." They wanted me to join their church, but my mother said, "She needs to go to St. James," which was the Methodist church not too far from our house.

We lived with the Turners for about four years. While I was there, my mother's father died in Texas. My mother went back to where he had been, but he was gone when she got there. We didn't hear from my father for a while. When I was nine years old, I got a letter from him, and I was delighted to get it. He found out where we were from his sister. I asked my mother if I could write him back, and she said, "Yes, if you want to. He's your daddy and you love him and he loves you. Answer the letter if you want to." I was up late answering the letter and Mrs. Turner came through and she said, "Oh my Lord, child. It's ten o'clock. You should have been in bed. You can do your homework tomorrow." And I said, "It's not my homework." She asked, "What is it?" I said, " I'm writing a letter to my daddy." And she said, "I wouldn't answer it if I were you. He's a bad man. You and your mother never hear from him. He doesn't help your mother out and she's working so hard." I believed her, and I didn't send the letter. I wanted to write to my father. I was trying to find him so that I could get him and my mother back together. I wrote to my mother's niece Maxine in Texas, my aunt's daughter, and "Max" wrote back and said, "I'm not sure where your father is, but his sister Maude can tell you. She's in Ft. Worth." She gave me her address. I sent a letter to my Aunt Maude, and she sent one back. That's when I learned that my father had fallen off a scaffold and broken his neck. He was dead when they got him to the hospital. When we got the news, my mother, stoic that she was, never broke down with me, but I know she cried. I think we both cried. I'm pretty sure she cried when I wasn't around. This meant that she really had to go it alone. She was **willing** to do it, but she was now **forced** to do it alone.

My mother was about as bold a critter as I ever knew in my whole life. When I was twelve, she was dating, and the men would come to the house because she didn't want to leave me alone at night. For a while, she was engaged to one man, and then he didn't come around anymore. I heard one of the ladies in the neighborhood having a conversation with my mother. They called each other by their last names. She said, "Williams, we don't ever see Mr. So and So. What's wrong? I thought you and he were gonna get married." My mother said, "I told him to get his hat and coat and go and don't come back. I didn't like the way he looked at my young'un, and I didn't wanna have to kill him." One day, I came home from school, and she was home early. I think I was about sixteen or seventeen at the time, and we were still living in Cleveland. You know how men can stand around (women, too) in groups, three or four people just laughing and talking together? Well, some men were standing out there, out front. My mother came into the house and she called, "Hey, baby." And I said, "Hey, mom!" I didn't hear anything more from her, so I went on with what I was doing. And then I heard her voice raised: "I hear there's a man around here who's been saying what he's gonna do with my kid when he gets his hands on her, and he better pray to God he never gets his hands on her because I'll kill him! I'll kill anybody that messes with my child!" She finished and she came on inside, and I said, "Mom! Why did you do that?" She said, "Because I meant it. Do you understand that you do not have to tolerate anybody messing with you because I will hurt them." My mother was my guardian angel. My daddy would have been, but he wasn't there. I have understood her since I am now older and have children of my own and my grandchildren, too. I have the same philosophy as my mother. If anybody bothers my kids, I'll kill them. I'll put a hurt on them!

I have two children, and I sent them one summer to visit my mom. She always wanted to own a house, and after the last trip we made to Texas, I asked her, you know, what part of town she wanted to buy the house in. I told her we were going to visit her the next summer and help her find a house to buy. We were going to hire somebody to do some work on the house, and we would do some work. We returned home to Atlanta, and I bought some dishes that I knew she would love. Beautiful china service for twelve. Silver to go with the china. Stemware. And a few other things. I never got a chance to give my mother what I had bought her because she had a stroke and was home alone for a whole week before she called my cousins. They asked her, "Aunt Lil, why didn't you call us when this happened?" My mother said, "I thought I was gonna get better, and I knew you were gonna call Atlanta and that gal would come flying out here, leave those children, take them out of school." She was looking out for my children. My mother died in 1955, two Saturdays before Easter.

I used to roll around on the ground with boys. I used to fight with boys. I climbed trees with the boys. I built tree houses with the boys. I raced with them. I wrestled with them. Every now and then, I'd get in a real fight with a boy and some neighbor would say, "Don't you dare hit that girl!" Boys would run along and pat me on the bottom, and I'd turn around and whop! I often did not have a regular boyfriend because of my mother's teaching: "Don't do this, don't do that."

When it was time for me to go to college, I couldn't get my mind made up as to whether I should go to Western Reserve in Cleveland. My mother kept saying, "You need to go South because you're a southern-born child, but you have never lived in the South. You don't know anything about the South. All you hear is what other people have to say. You need to go and see for yourself." "Uncle Buck," my mother's brother, had come to Atlanta to attend Gammon Theological Seminary. Gammon and Clark adjoined, and the only divider was Magnolia Walk, a curved, winding driveway lined with magnolia trees. I chose Clark College in Atlanta, Georgia. It was a bit of a surprise to my mother, but I had friends here in Atlanta, at Morehouse, at Spelman, at Clark, at Morris Brown, and I decided that I would come to Atlanta because I knew someone in school here. Interestingly, I did not know at the time that the fates had determined this was the best place for me.

I started at Clark in 1939 in the second semester, and I was put on probation shortly after the school year had begun. I met two young women who had been attending Clark. They were freshmen. I was a latecomer. I made friends with them. I did not know their history, and I wasn't trying to find out. I had made friends. One day, when we were supposed to be at vespers, we went to the AU Center to visit a Clark student who lived across the street from Morehouse. She wasn't at home, so, without entering, we turned to the leave. As luck would have it, a Clark faculty member spotted us. She did her duty; she turned us in. All three of us were sent to the academic council, which was an inquisition. The other two girls were suspended and sent home. I was put on probation because my mother was a maid and the council knew how she would feel if her daughter were suspended. I couldn't have visitors, and I couldn't leave campus. The only thing I could do was go to class and go to the library.

Mrs. Georgia W. Allen

I was about eighteen or nineteen when I met my husband. Thaddius Allen. He was seven years older than I, and I thought he was pretty old. I met him when I was given a part in a play, and he was this six foot tall, good-looking guy I was playing opposite. We were engaged after one semester. When I told my mother, she nearly had a fit. She said, "I thought you said you were not gonna get married! I thought you said you hated the boys!" I told my mother that Thad was different. I said, "He's a nice guy, Mom. I like him because he makes me feel like I don't have to fight." She didn't say another word. She got up and walked out of the room, and when she came back in, she started on a different subject altogether. We were married when I had one full school year left to get my degree.

Sometime during that year, my mother's neighbors called me and told me that my mother was very ill. This was in November in 1941. I had married in June of that year. My mother was living in Cleveland and, of course, I went to see her immediately. When I opened her bedroom door, four women were seated facing the door, and my mother's head was turned toward them. When I opened the door, all these heads turned. My mother saw those heads turning, and she looked to see what was going on. She stretched out her arms, and we started our hugging, kissing, crying, and carrying on. Two of the women were waiting to see how pregnant I was. They thought that if I had to get married in June, then I was probably showing in November. I kept my coat on in order to tantalize them. I was wearing a slim knit dress, and I twirled round and round, flattening my dress out across my tummy. I could see the disappointment on their faces. They would have been happy if they had known I was pregnant, and I was. My baby girl, Judi, was born in August of 1942. I stayed with my mother for a week, and during that time she asked me a lot of questions. One of them was if my husband had ever hit me. I said, "Mom, you know if he had ever hit me, I would have broken a chair or something over him when he was asleep, and then I would have been back here!" I learned from her not to take crap from any man. Let a man hit you? No! My husband and I have been married for sixty-three years. Sixty three! We married on June 4, 1941, and we have two children: a daughter named Judith Myrna and a son named Henry Burkley.

I worked for twenty-seven years in the Atlanta Public School System teaching English. Actually, I taught English, yearbook, African American studies, and drama. I taught everything, and I directed plays. During the summer, I would go to New York and work. I went to Connecticut several summers and stayed with my husband's two nieces and worked in restaurants in order to earn money to go to see plays on Broadway. I had an offer to be in a play, and I thought about accepting, but I had to turn it down because it was time to come home to my family. That's another thing. My husband was really great. When I went away, he was here with the kids. When he went away, I was here with the kids. He went to the University of Chicago in 1956 on a one-year grant to study mathematics. I went to Santa Barbara for a summer in 1968 and I returned there to study at UC Santa Barbara. That's where I earned my Master's in 1970. In 1974, I was one of twenty-five Atlanta Public School teachers selected by UCLA to go to West Africa. That was something my mother had expressed a longing to do: to see the place where our people came from first. I would go back to West Africa if I ever got the chance.

I went to Tallahassee for four or five years to direct plays at Florida State University, and I taught at the University for one semester or two. I went there because my daughter was working on a Master's degree in playwriting. She had written a play about African Americans, but there were no African Americans in the department, and only an African American could direct the play. My daughter said, "Well, my mother can direct it." So, I went there and I directed Judy's play.

My son was in the Air Force in Thailand, and I'm so grateful that he wasn't in Vietnam. And of course I am thankful that he came home from the War intact. My heart bleeds for parents who have children in the war now because I know the fear and worry about losing a child to war.

I loved teaching. I loved it. I started at W. H. Crogman Elementary School and from there I went to Turner High School, where I taught for ten years, before being transferred to Harper High. I left Harper and went to Boyd Elementary School and, after two years, I was

Mrs. Georgia W. Allen

transferred to Jean Childs Middle School, but it was then called Southwest. I spent one year there, and then I took myself on home. I ran into one of my students recently, and he said, "Mrs. Allen, we talked about you and said you were mean, but we loved you." And I said, "You didn't know that I loved you, too, and I wanted for you what I wanted for my own children." I feel good about what I accomplished in my twenty-seven years of working with public school kids.

I really admire my mother and realize that I have so much of her in me. I do understand now, at this age, why my mother was patient with me. Just like my mother, I wanted success for my children. I wanted joy and peace and happiness for my children and my grandchildren, and I want it for you, too.

MRS. CORNELIA BAILEY

Sapelo Island, Georgia

Author, Activist, and Griot

I have been called the Griot of Sapelo and I think that is an honor, but I want you to know that I tell my stories because I don't want them to be lost. Telling the stories is one way of saving Sapelo, and if we don't do what we can to save Sapelo, it will be taken over by developers and if that happens, what you see here now won't be here. Where you are sitting now could be where a condominium would be built. I don't want to see Sapelo become a community of condos and golf courses.

Mrs. Cornelia Bailey

Sapelo is a beautiful island. You know that because you have had a chance to see for yourselves, and there is still a lot you haven't seen. There is a lot you won't see because you won't be staying here on Sapelo three hundred and sixty five days a year. You are here for a few days, and then you are back at school. But you've seen enough to know this is a beautiful island. You liked the ferry ride. I could tell that from all your excitement and from all the pictures you were taking. I don't think you saw a porpoise when you rode the ferry. You saw seagulls and pelicans, but I don't think you saw a porpoise, but sometimes you can see a orpoise, or more than one, following the ferry.

Your professor told me you are going to the ocean tomorrow. That's what the Spelman students did when they came last year. They woke up in the dark of night. [Laughs] That's what you will do. You will wake up in the dark and go to the ocean and be there at sunrise. My son Maurice will take you. Some of you might have a hard time getting up in the dark of night, but you won't mind once you see the sunrise over the ocean.

Sapelo is an island, which means that it is surrounded by water, but would you believe that we children were told to stay out of the water, not to go near the water. Visitors who come to Sapelo assume that all of us are great swimmers because of the waters, you see, but people on Sapelo used the water. The water wasn't for fun. It was for getting you from one place to another and for getting food for your family. People on Sapelo had a fear of getting into the water and I think that was passed down for generations. They didn't trust the water because that's how they were brought from their homes in Africa to be slaves here.

I have lived all of my life on Sapelo. I died on Sapelo and then I came back to life. [Laughs] I got sick from eating tiny green pears from a tree that was near our house. You've read the book, so you know the story. You know that Papa measured me and took the measurements to the carpenter. His name was Mr. Freddy and he made my casket out of pine. Mama lined it with clean sheets and then she made a pillow for my head to lay, so that I would look like I was sleeping. You've read the book, so you know how my Mama's sister, Aunt Mary, packed my nose and my mouth with garlic. She put garlic everywhere she could.

[Laughs] And that's how I came around. Sometimes I think I came back to life so that I could save Sapelo. That's my mission: to keep Sapelo from dying.

The oldest person on the island right now is Viola Bailey, a cousin of ours. She lives about five minutes east of here. That's how we tell direction around here. She was born and raised here and then she moved. Larry Johnson, the young man that took yon on the tour. His father is the oldest man on Sapelo. He's ninety-one. So they are the two oldest on the island. His eyesight is failing so he goes off a lot to the mainland.

The Baileys on Sapelo Island are connected to everybody else and everybody else is connected to the Baileys. The only persons here that don't have a bloodline are the ones who got on the island through marriage and we have two of those, but everyone else is kin. You can not marry your first cousin or second cousin in the state of Georgia. They will let you marry your third fourth and fifth cousin. Basically we are all cousins. We can go down the line and find out we have the same great grandmother or great grandfather. Everybody knows they are kin.

We live in a small community. When I grew up, there were five communities and now there is only this one. Just like the mother country of Africa, there's a little tribal leadership here on Sapelo. Although we are all kind, when there were five communities people knew each other and they married across communities. There is a certain distrust, you know. I have this and you don't have this. At times it still pops out even if you don't want it to. It shouldn't be, but we still have this kind of attitude. You love each other, but you don't particularly like each other all the time. That's the short way to explain that.

Africanism and Muslim. We mix them all together and come up with our own blend. That's what we say on Sapelo. We have our own blend. Really, we have our own blend of everything, and it's special, which means you can't find it anywhere else. We are called Geechee and we are called Gullah. If you live on the Georgia Sea Islands, people call you Geechee. If you live on the South Carolina islands, people call you Gullah and then there are people in places like Charleston that call themselves Geechee. Both of the names are used, and

Mrs. Cornelia Bailey

it really depends on what the people themselves prefer. It's your preference and for me the preference is our traditional name and that name is Saltwater Geechee. So, if you want to know how I want you Spelman students to describe us, or what I want you to call us, I would tell you "Saltwater Geechee." We here on Sapelo think the words come African words. There is Kissi, pronounced "Geezee," and there is Gola. Those are the two West African tribes people came from when they were brought to the island as slaves. There is some thinking that the names "Geechee" and "Gullah" came from those tribes. You know, the way they got to be pronounced changed because the people were here and not in West Africa.

There used to be five Geechee communities on Sapelo and there were more than four hundred and fifty people in those communities. But a lot of people have left Sapelo and so we have only one community on the island. So you understand why I am trying to do what I can to save our island. That's one of the reasons I wrote the book and that's the reason I go around to a lot of places and to organizations talking about Sapelo.

People on Sapelo had a lot of beliefs, and those beliefs touched every part of their lives. You might call them superstitions, but beliefs might be a better word. There are things we just believe in because our ancestors believed in them and they believed in them because they worked. And even if they didn't work in the way you think something should work, they were a part of our culture and many of the things in our culture came down to us from our African ancestors. I grew up believing in spirits. Hasn't everyone had a spirit that came to visit them? [Laughter] Yep. That's a normal thing. We believe in spirits. You talk to them. They are here with us all of the time. They re the spirits of our loved ones. You don't throw water outside after dark because you could be accidentally throwing water on the spirits. If you were evil in life, I suppose you are an evil spirit. Just because you died doesn't mean that your spirit is good. There are evil spirits walking around. At funerals, we pass the youngest over the casket, and that keeps the spirit from taking them. We pass them over the casket or over the grave. One person passes them over to someone on the other side. The spirit will be restless if you don't. When you are carrying a new baby out of the house, you speak its name before you leave the house. When you reach where you're visiting, before you leave, you should call the baby's name. That way, you take its spirit back home with you. Even though it's a live kicking baby, you are supposed to carry the spirit by calling it. It works. Some people have had to leave and come back for not calling the baby's spirit.

You know, we have this culture and when scientists come, we tell them about it. My grandmother always said that she wouldn't mess with those buckra people. Everyone believed in the hag and that the hag would ride you, but now the scientists are now telling us that it's poor blood circulation. All of a sudden that part of life is gone. The jack-o-lantern we used to see was also explained away by the scientists. They said it was low lying heat and sulfur. After that, no one has seen jack-o-lantern.

We have lost a lot of our traditions. What's normal to us is not normal to you, and you are not accustomed to what we are accustomed to. You might ask where we got most of this and we can't tell you about all of it because we have lost so much. Traditionally, we do a few things here on the island that they don't do on the mainland. For example, we smoke fish. Some of the dishes we cook are traditional. Some of the folklore and belief systems are traditional, and you won't find them being observed on the mainland. Even though we have cable and satellite and internet, we keep many of our traditions. There are just some things that you don't get away from because they are a part of you. They are just here, you know? For example, I can't interlace my hands on top of my head like this. It's a sign of mourning and death. You see, in some of the older cultures in the world, women mourned by putting their hands on top of their heads. When you see the children doing that and you tell them to stop it, you should explain to them why they should stop. I am talking about traditions that are being lost because we now tell children "don't do this" and "don't do that" without telling them why.

The children attend school on the mainland. They ride the ferry over every morning and it brings them back in the evening. Traveling to school does have an effect on them. I would kind of say none, but then that would be a lie. It does have an impact on them because they have to change themselves between here and going across the water. They always talk about

Mrs. Cornelia Bailey

what friends over there can do, can say, and how they can dress. And I tell them, "You're not going to wear that. You're not going to talk that way inj my house." They respond by saying, "My friend I stayed with last week, his mother let him. . . . . " And I say, " I don't care what his mother allowed him to do. You're not doing it here." They are pull back and forth between two worlds. We see that as they get older, they appreciate the way we raised them.

When our children cross the water, go over to the mainland, the culture there has an impact on them because it is different from Sapelo culture. So, they have to change themselves as they cross that water. There are things that they can say and can't say on the mainland that they can say here on Sapelo. I don't care what their mother lets them do here. They have to go back and forth between two worlds, and that has its challenges. I know when my kids first started going to school, they knew how to handle themselves so it didn't matter. I remember when my kids first started going to school on the mainland when the school closed here. That was in 1978. They went to school, and they were teased a lot about where they came from. I remember when Jimmy Carter came here when he was President. The kids said that he came to stay with them on Sapelo. [Laughs] How could the kids on the mainland top that? [Laughs] Helicopters were flying over the island. The FBI came, and they were riding around Sapelo dressed, but we didn't know that this would be the route for the helicopter. We didn't pay them any attention. As long as they don't bother us, we weren't concerned about them. My father said, "I see 'em and I don't see 'em; I hear 'em, but I don't hear 'em; I know 'em, but I don't know 'em; and some of 'em I don't want to know." [Laughs]

Some things the people not from here just can't know. There's a lot they can't know. A lot. There's one thing that we would hear from my father when we were growing up on Sapelo. He would tell us, "A poor man only has three things going for him: God, his word and a piece of land." He didn't make a rise about whether a poor man was a White man or a Black man. Regardless, you have God on your side. You're supposed to keep God on your side. When we were growing up on Sapelo, we were taught that your word was your bond. You don't need a piece of paper to tell you have the land. You have the land because that's what God wanted you to have in the first place. And we mess around and get rid of our land over foolishness and sorriness. My father said, "When you word is not worth much because your fellow man won't take you seriously, the only thing you've got left is God. If you lose Him, you're really in trouble."

I am concerned about Sapelo. I really fear for my island because we are losing people and because so many developers are coming. Some people just chose to leave Sapelo. Some of them didn't have any other choice. Economics is what makes people leave the island in the first place. Now is the time to get people to move back because now we have fewer people here and that means we're gonna have outsiders wanting to come in and buy land. Some people have signs in the yard saying, "Don't ask. Won't sell." White people actually come on our property and knock on the door. They ask," How much property do you have and would you like to sell some?" I have had tourists get off the bus and say, "Mrs. Bailey, how much property do you have?" I say, "Just enough for my grandchildren and great grandchildren and my great great-grans." Everything has a price. I said to one man, "Can you pull out, at this moment, ten million dollars?" He was shocked. I said, "That's what I mean. I don't want to sell my property." They try everyday. We have received forms in the mail from developers in Atlanta. "Do you have any property you'd like to sell?"

Sapelo is like Custer's Last Stand. They are waiting. We have a few of them in the community already and that's a few too many. One lady told me that it was racist for me to think that way. "Cornelia, that's racist for you to think that you don't want any whites in the community." I said, "Give me a moment. Your people practiced racism for four hundred years. I do it for ten seconds and its racism. Come to think of it. I like it." If you are not in the bloodline of anyone here on Sapelo and you buy property on the island, you would be an outsider. I don't care if you lived here for fifteen years, you'd still be an outsider. No matter how much we might love you and no matter how long you've been here, you will be an outsider. You will be described in that way. We know everybody and that makes things easier. Now I'm on the stomping block trying to get anybody on Sapelo who wants to sell their property to sell it to an outsider Black, not an outsider White. They will sell to a White person before they sell it to a Black person. That kind of mentality is here and it hasn't changed much, so that means that we are losing acres.

You asked me about researchers coming to the island. What kind of researchers? Back up on that. I dislike White researchers coming to research my culture. They know how I feel because they can feel how I feel. If they can't feel it and they are too blockheaded to know, I just tell them straight up. I don't have time for all the niceness. I just have to say what I feel. We have researchers that set up shop here to do marine biology research. They come and they go. They are researching the marsh and creeks and the rivers. They get tired of it or they get transferred someplace else, and they're gone. None of them are permanent. They are not landowners. We don't count White folks. We only count people that are here three hundred and sixty five days a year and are landowners. So, we don't count nobody else. A White person who is a landowner, I still don't count. You know, it's funny that White people, when they interview me will ask me what I missed by growing up on Sapelo Island rather than on the mainland. I tell them I didn't miss anything. I had everything I needed. Everything! Besides, you can't miss something you never had.

MRS. LEILA BARFIELD

Anderson, South Carolina

Teacher, City Council Woman and Vice Mayor

When the slaves were first freed, they started walking all across the South to different places. And my great grandparents – this is on my mother's side – came through Atlanta and they passed a market that had a sign up front. My great grandfather could read, and he read the sign and it said, "Beal's Market." So he took that for his name, and that's how the family became Beal. They were slaves in Georgia, and they walked all the way to Anderson.

Mrs. Leila Barfield

I was born in Anderson, South Carolina on June 16, 1921. I was born at home, but I was delivered by a doctor and also by a midwife. My grandmother on my mother's side was the midwife. Her name was Leila, and she later became a nurse. Both of my parents were born in Anderson, South Carolina.

My mother's name was Leila Williams Milford, and my father's name was Eugene Milford. They met in Anderson and they courted through grade school and, I think, through high also. That was during the time when schools had three grades in one room. That was probably in the late eighteen nineties. There were four girls in the family: Sarah, Alice, Lougenia, and me. Sarah was named after my mother's sister. Alice was named after my father's mother. My father named Lougenia. There were three Lelias in my family: My grandmother Leila, my mom Leila, and I'm Leila. And, oh, yes, I had an Auntie named Leila. My father nicknamed all of us. He nicknamed my sister Sarah "Honey Love." He nicknamed my sister Alice "Sweet Thing," and she was a very sweet person. He nicknamed my sister Lougenia "Skeeter" because she was always so skinny. He nicknamed me "Butch" because he said when I was a little thing, I would say "Butcha. Butcha. Butcha. Butcha." [Laughs]

My father's parents were from South Carolina. They had eight children and my father was oldest child. I don't know how they got the name Milford, but there was a White family in Anderson named Milford who said that my family was probably related to them. My father's parents had a large farm in Anderson, and they hired a lot of people to help take care of the farm. But when my grandfather died, and that must have been in the eighteen nineties, my grandmother felt that my father should take care of the farm, so he became the man of the house, and that's probably why he went only to the eighth grade. But, you know, back then, going to the eighth grade was like being in college.

My mother's parents were also from Anderson, but her grandparents were from Georgia. Actually, they were in slavery in Georgia. Her grandfather was a slave, and his wife Catharine was the master's child. They were house slaves. Let me tell you the story. When the slaves were first freed, they started walking all across the South to different places. And my great grandparents – this is on my mother's side – came through Atlanta and they passed a market that had a sign up front. My great grandfather could read, and he read the sign and it said, "Beal's Market." So, he took that for his name, and that's how the family became Beal. They were slaves in Georgia, and they walked all the way to Anderson. They would walk until they got tired, and the older ones would carry the little ones. Isn't that something? We can't even imagine that, can we? That was my great grandparents on my mother's side. They were the ones who had property, but I don't know how they got the property, and I don't know how my father's parents got property either. I never asked. I just know that both of them owned property in Anderson. Back then, Anderson was a small town, something like Decatur, and it was mostly Black. What was amazing is that most of the Black people in Anderson were homeowners. I don't know how they got to be homeowners, but they were. What was also amazing is that Blacks and Whites lived in the same neighborhoods, and this might be hard to believe, but we had good relationships with the White people. I grew up playing with White children because they were neighbors. Now, when we went to school, all that changed. They went to a school for Whites, and we went to a school for Blacks. That was a big hurt. A big hurt.

My father was a barber and a chef. I don't know how he learned to cut hair, or how he learned to be a chef. I do know that when we lived in Anderson, we would go to Clemson College every summer. The College wanted my father to quit his job in Anderson and move to Clemson to be the cook, but he would tell them he couldn't leave his family. He would work there only during the summer, and all of us lived on the campus of Clemson College in students' facilities. We moved to Atlanta in 1919, and I was five years old at the time. The reason we left is that my parents thought the four girls would get a better education in Atlanta. My father and mother had friends who had already moved to Atlanta, and the friends encouraged them to move here. So, we moved, but both sets of my grandparents stayed on in Anderson, and we would go back and forth to visit them. We spent our summers with them. We would take the train from Atlanta to Anderson to spend the whole summer with them. I

Mrs. Leila Barfield

remember when we would go on the train, we had a lot of food. We weren't allowed to go to the club car because we were Black. But White conductors were very good to us because they knew us, you see, because we would travel to Anderson every summer to see our grandparents.

I loved going back to Anderson because I loved my grandparents, and I was very close to my grandmother on my mother's side. Her name was Leila. I would go to church with her. I didn't mention that my mother's father was a minister and when he would take me to missionary meetings, I would come back home with lots of money because I was the pastor's granddaughter. [Laughs] We spent the whole summer in Anderson, and we played real hard. We played hopscotch, and we played a game where we had to sing about putting "your right hand in and your right hand out" and then we would sing, "shake, shake, shake. That's what it's all about." I don't know that I can say I missed Anderson because it wasn't that far away and, as I said, we spent our summers there. So, you can say, that I grew up in Anderson and in Atlanta.

I was too young when I moved to Atlanta to compare it with Anderson, but my life didn't change that much, not right away, because I was still with my parents and my three sisters and, as I said, I was in Anderson every summer. But I was probably excited that Atlanta was larger than Anderson and you could do more things in Atlanta than you could in Anderson. What I will say about moving to Atlanta is that I had to learn about Blacks and Whites in a way that I didn't have to learn in Anderson. In Atlanta, you know, we had to deal with Blacks being here and Whites being there. We didn't have that in Anderson because we had White neighbors. That wasn't the case in Atlanta. The neighborhoods here were all Black, and there were the signs, you know, "For Colored." Segregation was just different here than in Anderson. Today, Blacks can go to the Fox Theatre and right walk through the front door, but when I was growing up in Atlanta, we couldn't do that. I will never forget the time we went to the Fox with my father. Every Sunday was his day off, and he would always take us somewhere together as a family. This particular Sunday he took us to the Fox Theatre. While they were getting the tickets, I just wandered into the main room, and the White usher there was really nice to me. I guess White people treated you according to the way you looked, and I was real fair. So the

White usher was nice to me. He said, "Have you lost your parents?" And I said, "No." He said, "Well, I'll let you go around, but I'll go with you." He let me look all around at the bright lights and then he took me back to the front door. He said, "I bet your mom has been looking for her little girl." He took me to my parents and my mom thanked him and then we went on to where the Black people were. We had to go up a lot of steps to a place that was very high. They called it the buzzard's roost. My father didn't like that. He didn't like that at all. So, from then on, he didn't take us to the Fox. Both of my parents were very proud, but they didn't teach us to hate White people. They would say something like "God loves all people," but there is time when it is not room enough for Blacks and Whites to be together, but you have to love everybody." That's the sense that I grew up with here in Atlanta about White people.

I had very happy experiences growing up in Atlanta. I really did like to skate. That's what children did for fun. We didn't have a car. There were trolleys and streetcars at the time. We lived on the Westside on Beckwith Street, and my sister Alice was good friends with Lena Horne. I never remember Lena having a father. She and her mom lived down the street from us, almost at the end of the street. I had close friends, but not like Lena Horne was a close friend to my sister. When I moved to Lawton, Oklahoma, Lena came to do a concert, and she said that she would be available to talk to people after the show. I told my friends, "Let's wait. I want to see her." They didn't think I knew Lena, and they were surprised that Lena remembered me. I asked her, "Do you Remember the Milford girls?" Lena said, "Oh, yeah. _____ Beckwith Street." My friends were shocked.

My father was very strict. He did not allow us to read the funnies in the Sunday paper. We would get up on Sunday going to Sunday school and to church and, at night, we would go back to church. We had a fence in the front yard and a fence in the backyard, and we were supposed to stay inside the fence. Anybody in the neighborhood could come in and play with us, but we couldn't go outside the fence. As I said, my father was very strict, and he loved his four girls. There was a professor named Grace DeLong who taught biology at Spelman and who lived in the neighborhood and she would say to my mother, "Give me Sarah and Leila." She

Mrs. Leila Barfield

wanted to take us home with her. My mother would say, "When my husband comes home, if there aren't two little heads in the first bedroom and two larger heads in the next bedroom, I wouldn't have anywhere to stay. Oh, I can't give you my children." [Laughs] Ms. DeLong would take us home with her, but we couldn't spend the night. [Laughs] Oh, no! My father had to see those four heads in those bedrooms.

My mom was a very quiet and very proud woman. She kept us well dressed. We had a seamstress who lived around the corner from us and who made our clothes. My mother didn't work because my father said he didn't want us coming home to an empty house. She had to be there at all times to greet us and give us our dinner and whatever. I was the baby of the family, and I guess everybody spoiled me. [Laughs] My mother was so dear. She spent a lot of time with us, doing special things. I remember she had us in a club and we would have to elect officers just like real clubs and read the minutes like they do in real clubs. It was more like a saving club for Christmas, you know. There were seven members in the club: my four sisters, my mom and my dad, and a girl down the street my mother kept. The first time I had to serve refreshments at a club meeting, my mom bought this box and she said, "The best thing for you to serve would be jello and cup cakes." And she put me on this box and showed me how to stir jello. I think my interest in politics started back then.

I went to E. A. Ware Elementary because the school in our community had burned. That was the Ashby Street School, and it later reopened as E. R. Carter. After elementary school, I went to Booker T. Washington High for one year, in the eighth grade, but when my sister Sarah graduated from Washington, my father didn't want me to go there alone, and that's why I went to Atlanta University Laboratory High. It was located in Giles Hall on Spelman's campus. I made two grades in one year. They thought I was smart. [Laughs] I went there from the ninth grade to the twelfth grade. The thing that I really remember the most is that Washington High dismissed thirty minutes before we dismissed, so the boys would come to Lab High and walk us home and carry our books. I graduated from Lab High in 1937.

The next year, I started college at Spelman. I never thought of going to any other college because most of my friends were going to Spelman. I lived in my family's home on Beckwith Street, which is not that far from Spelman's campus, so I walked to school with other children in the community. I was very excited when I started at Spelman. Oh yes, indeed! I was the first one in my family to go to Spelman! I majored in home economics, but only because my friends majored in home economics. I switched to sociology and psychology only because the sociology teacher asked me to change. [Laughs] I met my first husband when I was at Spelman. He was a student at Morehouse and I was attracted to him because he was handsome. In fact, he was called "Gable" because he looked like Clark Gable. His name was Curtis Joseph Terry, and we dated for two years before we married. We married in 1942.

When I became pregnant with our first child, I was excited, but I was frightened. I was frightened because I wasn't too familiar with sex. That's the first thing. My sexual life hadn't been pleasant because I was a virgin when I was married. During that time, children weren't free the way they are now. You know, you can see a baby being born on television, but we didn't have television. We had a lot of classes on hygiene, but not on sex education. I was always embarrassed when people talked about sex. Yes, girls did become pregnant out of wedlock, and sometimes they had abortions by a private doctor. They were ostracized, but the boys were not ostracized. I'm trying to remember the name of the woman who told us this. She was a teacher at Lab High, and she would tell us that boys can do anything and be forgiven. And she said that being a girl is like wearing a white dress and having a mud stain on it. You can't ever get it out. She told us this when we were in the twelfth grade at Lab High. When we started our cycle, adults would tell us that we could get pregnant, but we weren't taught anything about sex. So, I was afraid when I became pregnant and also I thought I was too young. Unfortunately, I lost my first child.

When I became pregnant with my second child, I was excited, but I was still frightened. I had a hard pregnancy. When I went into labor, the doctor gave me a shot in my back, called twilight sleep. I was in twilight, but I could hear them talking. One doctor said, "Where's the needle?" Another doctor said, "Oh my God, we broke that needle off in her back." So, they

Mrs. Leila Barfield

took a knife and had to run it up and down my spine to find the needle and when they found it, they had to cut it out. I didn't have labor pains because of the twilight sleep. I just turned over and went to sleep. The doctor said, "Oh, darling, you can't do me this way. You can't go to sleep. You have to cooperate with me." He told me that he would tell me every time I had a contraction and that he would want me to push. I didn't feel any pain. I was glad about that. The baby was a girl, and I named her Jean Elizabeth: Jean after my husband's sister and Elizabeth after my sister. Three years later, I was pregnant again, and I was really frightened because the problem with the needle had affected my back. You know, the doctors told me I shouldn't lift more than five pounds, but who can live without lifting over five pounds? My second child was a little boy, and we named him William Curtis Terry. He was so sweet.

Becoming a mother didn't change my life too much because I went anywhere I wanted to go and then, too, my mother would come and stay with me. I didn't work. I stayed home until my children were school age, and I enjoyed every minute I spent with them. My mom stayed home with us. And, you know, I handled race the same way my parents did. I tried to protect my children from racial indignities. There was a pretty café in Rich's that was closed to Blacks. When I would take my children shopping (and this was in the fifties), I would call the café and get the menu and then I would prepare food that was on the menu. When we would be in the store, my children would say, "Momma, we want to go in there and eat." I would say, "Well, let's see what they have." I would look at the menu and I would say, "Well, you just had that." I didn't go to work until Jean was five and William about two. My first job was teaching at Bethune Elementary School. After Bethune, I taught at Ashby Street Elementary School. I taught in the Atlanta System for thirty years. I enjoyed teaching very much because a lot of the kids I taught were under-privileged, and I wanted to help them.

I moved to Lawton, Oklahoma in 1991 when I married Quay F. Barfield. He was a civil servant, and I met him through a friend of mine when Quay was visiting here in Atlanta. I had no interest in meeting anybody because I had been single a long time and I had five grandchildren. Really, I couldn't think of anything I would rather do than be with my children and my grandchildren. But my friend insisted, so I went ahead and met this man she wanted me to meet. Quay and I courted for two years, from 1989 to 1991. We married in 1991, and I moved to Lawton to live with him. Lawton is a small town, and it is about forty miles from the all-Black town White people burned down. Was it difficult for me to move to Oklahoma? Yes! But I was back and forth to Atlanta so much that some people didn't know I was living in Oklahoma. Lawton was pretty much like the Black community I knew in Atlanta. The people were very proud of their neighborhood, and they let their voices be heard. That's how I became involved in politics in Lawton. The people in the neighborhood were battling the city about a wall that would be at the back of our houses, and someone said, "I know who will beat this guy. Leila Barfield can do it." So, they asked me to run against this guy who was making the proposal. He was White. I said, "Okay, if you have that much confidence in me, I'll go ahead and run." And I did, and I won. One of my neighbors said, "You beat him like he stole something." [Laughs] I was the first Black woman to become a member of the Lawton City Council.

Whenever the people didn't want something to happen, I would get my speech together and we would vote them out. A man who took pictures for the City Council said to me one day, "Mrs. Barfield, I like the way you stand up for your people." I think what impressed him was the time I stood up for a Black man who was in a wheelchair. He came to the council for damage some walls had done to his property. About six months later, a White man came with the same complaint and the Council said, "We'll pay it." And I said, "Oh, no you won't. There was this Black guy that was here with the same complaint. He was in a wheelchair. You all denied him." And I told them that if they voted to pay the White guy, they would have to pay the Black guy." They voted against the White man. I believe you have to stand up for your people.

I enjoyed being a politician. What I liked most about it was working to get Black people together. My husband and I would go all through the neighborhood telling people what we wanted them to do. There was this one lady who said, "Ain't no need of going down there.

Mrs. Leila Barfield

They gonna do what they want to do." She was talking about going to the City Council. I said, "Yes, they will do what they want to do if you let them. One vote will count." I believe that. One vote will count. I think the club my mother had, the one I told you about, had something to do with me going into politics because we would study about voting and electing officers. In Lawton, I would tell all the people who would give me money for my campaign, "Now this does not mean I am going to vote for your project. I will vote for what is best for the city." One of the richest men in the city would give me a large sum of money, but that money didn't tell me how to vote. I voted for the people. I voted for what was right and what was best for the people.

My husband was very supportive, and he would go around and ask people to vote for me. Let me tell you this. My husband had a policy with State Farm Insurance Company, and when the agent didn't make a contribution to my campaign, my husband cancelled the policy. [Laughs] Both of us are Democrats, but there is a funny story about me and the Republican Party. Before I moved to Lawton, a professor at Morehouse, who was our neighbor in Atlanta, would ask me to attend political meetings and take minutes. He was a Republican. He thought I was a Republican. I never told him I was a Democrat. But when the club voted to send me to Washington to be a delegate, I said to myself, "You gotta get out of this. You have to tell Mr. _____you are not a Republican." He was really surprised that I was a Democrat. The first presidential election I voted in was the one for Kennedy. I have always been a Democrat.

Sometimes I can't believe I actually served sixteen years on the City Council in Lawton and two years as Vice Mayor. That's a long way from Anderson, South Carolina. A White woman told me once, "Mrs. Barfield, you must write a book about your experience. I don't care if you bring in your childhood, but you must write about your experience as the first Black woman on Lawton's City Council." She told me, "You are a strong Black woman." I think I got my strength from my father and also from my mother. I believe Black women are courageous. We don't have any fear of standing up for what we believe in.

I lived in Lawton for seventeen years. I returned to Atlanta in 1996 because my husband came down with Ahlzeimer's and I wanted to be with my family as I was caring for him. The people in Lawton were sad to see us leave, and I was sad to leave, but it was best for me to go where my family was and that's why I came back to Atlanta. I had a good life in Lawton, but I am glad to be in Atlanta as I care for my husband. This is home. Atlanta is home. And if I weren't here, I wouldn't be able to talk to students like you. I don't think Spelman would be sending you to Lawton, Oklahoma. [Laughs]

I have enjoyed this oral history experience. It has brought back so many happy memories. So many. Sometimes when I talk with you, I cry. Sometimes, I laugh. Sometimes, I sing. Just talking with you about my life in Anderson and here in Atlanta and in Lawton makes me happy. I realize how successful I have been and how blessed I am. I am a blessed woman. Yes, I am a blessed woman.

MRS. JULIA BOND

Nashville, Tennessee

Librarian

We didn't live close to other Black children because we lived in a White neighborhood, so it was a matter of children coming to visit. You know, we had to make special arrangements. It wasn't easy to get to us, but living in the neighborhood had some advantages—you know, like deliveries and getting things that you needed. But it was isolated. It was lonely. We didn't have any playmates on the block. The children didn't play with us because we were Black.

I was born on June 20, 1908. I had a family gathering on my ninety-fifth birthday. All my children were there: Jane, Julian and James. We had dinner at a restaurant called Mary Mac's. That was exciting. I'm ninety-seven now. I was born in Nashville as Julia Agnes Washington. My father, George E. Washington, was a mathematician and a schoolteacher. He taught in a high school in Nashville. That's where my mother met him. He was the principal of the school, and she was a student. [Laughs] Her name was Daisy Turner, and she graduated from Fisk. She taught in the blind school in Nashville. She could read Braille, but she didn't continue teaching after she was married. They had four children. The first one, Henry, died in infancy. And then Alvin was born, and then me, Julia; then Marguerite; and then Joe, who was named after my Grandfather Joe. I was named for my father's mother, Julia. I don't know where they got Agnes. [Laughs] My brother Alvin became a doctor and moved to Syracuse. My sister Marguerite became a social worker and moved to Los Angeles. My younger sister is a retired schoolteacher, and she lives in Cleveland now so that she can be close to her daughter. I keep in touch with her. She is my remaining sibling.

We lived in Nashville, but I don't remember there being a special name for where we lived. It was just in the suburbs of Nashville, and there were Whites in the community. When I was growing up, we were made to go to my grandmother's Sunday School. I think it was Methodist. When we really started going to church, we went to the Congregational church. That was my mother's church. I didn't sing in the church choir. I can't carry a tune, but I could play the piano. It wasn't a personal interest of mine. It was just something children had to do, but I did enjoy it. I took lessons for a long time. I had a private teacher who would come to my house. She lived down the street from my grandmother. She was German, and she came to my house and taught me piano. Her name was Mrs. Schwartz, and she was pretty strict. She had other pupils, and they would go to her house for their lessons, but she came to me. I guess because I was Black. I was the only Black piano pupil she had. That was in Nashville in the twenties.

Mrs. Julia Bond

I learned to play the piano, and I learned to sew. People didn't buy as many dresses as you do now. When I was growing up in Nashville, the sewing machine was open every day except Sunday. Something was being sewn all the time. At home. Everybody had to sew. I think people made everything except men's shirts. They may have made those, but I don't think so. My grandmother taught me to sew. People didn't buy much from stores. It was just the way then. Everybody could sew. Sewing probably helped out a lot during the Depression, but the Depression didn't affect my family that much because, fortunately, my grandmother was well to do, and she saw us through the Depression. She inherited money from her husband who was a florist with a big flourishing business, and that's where all the money came from. My grandmother was able to send all of us to college and to graduate school. She sent us all to college and to graduate school.

How did my grandfather get to be a florist? Well, he was the son of a florist. His father was a Frenchman who came here from France and settled in New Orleans, where he peddled coal. And he left New Orleans and moved to Nashville, where he established a nursery. My grandfather was the son born to my great grandfather and a slave woman. My grandmother was Black. She was a slave. My grandfather was biracial. My grandfather inherited his father's florist business. He had a large establishment of eleven greenhouses. There's a big picture of it in the basement. So, yes, my grandfather's father was White, but that was true of most people of that generation.

My grandfather was unusual in Nashville because there weren't many wealthy Black families in the area during that time. His name was Joe Brown. When he died, the florist business was sold. That was according to his will. It was sold, and my grandmother came to live with us, but she didn't stay. She bought back the farm and moved there to live. She took me to live with her. I must have been about seven or eight. I guess she took me because I was the oldest girl, and someone needed to live with her so that she wouldn't be alone in the house. I enjoyed living with my grandmother. It was a very pleasant time in my life. She was very kind to me, and the house was a big place. I had lots of space to play, and there was a swing, which I loved. I lived with my grandmother through college until I married.

There were about five houses where I lived, and in one was a White family called the Webbs. I don't think they liked Black people. In another was Mrs. Schwartz, the music teacher. She was very pleasant. And there was another White family, and their little girl Lorraine and I played together every day. From morning until, you know, bedtime, we played together. And there was another White family in the community. The Fly family. Mrs. Fly and my grandmother were very good friends, and they visited back and forth. But, you know, their relationship was different from what a relationship with a Black person would be. It wasn't exactly the same. But with Lorraine, there was no difference between us. We were children. I think we were too little to go to school. We played together, and we didn't see any difference. And with Mrs. Schwartz, the music teacher, there was no difference, but the Webbs, who lived across the street, didn't care for Black people. We didn't have any encounters, but they didn't care for Black people.

When my father died, my mother and my siblings went to live with my grandmother. That was in 1922. So, we were all together. His mother lived with us, too. [Laughs] There were a lot of women in the house. They sent my brother away to school, to Howard, because he was living with five women, and that was too much. But we all got along well together. When we were children, my brother and I would never fight over anything except a book. [Laughs] We loved to read, and we would go to the library, the circulating library, to get books. It was some distance from home, and so we walked there. I was close to my brother, and he nicknamed me Jimmy because he wanted a boy to play with. [Laughs] So, I was a little bit of a tomboy because I played with him. You know, we would pretend that we were on a ranch riding horses. My sisters didn't play tomboy as much as I did.

One of my fondest memories of growing up in Nashville with my siblings is going to birthday parties. I remember when I was seven and when I was eleven, my mother gave me a birthday party and, of course, she decided who would come to the party. We didn't live close to other Black children because we lived in a White neighborhood, so it was a matter of children

Mrs. Julia Bond

coming to visit. You know, we had to make special arrangements. It wasn't easy to get to us, but living in the neighborhood had some advantages—you know, like deliveries and getting things that you needed. But it was isolated. It was lonely. We didn't have any playmates on the block. The children didn't play with us because we were Black.

We were in the neighborhood because my grandmother was well to do, but she wasn't flagrant with her wealth. She did modest things. She wasn't an educated woman. In fact, she went to about the fifth grade, but she was an intelligent woman. My grandfather wasn't educated either. Most people of that generation weren't educated. They probably went to grade school. My grandmother used her wealth to take care of all of us. She sent us to college and to graduate school. She lived to be almost in her late nineties. I was grown and had children when she died. She didn't do anything with her money except spend it on us. When she died (and this was in my grandfather's will), the money was to go to Fisk. That was the largest gift Fisk had ever received. I don't know why my grandfather chose Fisk except that he loved the College, and there wasn't any other institution in Nashville, except Meharry. I don't know. A lot of the teachers from Fisk did come to the nursery, you know, to get flowers and to visit.

I met my husband when I was twenty years old. He was teaching at Fisk in my senior year. Let's see. That must have been in 1928 because I finished high school in 1925 and Fisk in 1929. He was a very popular teacher. Students flocked to his class because he was young and single and eligible. But I didn't . [Laughs]. His father was the minister of the First Congregational Church in Nashville. In fact, his father performed the ceremony when my mother and my father married, so Mother had a good disposition toward my husband because she knew his family so well and she had known him when he was a child. As I said, when my husband taught at Fisk, everyone wanted to be in his class. I didn't take his class, but I guess in the course of things you just meet most people on a small college campus, and Fisk was small at the time. He started coming to see me at my grandmother's house in Nashville. That's where I lived, with my grandmother. He would come to see me and we would sit in the swing and talk. [Laughs] I don't remember how he proposed to me, but I was not surprised. [Laughs] I thought probably, yes, he would propose. He was so intelligent and so well read. He was so different from most young men who didn't read anything.

When I graduated from Fisk, I went to the University of Chicago to study English. That's where my husband got his doctorate. He came to visit me during the Christmas holiday, and we married. Since we intended to get married, I guess we thought there's no need in putting it off and so we went one day and got married. It wasn't really spur of the moment. We had planned to marry. Of course, we didn't have a honeymoon because both of us were in graduate school. When he told his mother that we had married, she insisted that we have a ceremony in Nashville. She said she had a friend who got married, you know, away from home, and when she came home and announced that she was married, nobody believed her. So, she had to frame her wedding certificate and put it on the wall. [Laughs] But, of course, nothing like that happened to me. I had a second ceremony in Nashville. It was not a big church wedding. It was just a minister performing the ceremony in the living room. That was all. I didn't have any bridesmaids because, you know, I didn't have a wedding, really.

My husband finished and got his doctorate. I decided to stay home and not go back to school. I guess I was just lazy. [Laughs] You thought then that, you know, if you got married, you didn't need an education. You had a husband to take care of. My husband worked, and I didn't do anything. We didn't have children for a long time. We had our first child, Jane, after we had been married for eight years. She was born in Nashville at Meharry Medical College. She was named after my husband's sister Jane and my sister Marquerite. When my husband was teaching at Fisk, Julian was born, and he was named for me and for his father. His name is Horace Julian. My son James was born in Fort Valley, Georgia. He is named after his paternal and his maternal grandfather, James George.

All of the children were born when my husband was working at a college. When we left the University of Chicago, he worked at Fisk; and when he left Fisk, he became President of

Mrs. Julia Bond

Fort Valley State. People ask me what it was like to be the President's wife, and I tell them that I had to be the hostess for the campus. In those days, they didn't have any buildings for receptions or places where people could be entertained. The president's wife would have to have activities in her house because that was the only place for such things. You had to have a nice dress for activities, and sometimes you would have someone make your dress. There were dressmakers who were really good. Back then, there were lots of people who could sew.

We were at Fort Valley for four or five years. I don't remember how long exactly. We left Fort Valley and went to Lincoln University, where my husband was President. I was hostess again. It was exciting. We met interesting people at both places. Mr. W. C. Handy came and E. Franklin Frazier and Langston Hughes and Albert Einstein. Then, they were just contemporaries. They weren't as famous as they are now, but it was still exciting having them as our guests. Langston Hughes was a nice man, a regular person. Mr. Handy was blind, you know, and he had a lot of people who traveled with him and helped him. I have forgotten the name of the woman who stayed with him, but she would put his food on his plate and tell him this is a potato, this is meat, and this is bread. He had to have somebody with him most of the time.

We moved to Atlanta in either 1956 or 1957, when my husband came to work at Atlanta University. That was after we left Lincoln. We had never lived on a campus where there were graduate courses and I said, "Oh, I think I'll take some classes and what shall I take?" And I said, "Well, maybe I'll try library science." I took one course, you know, and then another until, eventually, I got the degree. It was not a conscious decision to get a degree. I just sorta drifted into it, and I enjoyed my work.

I can't tell you when I finished library school. It was probably in the sixties, but I just can't remember. I was a librarian at Atlanta University, and I enjoyed doing that. I liked working with college students. When I retired as a librarian in 2000, they had a big retirement party for me. The library was right there in Trevor Arnett. It isn't there anymore. I think it's Woodruff now, and it belongs to all the schools. Originally, the library was at Atlanta

University, but I believe it belonged to all the schools while I was there. Undergraduates, as well as graduate students, would come to the library. Rather than buy separate libraries for each school, it was thought better to consolidate and cheaper, too. I worked in reference, and I liked that. Students would come to the desk and ask a question and if it were very difficult, we would find someone who knew the most about it. But, generally, most of us could answer the questions. If there were a very difficult question, we would keep it and work on it two or three days. Several people would work on it. The library was in the Atlanta University Center. The library school at Atlanta University had a good many White students. I don't think many other divisions had White students.

When we were at Atlanta University, my daughter Jane went to Spelman, and my son Julian went to Morehouse. Julian and James, you know, joined the Student Non-Violence Coordinating Committee. They were in the Civil Rights Movement. The young people were very courageous, and they were independent. We as parents didn't have direct involvement in the demonstrations. We did whatever the young people asked us to do, which was to feed people or to sleep people. That kind of thing. They could come to the house. Maybe fifteen or twenty of them were involved, but they wouldn't all come to the house at one time. We did whatever we could to help.

I don't remember participating in any demonstrations because, you know, it was mostly a young people's movement. Older people gave money and support, but they didn't, you know, demonstrate because they would lose their jobs. It was risky. You would lose your job and people would, you know, throw things at your house or do something to your car. You didn't know what would happen. But everybody was a part of the Movement, you know. It was just a part of your life. I thought it was wonderful what the young people did, that they would stand up like that. Of course, I was afraid sometimes because people would call and threaten us. You know, it was frightening. The students were routinely arrested. Sometimes they were beaten, you know. We would have to go down to the jail to see if anybody we knew had been arrested. I can remember once when my husband had been away on a trip, he came home and opened the

Mrs. Julia Bond

door and I said, in a crying voice, "Julian's been arrested." So, we went downtown and paid the fine. It wasn't pleasant, but we knew the young people had to do it, and we had to support them. Mr. Paschal supported them by giving them a free meal after every demonstration. Paschal's was the restaurant most people went to. It was a favorite place because there weren't many others that served Blacks, and the food was good. Mr. Paschal would feed the students for free after each demonstration.

You know, the Black community was very close and very small then. It wasn't a matter of living close to people. It was just knowing people through churches or meetings or whatever. It wasn't just that you knew your neighbors. You knew everybody all over the city. That was because we were segregated and wherever we were, we would have to be together, you know. It's different today because we're integrated. We don't have to be just with each other. We're not segregated. I think it's better. I don't know that it's really good, but it's different and better. It's certainly not good to be segregated. But there were some virtues connected with it. We got to know each other and depend on each other and support each other. It made us close. Closer than we would have been if we hadn't been segregated. We couldn't live next to White people. We would move or we would have to move when they found out we were Black. We enjoyed living in Atlanta. My husband liked his work at the University and I liked my work at the library. We had many friends together, and then I had friends in the Chatauqua Reading Group, which is a group supported by the Highlights Foundation. It produces Highlights, the children's magazine you might have read when you were a child.

When we came to Atlanta, we lived in college housing. This is the first house we owned. My husband bought the land, and there was nothing on the block then. Not a building except the frame building next door. We put in a bid for the land. It was government land, you see, but we thought the land we had bought was way up the way where Spelman's chapel is located. We didn't know what we had bought until we got here and found the lot. It was zoned for two units. My husband said, "Well, it's zoned for two units, so I'll build two units." So, he built the apartment upstairs. It's been nice living here. Of course, when we built this house, this area was just a grassy plain with trees. It was a muddy path up to the back gate to Spelman, and we called that "the back gate." You know, nothing was cultivated. There were no buildings on this street except the frame house next door, which Morehouse College now owns. The neighborhood was quiet then, and we never thought it would grow to be like this. Noisy and crowded. The college has grown. There are many more buildings now than there were when we built the house, and there are many more students at all the schools. So, it gets noisy around here.

I had a garden for quite a while. It was in the back of the house, and I grew vegetables. Beans. Tomatoes. Squash. I was a pretty good gardener. When my husband was alive, he liked to garden. He died in 1973 from emphysema. At that time, there was still some segregation, but he went to Emory Hospital. When my husband was sick, I retired from my work at the library because I needed to take care of him. When I retired, I asked James to leave New York, where he was living, and come home to Atlanta because I needed him. He came, and he has been with me ever since.

I've been very fortunate to have lived in different cities and to have traveled to countries outside the United States. The country I would like to visit is China. It's just so fascinating to read about. I love to travel, but I doubt that I'll travel anymore. I just write letters to people, and I keep diaries and notes. I have kept a diary for a long time, off and on, but I'm not consistent. I like to write because it just seems a natural way to express yourself. I don't think I'm gifted at writing. If I were, I would have written something by now. I always hoped I could. I love to write letters, but I've outlived most of my contemporaries. There's nobody left to write to. I still read a great deal. Oh yes. I can read five books in a week. Any old time. [Laughs] Two a day sometimes. I'm a very fast reader. I don't have any special favorites. I just like fiction. Action. I like love stories and adventure. And everything. I just like to read. When I go to the library, I get maybe five or seven books, and I can read them pretty rapidly. But it's just hard getting to the library now that I don't drive myself. I go to the neighborhood library where I once worked. I enjoyed being a librarian, you know, helping people find what they wanted to

Mrs. Julia Bond

read. I remember one boy came in and I couldn't remember his name and he said, "You must remember me. I'm the one you found that book for." [Laughs] Of course I had found "that book" for hundreds of students.

What makes me happy is knowing that everything's going well and my children are okay. That makes me happy. I have eight grandchildren and seven great-grandchildren. I like ice cream a lot, too. [Laughs] I'm sad when somebody is in trouble or is hurt. A typical day for me is that I awake. I have breakfast and read the papers and probably read something else. Maybe I sit on the porch a little while if it's warm enough. I don't go walking by myself anymore. I wish I could. I'd like to walk up to the campus and sit on the bench. James and I used to walk up there every evening or walk around the block. You know, that was nice. For a while, a boy from Morehouse came to walk with me. The college would send someone, but they haven't arranged for that now. I look out of the window a lot.

I've wanted to do a lot of things, but it's too late now. I'd like to have left some mark. I'd like to have written something or done something that would be permanent, you know, something that people would remember. I wish I could have written a novel, yes. But I couldn't. I'm sure if I could have, I would have. It takes a lot of discipline. My greatest challenge has been surviving, I guess. I have done a lot of pushing, struggling and trying to be the best I can.

MRS. FAYE BUSH

Franklin County, Georgia

Community Activist

I guess I felt sorry for my father because he had diabetes. I would go to the field and ask him if I could plough for him. I did that when I was about seven or eight years old. I would try to plough because I felt sorry for him trying to work, him being sick. My father was a sharecropper all of his life. It wasn't easy being a sharecropper because you worked hard, and you never got what you deserved. You would have to give a certain part of the crop that you made to the landowner. It was hard being a sharecropper.

Mrs. Faye Bush

My full given name is Willie Faye Johnson Bush, and I was born on August 27, 1934 in Franklin County, Georgia. That's about fifty-two miles south of Newtown. My mother's name was Maggie Johnson. My father's name was Ace Johnson. My parents were sharecroppers, and that was a very hard life. I had two brothers and three sisters. I don't know how my parents met, and I don't know anything about how my mother was when she was pregnant with me or anything about how she delivered me because, back then, they kept those kinds of things a secret. They didn't tell you anything about that. They told you the doctor brought you in the little black suitcase. [Laughs]. And, you know, it's amazing, but we didn't pay women who were pregnant that much attention. We didn't notice when they were getting big because we thought the doctor brought babies in a little black suitcase. [Laughs]

I was kind of tomboyish when I lived in the country. My sister Drewnella painted her fingernails and looked pretty. I rode the wagon, and I did mischievous things. I was always wanting to do things in the field and that kind of stuff during the time when I was growing up. They called me Butned. [Laughs] I can't spell it, but it's pronounced But-Ned. [Laughs] They called me that because I was so mischevous. I stayed into stuff all the time. I played with dolls and things like that, but I also wanted to do things that men did. You know, like saw wood, cut wood, plough, and pick cotton. I guess I felt sorry for my father because he was sick. He had diabetes, and I would go to the field and ask him if I could plough for him. I did that when I was about seven or eight years old. I would try to plough because I felt sorry for him trying to work, him being sick. My father was a sharecropper all of his life. We grew corn, cotton, wheat, and also we grew sugar cane. We made our own syrups, you know. It wasn't easy being a sharecropper because you worked hard, but you never got what you deserved. It was hard being a sharecropper. But it was good growing up in the country because, back then, you had the love of your parents. You were close because you lived distant from your neighbors. When you sat down at the table, you always delivered a blessing. My father would sit at the head of the table, and we would bow our heads while he said the blessing.

Families were real close in Franklin County. Only about five or six hundred people lived there when I was growing up. We didn't have any stores like the ones you see in Newtown. We had little bitty stores, and they were all run by Whites. We would walk to the stores. In fact, we walked just about everywhere we went. We would go to the stores to buy eggs and salmon and bacon and fat back and sausage. We didn't buy vegetables because we grew our own. We also raised our own hogs. We had a wagon and that's what we would ride when we would go to Lavonia, Georgia. That's where we would go to shop for clothes. Lavonia was about thirty miles from where we lived in Franklin County. All of us rode the wagon. But we didn't buy too much when we went to Lavonia because my mother made our clothes. She would make them on a pedal sewing machine. She also crocheted and she quilted.

We got our water out of the well. You would have a bucket and a rope, a bucket on a rope, and you let it down in the well and you would wind it back and that's how you got your water. When the bucket came back up, you would have your water in it. Boys and girls would draw water out of the well. And we didn't have to boil the water because it wasn't like it is today where you have all the chemicals. We grew all of our food, you know, and we didn't use anything that was contaminated like it is today.

Our next-door neighbors in Franklin County were Whites, and we would share food with them. They were sharecroppers, too. Everybody in the country was a sharecropper. We were real close to the White children, and we played together until we got to a certain age. We got to where we couldn't play with each other. It made me think about the Dr. King story because, you know, we played together with our White neighbors until we got to be a certain age and then everyone went their separate ways, but you didn't understand what was really going on. I was a teenager, maybe about thirteen when this happened, and, really, you didn't think much about it. You didn't understand it, but you didn't question anybody back then why things were like that. I can remember the time when the storm used to come up and we used to have storm pits. We used to all go in the storm pits together, Blacks and Whites. And when it came a storm to kill us, we all would have died together. But then all of that changed when we got to be a certain age. We never understood why, you know. I mean, the children didn't understand, and your parents didn't get into too much of that to try to explain it either. I don't remember any racial incidents happening in the country, but I know the Klan was there. Well and alive. We didn't know who they were because they wore the hoods. They could have been your next-door neighbors for all you knew. That's the same thing that's happening now. You might know one or two of them, but there are others behind them you don't know.

We had a pretty small church, and it was called Harricane Grove. We had to go miles to get to the church, and the schoolhouse was in the yard of the church. People in the country were serious about religion back then because they were having a hard time, and they believed God would make it better for them. One Bible verse I remember and it's my favorite one is *God sent his son into the world not to condemn the world but the world through him might be saved.* When you joined the church, you were baptized in a little stream of water. They would dam it up and make a little pond out of it and that's where they would baptize you in. We would be baptized in blue jeans or pants of some kind because the water would get muddy with so many people going in it. You would be dipped in the water and then when you got back to church, people would sing songs. We didn't have a piano in the church. We used our hands, and we used our feet. You know, we would stomp on the wooden floor of the church. One song I remember they would sing after somebody was baptized was "Amazing Grace."

We had dirt streets when I first came to Newtown, and that was in 1948. I was fourteen, and I moved here to further my education. My sister moved to Gainesville, which was Newtown for us, when she was eighteen, and she got married. I remember when my sister had gotten pregnant with her first child. I didn't pay her any attention because I didn't know anything about her carrying a baby. You know, I didn't think that way. The only time we heard about how you got a baby was in school. Our teacher would talk about it a lot and talk about how you shouldn't date guys and take gifts from them, expensive gifts, because they would be expecting more from you. They did a lot of teaching like that in school. My parents stayed in the country until my father passed and then my mother and my sister and my brother moved here, too. As I said, I moved up here from the country after I finished the seventh grade, and I moved to get an education. Back there in Franklin County, our school only went to the seventh grade. It was one room and all the grades were in the same room. When my mother came here, she worked at the poultry plant. When I came here, that was a big change in my life, you know, because I had to get adjusted to city life, which was better than country life. I went to Saturday school to make friends because I didn't know anybody, and it was kind of hard. I can remember the time when I was ashamed to eat in front of the other kids. I would walk all the way home just to eat lunch. They made fun of me, you know. They made fun of the way I talked, you know. "Country girl." That's what they would call me. But when I got to know more kids, it was all right.

We had lights and running water here, but when we lived in the country, we had wells and lamps and things of that nature. It was very different in the city because you had water and lights, and you didn't have to worry about going to the well to try to get water. I told you how we would get our water from a well, and it was good, clean water. And the houses were close where in the country the houses were far apart. Here we could walk to each other's houses. We had to walk to school, though, and that took us about an hour. Black kids walked, and White kids were bussed. They would pass us as we walked and they would call us names and try to spit on us, you know. We would just keep walking. Only White children rode the bus, and I think poor White children rode the bus, too, because I didn't see any White children walking to school. Only Black kids.

When my sister Mozetta moved here, she worked at restaurants and in private homes. She was what you would call a domestic worker. She never talked much about her work except to tell me that she would clean up their houses, but still she couldn't go in the front door. She had to go to the back door, and she couldn't eat with them until they had finished eating. Then she could eat. I had the same experience when I worked as a domestic. Race was a little different in Gainesville because this was more of a city than Franklin Country. You still had some of the same problems like the Klansmen and jobs and all of that. Back then, the perfect

Mrs. Faye Bush

job we had was doing poultry work in the poultry plants. They didn't pay you that much money, but a little bit of money would go a lot further back then because things were less expensive. A lot of people worked in private homes, you know. I worked in private homes after school. I worked for two White families, and the relationship was all right. You just fit in their ways, the way you had to go to the back door. You couldn't eat with them and all of that. But as far as them being nice, they were pretty nice people. I would use the money I made to pay for school expenses, and I would help my mother some, too, because my father had passed and she was the only one working. When I came here, I lived with my sister and then when my mother moved here, I moved into a house with her.

My first job was working in White people's homes, and then I got a job at Georgia Broiler. That was a poultry plant. I worked in the poultry plant in the fifties. Blacks and Whites and women and men worked in the plant, but it was mostly Black people working there. At that time, we had to do most of the work by hands. We didn't have the machines they have now. We worked standing in water. It was hot in the summer and cold in the winter. One time we walked out because it was so hot in the plant. Well, what they did was to bring in blocks of ice and put it in the building. They put the fear in you about losing your jobs, so we went back to work because we didn't want to lose our jobs. The only time we could go to the restroom was on break time. And when we went, we had to carry a stick. If the stick was gone, you had to wait. We worked side by side with White workers, but we had to drink from Colored fountains and they drank from White fountains.

I met him, my second husband, Howard Bush, when I was working at a café on the south side. His sister introduced us. He was from Commerce, Georgia. I had three children when we met: Gregory Mize, Jackie Loretta Mize, and Jonathan Craig Butts. When Gregory was born, I had natural birth. There was one Black doctor here. His name was Dr. Butler, and his office was in Athens. He didn't live in Newtown, but he served all the Blacks. It took me all day to have Greg. I went into labor that morning, and I labored all day until about five o'clock.

Neighbors were just rejoicing over the child that was coming, you know. My mother and a neighbor named Miss Castleberry. They would come over and tell me to bear the pain. I would just say, "Ahh." [Laughs] They put me on the bed and every time I got a pain, they would pull down on my arm, you know, and tell me to breathe out. And, finally, at five o'clock (I'll never forget this), the doctor was running from my house to the house across the street because the house across the street had a television and the World Series was on. So, he would go over there and watch a little bit and then come back and check on me. I delivered Gregory during the time when the World Series was going on. The Dodgers was playing, and they won. Joe Black was the pitcher. The doctor told me if I named my child Joe Black, he would send in his name and every World Series I would get something. I said I don't want my child named no Joe Black. [Laughs] As I said, my son was born at home because, at that time, Blacks couldn't go to the hospital and have babies. But Jackie and Jonathan were born in the hospital. It was a lot different when they were born because you got pain pills to numb you and all that. It wasn't hard at all. But, you know, I think a lot of the young people are having natural births again. I was looking at a show on the Learning Channel and I see that a lot of people have started to go natural to have a child naturally because they believe it makes them more healthy. The same thing with breast feeding. I breast fed all of my children.

My life changed when I became a mother because I had more to focus on. I had children I had to raise and try to get them through school and I had to work, too. When I had Gregory, I had to stay in bed for nine days. I couldn't lift the baby for so many days. I couldn't lift water. Those were some of the things my mother taught. And she showed me how to do the navel, you know, to keep the baby from having a big navel. She showed me how to care for that. They used to have a band that you put around the stomach to hold that little navel in. They called it the "belly band." I remember when the nurse used to come by (because we used to have a nurse that would come by ever so often and would check on the babies for you), she would take the band off the baby's stomach and tell me he didn't need to wear it. As soon as she left, Mama would put the band back on his stomach. [Laughs] She showed me how to do that and

Mrs. Faye Bush

how to make a tea that would keep the baby's stomach from hurting. Basically, she just told me different things that I needed to do in order to take care of the baby. The tea was for colic. One was catsnip tea, which we would boil and strain and then dilute with water and put in the baby's bottle. My mother grew catnip. My mother believed in herbal things. Lord, let me tell you about castor oil. That's all she believed in!!! If you stomped your toe, they gave you castor oil [Laugh]. I don't remember growing up as a child ever going to a doctor. I was almost grown when I went to the doctor. My daddy used to get something like bone set tea and use pine needles to make tea out of it for colds. And he used to have a lot of different kind of things they used to rub in you. They used to take onions and make you a little pad out of that and put it on your chest. You know? Onions that you eat. Red onions. I remember seeing in California about two months when I went to a workshop there and there was a guy who carried us through the different areas to show us different kinds of herbs you can use and he said he believes in using natural herbs instead of so much medicine and pine needles was one of the herbs he showed us. And he showed us different kinds of barks, tree barks that you could get to make different kinds of teas out of. And you can make toothbrushes out of the barks. We didn't have toothbrushes while we were growing up. We would take a limb from an oak tree and make a toothbrush out of it. We brushed our teeth with baking soda instead of toothpaste. People didn't believe in New Year's washing. They said you washed someone out of the family. You know a lot of people still believe in some of that stuff.

I know you have read the book for your class, so you know how Newtown was created. It was built after the tornado of 1936, so it was twelve years old when I moved here. And then in 1990, we realized how many people in the community were dying and the way we noticed it was that when someone died, a young lady would go from door to door to take up money for community flowers. So, one of the gentlemen said, "Why don't you all start up a flower club?" So, that's how it started. It started in 1950. People would give ten cents a week for dues and we'd use that money to buy flowers and we also used it to do some of the work that agencies do now, like go in and bathe sick people and go to the store for them. We would go in and turn them. That's how the club got started. But, then, in the sixties, we got more involved into different issues like police brutality, the school issues and things of that nature. But we still did the same service that we had always done. When the policemen got to where they were arresting people illegally and they would just come and kick your door in and come into your house, we began to monitor that and speak out against it. And when they integrated the schools, we got involved in that issue because our kids were being uprooted from their school and going to a White school across town. We fought for recreation for our kids, too. We fought to have the old school become a recreation center. So, we kept meeting on that until we got them to do that. The club was all women, but we now have three men members, and they say the only reason they are in the club is to lift heavy stuff for us. [Laughs] There used to be a Newtown Men's Club, but it folded. I think we have stayed together because we have dedicated women who wanted to see a change. The men respect us, and they support what we do.

We did a door-to-door survey in 1990 and that's when we found a lot of people were dying from lupus and cancer and had respiratory problems and, you know, we noticed how many flowers we would buy for the people that died in the community and so we petitioned the State. And they came in and got information for us, and it was verified that the people had died from those different kinds of illnesses. Then, they came back and said the problem was our lifestyle. Drinking and smoking. But some of the people who died didn't even have a lifestyle, you know, because some of them died when they were young, from lupus. And you hear that in every city you go. Whites try to blame our dying on lifestyle rather than on the environment and all the chemicals they are putting into the environment. More White people smoke and drink than Blacks do. So, if the problem is lifestyle, everybody would be dying from lupus and cancer.

The fact of the matter is that our houses were built on top of a landfill. The old people told us this, but when we took this fact to the city, they denied it at first and the State supported the city. But when students from the University of Georgia did a soil test, they found lead and they found chromium and they found sulfuric acid in the soil, but the State was trying to cover

Mrs. Faye Bush

up for the city. And, then, there is pollution from factories, and that isn't just on our side of town. When the wind blows, it's on the other side, too. And we have a junkyard right in back of our houses. The closest factories are Purina and Cargill. And there is a scrap metal yard right at our back door. I think Purina came in the fifties, and, to tell you the truth, it has done more damage to us than the other factories because the grain dust used to be so heavy over here that when we came in from play, we would be covered in the dust. And the odor was real bad. The funny thing is that the factories never hired many people from Newtown. When the factories came, people thought there would be jobs, but the factories didn't hire that many of our people. They didn't have that many employees anyway, and they brought workers with them.

The regulation has gotten better. The companies had to change a lot of the ways they were emitting pollution into the air. They say they are staying within the guidelines, but if they are staying within the guidelines, why does Newtown have so much more over here? Sometimes, workers in the companies give us information. Like one company that had a spill and denied it? One of the workers told us the truth, and that meant almost getting fired. We filed a lawsuit against the company, but it was too late for us to do anything. We had to prove the amount of the spill, and we had the evidence, but the jury didn't want to work with us. So, it's still hard. There is still a problem. So, we need you young people to keep fighting.

All the plants we used to use to help us get well I am afraid to use today because the soil is contaminated. That's why people have miscarriages and breast cancer and lupus. I now boil my water, my drinking water, most of the time. And, then, there's the noise from the feed plants and the noise from the train that goes in back of us, close to where we live. It runs day and night, and that noise contributes to high blood pressure. So, we have been fighting against this pollution. We have been fighting since the seventies. This has been a major project of the Newtown Florist Club. My mother was one of the founders of the club. The other founders were Miss Ruby Wilkins, Miss Colina Castleberry, Miss Cecil Cleveland, Miss Laura Barnette, Miss Ruth Cantrell, Miss Elzora Davis, and my sister Mozetta. I became the president of the florist club in 1990.

The saddest moment in my life was when my son Gregory died. He died this past February. What got me through it was that they discovered my sister Mozetta has a tumor on her brain. Focusing on her got me through it. The happiest moment was when our book was published. To see it come off the press and to know that people could hear our story, that was a happy moment for me.

Blacks are better off today in many ways, but in other ways we are going backwards. Racism is being dressed up. I don't think Blacks and Whites will ever live together in peace, not in my lifetime. We need things to change. I am worried about the younger generation because more Black women are going to jail than ever before. I think this generation is turning its back on motherhood and family, and we need to keep that link. I worry that they are thinking too much about professions and making money. But I have hope that we will make it as a people. That hope comes from within, and it comes from young people like you.

DR. JUNE DOBBS BUTTS

Atlanta, Georgia

College Professor

Now how did I get the name June? That, too, is an interesting story. When I was born, my oldest sister Renie, who was twenty years old at the time, was spending the college at Middlebury College in Vermont, and she sent a telegram home because I was two weeks old already and didn't have a name. Because I was born in June, she said, "Why not name her June?" That's how I got my name. I used to tell her, "Thank God, I wasn't born in February."

My father, John Wesley Dobbs, was born in Kennesaw Mountain, Georgia, in 1882. He had a sister named Willie, who was four years older than he. His parents separated when he was two, and he never saw his father. I knew my paternal grandmother. We called her Nanny, and when I was growing up, she lived within walking distance of our house. My father paid her mortgage, but he didn't really want Nanny to live with us. You see, she was not an easy woman. She would come through the house and say, "Irene (that was my mother's name), these children don't need these sweaters. There is a poor old lady down in the lanes." She called alleys lanes. They don't have alleys now, but people used to live in alleys. Beggars would walk through the alleys and not on sidewalks. They would come into your backyard and just stand by the window until you gave them something like water in a jar or leftover food. Nobody had much then, but I never heard of anyone who didn't give food to a beggar. So, Nanny would say, "Irene, those people down in the lane need these sweaters more than your children," and she would take the sweaters to the people.

My dad would say, "Don't criticize my mother. She is a product of slavery." And she was. She was born during the Civil War. My grandmother's name was Millie Minerva Hendricks, and her mother was a cook on a plantation in Cobb County, Georgia. The owner, a medical doctor, and his wife didn't have children, and both of them liked Minnie very much because she was so very cute and so very smart. When she started to grow up, they said, "She's gotta get married." When she was twelve, her biological father found a man who was free and made arrangements for him to become engaged to her. When they married, she was fourteen and he was twenty-eight, so they had little in common. They had two children, one of whom was my father. Neither the husband nor the wife—I should say father or mother—stayed with the two children. First the father left, and I don't know where he went, or why. The mother later left. The two children were left in the care of their grandmother, Grandma Judie Dobbs, who took care of many of her grands. This lady had been given her freedom when she was twelve and was told that any children she had would be free. She had twelve children, and the first one was Will, the father of John Wesley and Willie. Over a period of seven years, their mother Minnie would come back, often at Christmas, to visit. When Willie was thirteen and Wes was nine, she returned and took them to Savannah with her—to help her work.

My mother was born in Columbus, Mississippi. Her name at birth was Irene Ophelia Thompson, and she was the third of five children. Her father was the only barber in town, and he cut hair for White men. However, on Thursday afternoon around four o'clock, he would close the shop and that's when Black men would come from all over the county. He would keep the shop open for them until past midnight. You see, at that time, Black and White couldn't be together in the shop. Let me explain how they came to be in Mississippi. My mother's grandmother was an Irish immigrant girl who, somehow, came to Atlanta. She worked at the Kimball House in Atlanta and fell in love with a free man named Levi Thompson. They both worked at the Kimball House. Her name was Lenore. We don't know her last name. They went to Mississippi to marry because they heard that racial matters were a bit easier there, but when Mississippi passed Blue Code laws, conditions got much worse. By this time, they had four children. Two children remained Negro, and two passed for White. Kelly Thompson, my mother's father, did not pass for White. He married a free woman named Mattiwilda Sykes, and they had five children. My mother was the third child. She was color conscious, but she wasn't color- prejudiced like Nanny. She didn't look White, but she didn't look Black either. My mother wouldn't say the word "Black." She would say "dark."

When she finished the academy (high school), she wanted to teach, but her father wouldn't let her. He said, "You will get lost there in rural Mississippi." Hearing this story years later, I thought he meant she had no sense of direction. You have to understand that Black women had no recourse then. If a White man came up and grabbed you, what could you do? What recourse did you have? What recourse did your parents have? So in order to protect Irene, my grandfather sent her to Atlanta to help her older married sister take care of her children. Her sister eventually had nine children. Irene came to Atlanta in her late teens. She married my father when she was twenty-one and he was twenty-four. They were married on June 6, 1906. In fact they had just gotten married when the Atlanta Race Riot began.

You know, it's interesting that we talk about the riot, but rarely do we talk about what caused the riot. There was such a cover-up that it is hard to define what actually happened. As I understand it, there was a red light district on Decatur Street, and that's where Black and White prostitutes worked. The men who went to the brothels were White, but the piano players were Black. You seem surprised that there were pianos in brothels. You have to keep in mind that there were no records or DVDs at the time. Besides, Johannes Brahms used to play in a brothel. [Laughs] I think prostitutes who had been serving White men started having sex with Black men. The men started fighting, and the riot got under way. The men who were involved were not considered Atlanta's finest citizens. As it spread, the Klan got called in, and this is where there was a cover up. The riot lasted for four days. A French journalist wrote about the riot and sketched pictures that were printed in France. As a result of this publicity, Atlanta became international, but certainly not in a positive way.

I don't know whether or not my dad was in the city when the riots took place because he traveled a lot as a railway mail clerk on the Nashville and Atlanta. He was required to have a gun because he was chief clerk in charge, but he said that he never wanted to kill anybody. My father was intent on protecting Black women, and he felt that my mother's sister, nicknamed Nooks, really needed protection because her beauty attracted attention. Daddy said Mama was pretty, but he said Nooks was just plain beautiful. White men, driving in their carriages, would stop and ask her to get in. Daddy would sit on the front porch waiting for Nooks and if a White man started up the steps, he would stand up with gun in hand. My mother was ashamed to have that story mentioned because, to her, it was degrading.

My parents had six daughters spread over twenty years. No boys! And Dad was disappointed that all six of us were girls. During that time, women had their babies at home because what few facilities were available to Black women were usually death camps. People with severe diseases went there, and the facilities were so unsanitary. I was the youngest of the six girls. All of us have interesting names, and that reflects a tradition in our family, and probably in most Black families: naming children for people in your family or people whom you admired. The first daughter was named after my mother, Irene. The second one was named after our grandfather. His name was Will. Her name is Willie. And the third was named Millie for my father's mother. My sister Millie hated that name because it rhymed with Willie, so she changed her name legally to Millicent. We called her "Millie," and she liked that. She taught at Spelman. The first daughter, Irene, also taught at Spelman. After Millie, there was Josephine, whom we called Josie. She was named for my father's nephew Joseph. And then there was Mattiwilda. There's an interesting story about this name. My mother's mother had two names, Mattie and Wilda, so my mother dropped the 'e' from Mattie and put the two names together and made Mattiwilda. Isn't that creative? When I was a little girl, I called Mattiwilda G-e-e-k-i-e. I couldn't say the "Wilda" part of her name, so I would say "Weeky." I changed it to Geekie, and that became her nickname. I once said to Mattiwilda, "We're old ladies now, so don't you think it's childish to be called Geekie?" And she said, "No, I like it. I like it better than Mattiwilda." Now how did I get the name June? That, too, is an interesting story. When I was born, my oldest sister Renie, who was twenty years-old at the time, was spending the college at Middlebury College in Vermont, and she sent a telegram home because I was two weeks old already and didn't have a name. Because I was born in June, she said, "Why not name her June?" That's how I got my name. I used to tell her, "Thank God, I wasn't born in February." [Laughs]

I was born in a hospital, actually in an infirmary, owned by a Spelman graduate by the name of Dr. Georgia Dwelle. My dad and other men thought she was uppity because she married three times and never changed her name and also because she acquired a lot of money. She had a school of nursing, so she gave back to the community. My mother thought Dr. Dwelle was heaven on earth! Dr. Dwelle delivered Mattiwilda and me at the hospital. Josephine was born on Spelman's campus at MacVicar Infirmary. The older daughters were born at home. When my mother was carrying Mattiwilda, she was very depressed because, you see, pregnant women didn't go out in society once they were obviously pregnant. You were "confined." You stayed at home, even if you were married. So, as unbelievable as it sounds, pregnancy was considered shameful. Also, when my mother was pregnant with Mattiwilda, she was forty, and she felt so grossly big and so much older than other women who were pregnant at that time. A lady who had eight children, Mrs. Nabrit, a friend of Mama's, came to visit my mother and to talk to her. She said, "Mrs. Dobbs, this child is going to make you proud. All of your children will be fine, but this child you're carrying right now is going to make you proud!" The child my mother was carrying was Mattiwilda, and she makes all of us proud. She became the first Black singer in opera at several places and the third Black singer at the Metropolitan Opera House: Marian Anderson, Robert McFerrin, and then Geekie, in that order. I thought her voice was the most beautiful voice I had ever heard. When people passed our house and heard Mattiwilda practicing piano and singing, they would say, "That girl sho can sing."

My father could be an austere person, but he was very good-hearted. He had to stick to what he believed in. He made ninety percent of the decisions in our home, and if my mother disagreed, she would talk with him behind closed doors. I never saw her really argue with him and certainly not about anything pertaining to the girls. He had his own strict views, but when I was growing up, I thought he was very authoritarian. He did not let us play with boys. I'll give you an example. Once, when I was nine years old, my cousins, my best friends, my sister Geekie, and I went to a camp named after John Hope, President of Morehouse and Atlanta University. The camp, which was located in Fort Valley, Georgia, was for Black girls, and we were going to spend a month there. Two weeks after we had arrived, Dad happened to be in the area, and he came by to see us. When he saw boys at the camp, he asked, "Where did these boys come from? " I told him, "Oh, their camp is across the river, and we share the same dining hall, and then at night we all flip a coin to see who goes to the showers first." That night, we were back in Atlanta! My father was very distrustful of boys. As I said, he was very strict and my mom backed him up because she believed the man should be "head of the house."

Dr. June Dobbs Butts

My mother admired women who were educated. When I was in grad school, I was learning to do tests and measurements, and I did a lot of practice on children's intelligence tests and then adults'. I mean it wasn't all that valid, but I gave a test to my mother and to my father. He beat around the bush so much, he wouldn't give the precise answer, and he lost points for that. My mother came right to the point. Zip! That was it. Neat and clear. She was a very intelligent woman, and that was a shock to me because, at the time, I didn't think of her as bright.

Both of my parents were very good people and they were very wise and they were unpretentious. You couldn't faze them with styles and fashions. They were interested in the dynamics that were much deeper. My dad believed women should be educated in case their husbands didn't measure up, or died, and the woman had to work. He believed a woman's place was in the home. I think it might have been after I married, through my husband, that I realized my dad was very proud of me. He actually admired my asking questions and talking about "unpopular things." It embarrassed him, but he was proud of me. There is a story associated with how I came to know this, and it has to do with my honeymoon, which was at the Walluhaje here in Atlanta. Daddy told Hugh, my husband, that he would make him a Mason as quickly as he could. And I thought, "Not on my honeymoon." The initiation took two nights! Hugh had to spend time away from me at the Masonic Temple on Auburn Avenue. Much to my surprise, he was very interested in becoming a Mason and, of course, that pleased my dad immensely. A few days after we married, actually while we were driving to New York, Hugh said, "Your dad really loves you." I think my dad was determined that he would have no favorites, probably because he had heard about parents having favorites. He would often say, "I treat all my children the same, and I love them all the same." We would tease him and say, "Renie is your favorite." She could do no wrong in his eyes.

Mattiwilda attended David T. Howard, which was a public school across the street from my house. I was three at the time, but I would go to school with her and sit with her in her chair. The teacher would say sit "piece ways" in the chair. It was not uncommon then for younger children to go to school with older siblings. But that changed when a law was passed that required you to be at least six when you went to school. I enrolled at David T. Howard when I was five. Everything was going well until a girl I played with was sent home because she was five, and her mother, knowing my age, told school authorities I had to be sent home as well. My mother said I couldn't stay home. My father took out two loans and sent Mattiwilda and me to Oglethorpe Elementary School, which was a part of Atlanta University. She was in the fourth grade; I was in the first. I remember that there was a long streetcar ride from the northeast, where I lived, to the southwest, where the school was located. I would catch the bus in our neighborhood, and it would take me straight to school. I knew where to get off.

From Oglethorpe, I went to the Atlanta University Laboratory High School, which we called Lab High. It was located in Giles Hall on the Spelman campus. The kids who went to Booker T. Washington High School, the public school, would say, "Oh you go to the lavatory high school." Mattiwilda's class was the last class to finish at Lab High. You see, Spelman wanted its building back. Spelman was Ms. Read. Ms. Florence Read. I know you've heard of her. She was very dictatorial. She felt that Spelman needed Giles Hall, and the Black community should provide something else for Black children. If the city of Atlanta didn't have standard education for Blacks, Blacks should start a private school. She wanted her building back! So, she gave them a deadline, and then she reclaimed her property. When Lab High closed, we felt that was the end of the world.

With Lab High no longer in existence, I had to go elsewhere and elsewhere was Booker T. Washington High School because it was the only high school for Black kids in the city and in the county. Many of my friends went away to boarding schools up east, but my parents couldn't afford to send me away to school. Washington High was horrendous. It was so crowded. There were two thousand of us, and it was fully hell. I was very ready to leave Washington High. So, I took advantage of early admission into college. You see, there was an effort (this was during Word War II) to rush guys into the army and the way to do that was to give them an exam and if they passed, they would skip the twelfth grade and go directly to college. When women

Dr. June Dobbs Butts

started signing on for the women's military service, like the WACs, the exam was opened to girls. I took the exam and that's how I sailed into Spelman at the age of sixteen. That's how Martin Luther King went to Morehouse when he was really fifteen and a half.

I entered Spelman in 1944, and I finished in 1948. I was an honor graduate and President of the Senior Class. There were strict rules at Spelman. One was that visiting hours were over at five-thirty p.m. I had to live on campus my senior and when I would go home to visit my parents, I had to be back on campus before five thirty in the evening. And if you lived in the city, you couldn't go home every week. The result of so many of the restrictions was that we learned how to slip off from campus. We called it "creeping." We'd pretend that we were going to the AU library, and then we'd go into the most horrible little places—College Park and East Point and places around Morehouse. It was an adventure! We did a lot of creeping.

When I finished Spelman, I went to Teachers College at Columbia University. I entered in 1948 and I lived in the Emma Ransom House of the YWCA, located in Harlem. Mattiwilda and I roomed together and what is interesting is that we stayed in the very same room my sister Millicent and Josephine had stayed in when they lived in New York. Speaking of New York makes me remember the time Mattiwilda, my mom and I went to New York with my dad. I was nine years-old. We were at the YWCA going down the steps and Dr. W. E. B. DuBois was going up the steps. He was rushing. My dad said, "Dr. DuBois, I want you just to shake my little girls' hands." Dr. DuBois said, "I'm sorry, Dobbs. I haven't time." He tipped his hat and he zoomed on away. My dad was so crushed by that, so very crushed. I said, "Daddy, what's the matter?" He said, "I just wanted him to shake your hands." I said, "But, Daddy, he really didn't have time." I accepted that and let it go. I knew Dr. DuBois was a prominent person, but I didn't know whether he was White or Black. He didn't look all that White, but, then, I thought that a lot of people who were White were actually Black. I thought they were Black because they went to our church or they worked at A.U. or they were around us. From first grade on, I had White people who were my teachers, and I thought they were the "good White people" because White people in stores and on streetcars were not nice.

When I finished Teachers College in 1949, earning a Master's in vocational guidance, I remained in New York and got a job at the YMCA Vocational Service Center, but when my mother's sister died (we called her Aunt Sis), I returned to Atlanta to stay with Mama. Actually, I returned because Mama called and asked me to return. You see, she was having a difficult time with her sister's death, and she wanted me to be home with her. I was the only daughter she asked to come – perhaps because I was freer than my sisters. Mattiwilda was studying voice, and the other sisters were married. When my became stronger and was able to go on, I told my father that I needed to start looking for a job and, that summer, I sent out applications for a job. I was offered a teaching position at Fisk University. I went there in the fall of 1950.

I lived in Nashville from 1950 to 1953, and during that time I had a number of jobs in higher education. I taught in the psychology department at Fisk University, did counseling and worked part-time on a research project on norms for babies directed by E. Perry Crump, M.D., Head of Pediatrics at Meharry. The project was very interesting. Dr. Crump believed that Black babies were different from White babies, and he was trying to establish norms that reflected those differences. Bone formation, eye coordination, reflexes for grasping—these were some of the things he studied. I was one of his assistants. He asked me to stay on with the project when I went to Tennessee A & I State University full-time.

I was teaching at Fisk when I met Hugh F. Butts, whom I later married. Actually, I met him in the faculty dining hall at Fisk. He had finished Meharry in 1953, and we were married three days later, on my birthday. His parents, who were from British Guyana, flew down from New York for the graduation and the wedding. I will always remember how my mother helped me on my wedding day, which was also my twenty-fifth birthday. She made it very special for me by telling me, "You've got to honor yourself, not just your wedding. You're twenty-five, and that's a beautiful time of life." That was a very nice and generous attitude. I became pregnant with my first child in 1955, and I was very excited. I wanted natural childbirth because I didn't want medicine affecting the baby. I have three children: Lucia Irene, Florence Dobbs

Dr. June Dobbs Butts

and Eric Hugh. My husband didn't want a junior. I felt real privileged to be a mother. I had a good marriage, but a bad divorce. My mother died at the time that my marriage was falling apart, and I think that is one of the reasons I grieved her death more than I did my father's death. His seemed more natural. My father died in 1961; I divorced Hugh in 1971, and my mother died in 1972.

In 1973, I began teaching at the University of Massachusetts at Amherst in the Division of Health Sciences. I left the University in 1975 to join the staff of Masters and Johnson, the noted sex researchers, in St. Louis, Missouri. I was the only African American they had trained. After Masters and Johnson, I worked at Howard University College of Medicine for five and a half years. During that time, I came to understand the nexus of biology and culture, not merely on the professional level, but up close and personal. I had to face my own alcoholism, an addiction I'd been in denial about for most of my adult life. In 1988, I joined Alcoholics Anonymous. I'm very glad and grateful for these eighteen years in AA, and I'm proud to be a certified addictions counselor. You know, if alcohol were brought as a chemical to Food and Drug Association, it wouldn't be licensed for sale in restaurants. It's too powerful!!! I have had almost eighteen years of sobriety, and that makes me absolutely happy. But all you really have is one day at a time.

MRS. ANN COOPER

Bedford County, Tennessee

Community Volunteer

When I was born, my mother said to the midwife, "I can't think of a double name for her." And that old lady said, "Well, name her after me." She was an old White lady, and her name was Annie Lou Mullins. All those White people thought they were rich. I guess they were rich. There was one I thought was just pretty and rosy. She wasn't one of those burned, ruddy White women. She was just pretty and rosy. Her name was Miss Louise. I didn't like Annie Lou, but I liked the name Louise because I liked Miss Louise. After so long, I went and asked my mother if I could just take that "ie" off my name and add "se" and just be named "Ann Louise." So that's the name I go by. Ann Louise.

Mrs. Ann Cooper

I was born on in January 1902 in Bedford County, Tennessee, but my parents, I think, were born in Shelbyville, Tennessee. My mother's name was Mollie George, and my father's name was James Henry Nixon. The way my family name became Nixon is that when my father's parents were freed, the master said they could become Browns or Nixons. They chose Nixon. My parents had eight children, and I was way down, almost to the last. There were seven girls and one boy. My mother named the oldest girl Bessie Margaret. It's a double name, Bessie Margaret. The next one was Mary Elizabeth, and the next was Willie Lee and the next was Joyce Etta and the next was Grace. There might have been two Elizabeths. Grace was named Grace Elizabeth, and she is eighteen months older than I am. And then I came along.

When I was born, my mother said to the midwife, "I can't think of a double name for her." And that old lady said, "Well, name her after me." She was an old White lady, and her name was Annie Lou Mullins. Well, that's what my mother came up with. She named me Annie Lou. The midwife said, "Well, name her after me." All those White people thought they were rich. I guess they were rich. There was one I thought was just pretty and rosy. She wasn't one of those burned, ruddy White women. She was just pretty and rosy. Her name was Miss Louise. Well, I didn't like the name my mother gave me. I didn't like Annie Lou, but I liked the name Louise because I liked Miss Louise. After so long, I went and asked my mother if I could just take that "ie" off my name and add "se" and just be named "Ann Louise." So, that's the name I go by. Ann Louise. I was the baby for four years, and I was so spoiled. I don't know why everybody pampered me all those years, but it dawned on me that I was a baby for four whole years. My brother was four years younger than I. My older sisters pampered me, and I followed my mother everywhere she went.

My father was a sharecropper, but I didn't know anything about any sharecropping. I never heard of my father having to share anything with anybody, but I understand now sharecroppers had to give half of what they raised to whoever owned the farm. As I said, I didn't know what a sharecropper was. I remember my daddy would come home with a little money. Everybody had trunks then, not cedar chests, but trunks, and my father would put his little money in a trunk. It didn't matter how much because we had everything we needed. We had chickens, pigs, one horse, and one cow. We had all the milk we needed. At nighttime, we had a great big fireplace, and we would burn a big log that looked like part of a tree, you know. We didn't know anything about coal or anything. Whatever work he was doing, Papa would come home on time. We didn't have clocks then. We went by the sun. That's how we'd know when it was time for Papa to come home. Mama always had something good on the stove. Sometimes on Sundays, we would have chicken, and Mama would say, "Catch that chicken." We would wring the chicken's neck and put the chicken in boiling water and, of course, we would pluck away the feathers. I'm a little bitty thing watching them do this to chickens. Isn't that something? We had a garden, and we'd dig what we'd call new potatoes or red potatoes. We would dig them up. We would put them in a pan of water and scrape them. I never liked to scrape them. It took so much time for all of us. I remember Mama would sit us down with a pan of water, and everybody got to scrape.

My father's brothers lived near Nashville and were working in Nashville. They were trying to get all of us out of Bedford County, which was out in the country. However, we had all been born there and were the happiest family you ever heard of, you know? I remember there was a little White girl in Gallatin, which was thirty-eight miles from Nashville, that I used to play with. There were no other children for her to play with. Her family knew all of us in my family who were down there in Bedford County. So, they said to send somebody that little girl's age for her to play with, and I was the one chosen to go and play with that girl. One Christmas, Santa Claus brought her a pony, and she had to be taught to ride the pony. I rode on the back of the pony when she was learning. Many years later, after I had become an adult, I went to Nashville and I went to the house where the White family had lived and we talked about things that happened when we were small. I didn't recognize her, and she didn't recognize me, but I was thinking she was that little girl I had played with. So, finally, I asked her if Santa Claus had brought her a pony one Christmas and she said, "Yes," and I said, "Do you remember the little girl that rode behind you on the pony?" She said, "Yes." I said, "Well, that was me!" We had a great get-together off of that. We just hugged each other.

I wish I knew how my parents met. I guess they were very young when they married because my father's oldest brother signed for them. I got that in the research I did. I always wanted to know how we were living out in the country and my mother was having babies and her people didn't come to see us. I'm thinking that maybe she and my father got married so young that her family didn't approve of it. I wanted to know badly enough to get someone to do some research. That's how I learned that one of my father's brothers signed for them to marry. We don't know very much about my mother's background. All I know is that my mother was strickened away from home and never regained consciousness. I guess they buried her the next day. In those days, there wasn't embalming and all that sort of thing. So, they buried you right away. None of her family came to the funeral. I guess those who came to see her buried lived very near.

I had just turned eleven when she died, and she died on January 13th. She had made herself a nice dress and she had gone off to thank folks in the neighborhood for Christmas gifts, and she was strickened away from home. I wonder how in the world they brought her home. They brought her from up the hill or someplace. I didn't see them when they brought my mother home. So, I don't know how they got her home. All I can remember is they shut all of the children back in the kitchen. My daddy came stumbling down the steps and he was crying. He said, "She died." Well, how come Mama died, you know, when I'm Mama's baby? She never regained consciousness. I can remember seeing them putting my mother down in the ground. It was a black casket with silver handles and everything. And to realize that my mama was in there and they put her down in the ground. That's when I fell apart.

They had to decide what to do about each child, and they had to separate my brother and sisters and me. We went to different people. I was sent to Aunt Joyce, but she was not my blood aunt. She was the wife of my father's oldest brother, Uncle Jerry, and I don't know how Aunt Joyce and Uncle Jerry got together because he was a traveling man with race horses or something. She was not a blood relative, but she was the one I went to when my mother died. I had somebody to look into all of this, and that's how I found out where my Aunt Joyce lived when my mother died. When I learned about all this from some research I had somebody do for me, I thought, "This is where I grew up." And it was very exciting to me. The house was on Tenth Avenue in Nashville, between Eighth Avenue and Division Street. My aunt, you know, owned that house and that took care of her and my aunt's mother. We called her Granny. She was a big White woman, what they called a Mulatto, and they weren't the kind that got out and worked on the farms. They were house servants. Granny had one brother, and I have pictures of him. He was a handsome White man. I think maybe he went for White, but Aunt Joyce didn't go for White. She stayed in the neighborhood where her father had gone, and the house accommodated Aunt Joyce and her sister. That would be Aunt Bess. Aunt Bess was just an old White-looking woman, just what you would call a cracker, with stringy hair and always sunburned. She had a hump shoulder. She didn't look like Aunt Joyce. Aunt Joyce was a dressed-up lady all the time. I have pictures of her when she was really dressed up. [Shows a framed picture] Aunt Bess never looked like anything like that, but she was a nice person. She had to stay home to look after her mother. We called her Granny, and, as I said, she was a great big fat White woman. I thought she weighed about three hundred pounds. They said she was not White, but evidently Granny had been married to a Black man because Aunt Joyce had some mighty handsome, brown-skinned brothers. I have pictures of them, but I also have pictures of her White brothers. Handsome White men with "a drop of Black blood," as the saying goes. I knew a number of them. They would come from way out around California and places like that ever so often to see Granny. She was a member of the White church downtown.

Let me try to put this story together for you. Aunt Joyce's father was one of the old master's children. And when he grew up, he became the master's valet. The old master was fond of him. When he had twelve beautiful children, he told the old master that he wanted to leave the plantation so that his children could go to school and be able to get jobs. Old master gave him five hundred dollars and freedom. Understand, they were living on the plantation, and it seems that some were house servants and some were field servants. Aunt Joyce's father went

Mrs. Ann Cooper

to Nashville because the plantation wasn't so far outside the city of Nashville. He went to Nashville and bought a place, a residence, for his family to live in. That's why Aunt Joyce was in Nashville and that's where I grew up after my mother died.

Aunt Joyce had a daughter named Irene, and Irene was thirteen years old when I was born. So, she was already in school in Nashville when I got there, but Aunt Joyce took me under her wing. Her daughter Irene taught public school in Nashville, and Aunt Joyce was the maid for the family that owned the big bank in Nashville, First National Bank. So, she was well known at every department store. All I needed to do was say, "Charge it to Joyce Nixon." Nobody knew whether she was White or Black. She could call the Mayor of Nashville and all she had to say was, "This is Joyce. This is Joyce." I remember when the White family got an automobile and a Black man had to come and teach everybody how to drive. It was a Pierce Arrow.

When school closed for the summer, we went to the White folks' country home. It was located in Elmwood, Tennessee, and it was a big estate. Everything was there. Animals, chickens, peacocks, and a lot of land. Aunt Joyce was in charge of thirty odd servants, and the servants had their own living quarters and everything. Aunt Joyce and Uncle Jerry had their own place, and they had to share a bath that was down the hall. I'll always remember a big clock-like thing was out in the entrance in the back with all the room numbers in the house, you know. If a bell rang for number ten, you had to go. Aunt Joyce would let me go around in the house with her. She was a very special woman.

I was living in Nashville when I met my husband, Albert Berry Cooper, Jr. He was in dental school at Meharry. I was seventeen, and he had already turned twenty. He had been there at Meharry two years before I met him. They were drafting all those young men, taking them out of college, you know, and somebody had an idea that there should be a way for young men out of college to meet young girls. So, there was a dancing class formed in the afternoon, and my cousin Irene would take me to those dancing classes. I'd go on Saturday afternoons. One young man in this class would travel around in the summers, you know, and find out what dances were popular and then he would teach them to us. They weren't ballroom dances. They were more like the Electric Slide or something like that, you know. As a matter of fact, I just did the Electric Slide recently at a party for my birthday. I am one hundred and two.

Well, my husband saw me dancing with someone and by that time he was a junior, you know, at Meharry, and the young man I was dancing with just couldn't keep up. My husband came and took me away from him, and we danced. We were wearing high-top shoes then, and I had some dance shoes with light tan satin tops, laced up. I had little bitty feet and legs. My husband noticed that. That was in December. He asked me if he could have my telephone number and my name. I said, "Yes." My cousin, Aunt Joyce's daughter Irene, had a party every December, and I asked him to come if she would let him. He said he'd be glad to come, but then he called me and said he had a chance to go home to Georgia and he was sorry that he couldn't come, but could he come to see me when he got back? There was a woman that he had been carrying around, and I guess he felt obligated to her. She had gotten a job in Kentucky, and she had written him that she was coming home for December and she expected him to carry her around. Well, he felt obligated to her. I have to give him credit. As young as he was, he was still a gentleman. But my feelings were hurt.

My cousin Irene had married a young dentist and we were all living in the house and he was running my life, acting like my daddy, you know. Well, anyway, when A.B. [that's what I called my husband] came back to Nashville, we started seeing each other. And the more we saw each other, the more he decided he didn't want me to see anybody else. So, he said, "That's it. Shoo everybody away." Well, that went on until it was time for him to graduate. He didn't know where he was going. In those years, nobody had any money and nobody had any jobs. His father and his mother were Atlanta University graduates, and they had taught all around. When his daddy came to see him get that degree, he talked to a man who ran a newspaper here, a Black man, and had him stand for my husband to get a loan from Citizen's Trust. It had just opened up in 1921. My husband was probably the first one to get that kind of loan from Citizen's Trust.

Mrs. Ann Cooper

When my husband left Meharry, he made me promise to write him every day and all that sort of thing. Let me think now. I didn't hear from him, I think, for about ten days. Finally, he called and said, "I am practicing dentistry." He didn't let me hear from him until he was ready to go to work. The next month, he called and said, "I made five hundred dollars last week! Oh boy! We don't have to wait until Christmas to get married!" He was becoming a rich man now. [Laughs] Well, you know, practicing dentistry in those days, I guess, was about extractions and plate work, and I don't know what else dentists had learned to do. But, in no time, his practice had taken off, and he was doing well. [Takes picture from table] That's me with my husband. This is the picture he had to go and get for the graduation program when he finished Meharry. He said to me, "Now, you put on your prettiest dress because I'm going to take you with me to get your picture made so I'll have it to bring with me." And so, there we were, you see? He always liked me in red or something loud. I really don't know why. After we were married, he would come home at lunchtime, and he would say, "You are going to put on your loudest things." He was crazy about flowers and all colors. "So, go put on something red." This was my favorite dress. Maybe that's why I have preserved it. I just told Zelma [Payne] I hadn't seen it since my husband's death, and he's been dead more than thirty years. He died in 1967. This was my favorite dress, and I've taken care of it all these years. I saw it the other day and said, "I'm gonna put this on." So I thought I would wear it when you came over.

My husband graduated in 1922, we married in 1922, and I moved to Atlanta after we married. This is my husband's high school diploma. The date is 1916. That's sheep's skin, I think. He graduated from that branch of Morris Brown that was located in a town called Cuthbert. I never went there, but my husband's father and mother ran that school. I understand that when people finished that school, they came to Morris Brown. That's where Edith, my husband's sister, went to school and graduated. So, we married in 1922 and moved to Atlanta in 1922. When we moved to Atlanta from Nashville, we were living with a doctor and his wife and we were paying five dollars a week to live in a room and have use of the kitchen. I know folks cannot imagine how that is. You're cooped up in somebody's one room and you got use of the kitchen and the bathroom. But anyway, I thought, "Now here I am in this lady's house and I don't know anybody and don't have any interest in anything." I knew I needed to get out of there; I needed a job. My husband had always said he didn't want his wife to work because his father was an AME minister and wherever his father went, his mother had to go and live in the parsonage the church had for them. My husband, being the oldest child, had to stay home and take care of his siblings. His parents came home at the end of the week. So, that's why he didn't want me to work.

But what was I going to do? There I was in a strange town, a strange house, no friends, no nothing. But I insisted on getting a job, and my husband finally agreed to let me. I could type and take shorthand, Gregg shorthand, and my husband remembered the woman who worked with his parents at Morris Brown. She was the first Black librarian around here I think. Her name was Miss Alice W. Terry, and she had retired and was living in one of the Atlanta University buildings. She was the one who told me how I should go about looking for a job. I didn't weigh one hundred pounds. People would say, "You're too little to teach school." I didn't teach school. I hadn't been to college or anything. Back then, most women didn't go to college right away. They finished high school, but they didn't go to college right away. They married and started families. In those days, I think Tennessee's education was a little beyond Georgia's education because my cousin, Aunt Joyce's daughter Irene, had finished twelfth grade high school in 1908. She finished at Pearl High and then went to a school in Nashville called Walden University. You could go to Walden and take two years, and then you could teach in the public school system. So, that's what my cousin did. In Atlanta, women could get jobs in insurance companies, you know, and that's where I ended up working. I had to see how many weeks behind people were in paying their premiums. That's all you had when you got sick, you know? Your insurance would pay because we didn't have Medicare and all that. When the company saw that I could write in many different fancy ways, they started keeping me overtime writing names on policies. Now that is something that I enjoyed doing. I don't remember, but I'm sure I was paid a small sum weekly, and out of that I paid the room rent, you know, every week. I was paid five or six dollars a week and two dollars extra overtime writing those names on the policies. So, you see, I was making big money then. [Laughs]

Well, of course, by the time I got to enjoying work, I was pregnant and I was sick as a dog. They gave me medication, but I couldn't retain it. So, I had to come home. I think I might have been able to work, not a whole year. When I got pregnant the first time, and that was in 1924, my husband said we had to have a house. We bought one of the new houses that had been built over on Mason Turner. All of my children were born while we were living in that house: Gwendolyn Yvonne. We got her name out of a magazine my husband's cousin Ella Mae found. Joyce Nixon, who was named after Aunt Joyce. Albert Barry Cooper, the Third. He was named after my husband, who was named after his father. And Ann Marie. She was named after me and after Marie Brown, who was the wife of E. Franklin Frazier, who was head of the Atlanta University School of Social Work.

How we came to move to this house is interesting. It was built for a man who asked for so many changes that it cost more than he wanted to pay, or could afford to pay and when the house was finished, he wouldn't touch it. The house had been built, but the man didn't want it. So, somebody told us to look at this house. We did, and we liked it. So, we didn't have to build our house. We bought this one. Brand new. We've been here for sixty-odd years.

Well, of course, there was segregation when we first moved here. There was segregation everywhere in Atlanta. Hospitals didn't admit Black people. My first two children were born at home. It wasn't until my son was born that we had Black hospitals. We could go to White doctors, but we sat in separate waiting rooms and if there were no rooms, we would stand in the hall. I remember taking my daughter Gwen to a White doctor for breathing problems that came from her being born in an unheated house. We stood in the hall. This doctor had a colored receptionist and I went up to her and told her, "This is the last time I'm going to bring my daughter here. You tell that doctor I will not keep my daughter standing out here. You remind him that his services have already been paid for." She said, "I don't blame you." But there was nothing she could do. When I got home and told my husband what happened, he said I shouldn't have left and shouldn't have spoken the way I did. In Nashville, where I grew up, things never got so bad that you couldn't see a Black doctor. I wasn't quite accustomed to being treated like we were treated down here. That went on and on everywhere you went.

We used to have trolleys in Atlanta, and one stopped right up the street there at the railroad, where the trestle goes across there. When the trolley got here, you had to get off because the driver had to turn the trolley around and go back to town. Nobody colored much lived out beyond me then. Our house was the last one on the street. There are many houses now way up the street, but our house was the last one. So, I would be the last person on the trolley because this was the last stop and there were no houses past this one. This old White man who drove the trolley would hop out the front door and turn the trolley around. I would be sitting behind him, up front. So, one day he wasn't driving. There was a new man, a younger man. He went out the front door to turn the trolley around, and I went right out behind him. He said, "Nigger, you get back on that bus and go out that back door!" I thought, "I'm already on the ground." But somehow I never was afraid of them because I'd grown up with them, you know? I said to myself, "Now any other lady would just keep walking." He was talking about, "Nigger, you hear me?" I said, "You and who else gonna make me get back on the trolley?" How foolish would I look getting back on, running through, and getting out the back door? But, anyway, he thought he could make me do that. I told him, "Look, my husband will be driving along here after awhile. If he catches you near me." [Laughs] I didn't do what he asked me to do. He was an old cracker. I'm not sure how White people came to be called crackers. Most of the ones I knew were poor. I don't know where the name came from. Maybe because they had no color, and so they were like a soda cracker. But that's how it was here in Atlanta.

You know, we couldn't get a charge account in any of the stores in anything but your full name. When I would try to open a charge account at Rich's, I would get angry. The White woman would ask, "What is your name?" So, for example, you might say, "Well, I want it in

Mrs. Ann Cooper

Mrs. A.B. Cooper." "What is your name? What is that 'B' for? What is your name? Is it Annie Belle?" This would make me angry. In our Utopian Literary Club meetings, we discussed not giving them our first names, but rather the names that we wanted to be called. We decided we would give only our initials, but the White woman in the credit office would ask, "What's the 'A' for? What's the 'B' for?" and all that. No matter what your occupation was, if you were a Black woman, you couldn't get a credit card in your name with a title. That was to keep you down. To keep you low. Black women were out there teaching school, but nowhere could they get a sandwich and nowhere could they go to a decent restroom, and your card showed your first name and your last name. The White women would talk to us as if we were great buddies. Ann this and Ann that. I would ask, "Do I know your first name?" I called the credit department at Rich's and talked with a White woman and told her I did not want an account if it couldn't be in Mrs. Ann Cooper. We argued and argued and argued. We hung up. She called me back. Several days later, I got an account in the name of Mrs. Ann Cooper.

I had four children, and I was the only woman in the neighborhood after the thirties that didn't go out to work, but I was always into different projects. One was the Gate City Nursery Day Association. There were about forty women on the Board, and I was elected president of the Board of Directors. I loved working with the women. Another project had to do with helping girls whose mothers left them at home all the time because the mothers were working. This is where Grady Homes comes in. That was one of the first housing projects for Blacks in Atlanta. The story is that when they needed somebody to get into this project, a man at the Y said, "Call Mrs. Cooper." Well, here comes Mrs. Cooper. We had no money, but we were able, finally, to get into the United Way, and that gave us a little help. The only place we could find to have a girls club was in the basement of the Grady Homes Housing Project. The meetings were at seven o'clock at night, down in the basement. I can think of so many things going on in the city that I had to miss because I was bringing children back here. I had a clubhouse back then, and the girls were everywhere. I remember when Mrs. Roosevelt, wife of the President, came to Atlanta. Everyone was going to see her drive through, you know, but I couldn't go because I had a yard full of girls. We would take them to Mozley Park. That's up the street from here. And when they did well in school, we would honor them. By the time we organized our chapter of Links, we could get a small amount from the organization to give to girls who made good grades.

You know, I have been honored at so many places, and when I hear that I am somewhat of a legend in Atlanta, I have to say that I never thought much about being a legend. I enjoyed being with my family and my friends, and I enjoyed working in organizations. I was invited to a party Labor Day night and I thought, "Well, I came to Atlanta on Labor Day in 1922." And I thought, "Just look. I have been here all these years. I came here on a train on Labor Day. I had turned twenty. My husband came to the station to meet me. I was standing up and I could look out the window. He was running here, there and yonder, you know. Looking for me. Looking to see if I got off that train. That was in 1922.

MRS. MARY ELOISE STEPHENS DANSBY

Atlanta, Georgia

Teacher

I don't know whether they knew each other when they were at Morris Brown, but they might have because my father took shorthand and my mother took a secretarial course. That's why they both knew shorthand. Daddy would write postcards in shorthand and put them under a rock on my mother's lawn. One day my grandmother saw him doing this and she went outside and picked up the note. She couldn't read it because my father had written the note in shorthand.

I was born on January 13 in 1927 in Atlanta, and I have lived here all of my life. I'm like the motto for Rich's Department Store many years ago: "Atlanta Born, Atlanta Owned, Atlanta Operated." The full name on my birth certificate is Mary Eloise Stephens. I was named after my maternal grandmother, Mary Annalitha Liza Hill. I was born at home on Griffin Street, and the doctor who delivered me was a Spelman graduate named Dr. Georgia Dwelle. I believe she was the first Black woman doctor in Atlanta. She had a small hospital on Boulevard, but that is not where she delivered me. I was born at home. My oldest brother (and he was only four at the time) said that after the delivery, Dr. Dwelle asked him, "Would you like to have a little sister?" He said, "Yes," and then Dr. Dwelle said to him, "Well, you have a little sister."

My mother, Freddie Mae Grant, was born on the same street I was born on: Griffin Street. She had five brothers and no sister. My father, William Robert Stephens, was born in a small farming town called Newell, Alabama. He was the baby of seven children and, if I'm not mistaken, only my father and one of his brothers reached adulthood to marry and have children. The other brothers and sisters didn't and that is why we did not grow up with the experience of having aunts and uncles. I'm told a fever swept through Newell, and two of my father's sisters died within a week. One was thirteen, and one was fifteen.

My father moved to Birmingham when he was sixteen. That was perhaps in 1909. He went there because Birmingham had steel mills at the time, and Black men could get jobs in the mill, and that was what he did. He worked in a steel mill and attended high school in the city. My father told us that during recess, he would go to the home economics department and learn how to cook, and the rest of the boys would go outside and play ball. He wanted to learn how to cook, and I guess that explains why he was a very good cook. My daddy could really cook! He left Birmingham and moved to Atlanta perhaps in 1912. He enrolled at Morris Brown College, where he remained until his junior year in perhaps 1914 or 1915. When WWI started, he enlisted in the Army. When the War ended, he did not return to Morris Brown. Instead, he became a letter carrier at the Atlanta Post Office. My mother also attended Morris Brown, and she took a secretarial course. However, she was very talented in music. In fact, she started playing the pedal organ at the age of five. She met my father because his postal route included my mother's street. I don't know whether they knew each other when they were at Morris Brown, but they might have because my father took shorthand and my mother took a secretarial course. That's why they both knew shorthand. Daddy would write postcards in shorthand and put them under a rock on my mother's lawn. One day my grandmother saw him doing this and she went outside and picked up the note. She couldn't read it because my father had written the note in shorthand. [Laughs]

My parents married perhaps in the early twenties, and they had six children: William Robert, Grant, Mary, John Madison, Gwendolyn Yvonne, and Dollye Rebecca Jean. We said there were three groups of children. William, Grant and I, of course, were in Group I. By the way, I was Mary Jean for a couple of days and then my sister Gwendolyn was Gwendolyn Jean for a couple of days. My mother thought Jean was such a beautiful name. My brother John and my sister Gwendolyn were in Group I. The only one in Group III was Dollye Rebecca Jean. She was named Dollye Rebecca after my father's mother who died in 1931. I think my mother thought, "This is the last time for me to put a Jean in one of my children's names," so she named the last child Dollye Rebecca Jean. Dollye was born in 1940, five years after Gwendolyn. She was a baby of my mother's change.

Nine of us lived in the family house on Griffin Street: my parents, the six children, and my mother's mother whom we called Granny. For a short period, my father's mother lived with us due to her declining health. My daddy brought her from Newell to live with us here in Atlanta in the late twenties, I think. You know, there were no nursing homes back then, so you took care of your elderly parents. I'll never forget the evening my father's mother died. It was in the wintertime, and we were playing in the basement. That was a great place to be when it was cold because we had a big coal furnace that heated up the basement. Anyway, my mother called down to us and said, "Come upstairs. Your grandmother has just passed." I can still remember that day. My grandmother died in Atlanta in our house, and she was carried back to her home in Alabama to be buried.

I don't recall ever being bored when I was a child. You see, we made our toys. We converted Union Hardware skates into skateboards. We made small cars. We used skate wheels as the wheels on the cars, and clothes lines wrapped around castaway broomsticks as the steering rods. We made necklaces out of dried watermelon seeds strung on thread, and we dotted the seeds with fingernail polish. All of us had our chores to do. My brothers and I were assigned to clean the kitchen and wash the dishes. Sunday dinners were special because there would be more food and also my mother would make a delicious pound cake. Nine people would sit at the dinner table, and the family would talk about spiritual values, or moral values, and what was expected of us. And of course we were expected to attend church and to do well in school. All of us were active in the church. We didn't go to the church my mother attended, which was Friendship Baptist Church, because she stayed sickly, so we followed Daddy to a church called Big Bethel A.M.E. Church. That's where we grew up. When I was a child, my daddy went to Big Bethel every day. I didn't realize until I was older that Daddy had to go every day, especially during the wintertime. You see, he kept the church warm. This was during the thirties, and at that time the church was heated by a coal and wood furnace. My daddy was one of the persons who started the fire that kept the church warm.

Every Sunday after dinner, my daddy would take us for a ride in a 1920-something car—the ones we see now in museums. He would drive to Peachtree Road as far as we could go, and he would bring us into this neighborhood, which is now called Collier Heights. We would go out Bankhead Highway, which was then Georgia 78. That is the road we traveled when we would visit my father's parents in Tallapoosa, GA. So, I remember all of this section. I remember when it was a wooded area and, if I'm not mistaken, Highway 78 was a dirt road. It seems that fate would have it that when we were going to see my grandparents, it would always rain, and we would get stuck in the mud and we would have to get out and push the car. [Laughs]

Everything in Atlanta was segregated then. Only White people were employed as city clerks, bus drivers, policemen, and firemen. The only jobs we could be sure to get would be as elevator operator, dishwater, janitor, or maid. Everywhere you went in Atlanta, you saw segregation. I remember the time I went to City Hall with my grandmother. I was about ten years old, and she was going there to pay her taxes. I saw only White people. I guess maybe I thought, as a child, that this was just the way it was and the way it always would be. I remember when the first Black police force was created. That was in the forties, and eight men were hired. Of course we were very proud to have Black policemen, but they were restricted as to where they could patrol and whom they could arrest. Would you believe four Blacks were lynched in Monroe, Georgia, the year I finished college? And that was in 1946. Jim Crow was hard. My brother told me how he had worked at a noted restaurant when he was young man in order to make spending change. He's deceased now, but he told me about this eight or ten years ago. When he would leave work, his boss would give him a slip of paper confirming why my brother, a Black man, was in the neighborhood. That was his permission slip. He never told our mama about this because she surely would have said, "No, you are not going to work," and he wanted to keep the job. You know, in spite of all the discrimination, we were never taught to hate. We were taught that we were as good as anyone else. We didn't have that -- at least I didn't have that -- "I wish I were white" attitude. I never had that attitude.

We were really a self-sufficient and very creative people. What we were able to do with herbal cures was really quite amazing. Do you think people went to the doctor every time they got sick? Of course they didn't. For one thing, they didn't have the money and, for another, they didn't want to deal with all the discrimination they had to face, but mainly they believed they could cure themselves of most illnesses. People shared herbal cures and the different ingredients you needed. In my family, Daddy was the master of home remedies. Every winter, he made a concoction for your cough. It had cod liver oil and spirits and Rock Candy and other ingredients. People had all kinds of home remedies. When you stepped on a nail, you put a piece of fatback in gauze and put the gauze over the wound to draw the bad substance out.

And there was a certain type of tallow used for healing. Tallow is the grease taken off when you cook your beef or lamb roast. Our parents knew how to mix that grease with another ingredient and would rub the mixture on your chest. It was better than Vicks. And there was a remedy our grandmother would put into a bag, and she would put the bag on a string and we would wear the bag around our neck. It really smelled. Don't ask me how to spell it. [Laughs] It worked. And you know we can't forget castor oil. [Laughs] When you got sick, you'd have to line up to take that terrible castor oil. Some people could go to the backyard and select a plant for healing. They would take what they called polk salad (I think I am saying it correctly), which I heard can be poisonous if you don't know how to boil it, and they would pour off the liquid. The Scripture says, "The leaves of the trees bring healing to the nations." And then there's another Scripture that says, "Grass is for the cattle, and vegetation is for man." Even the dandelion is supposed to be good, but I don't know how to use the dandelion, so I leave the dandelion alone.

When I was living in the neighborhood (it's called Vine City now), Sunset Avenue was partially occupied by Whites. It ran parallel to Griffin Street. The area adjacent to Griffin going in the direction of Ashby Street (Joseph Lowery) was all Black. Eventually, Sunset Avenue became Black. There was a grocery store in the community run by a Jewish man named Lipsitt, who lived over the store with his wife and one son. The store was about three blocks from where I lived, and my mother would send me to the store to shop for potatoes, mackerel and other things. She would give me postal stamps, and I would pay for the articles I bought with the stamps. Isn't that something? I was bartering. My mother had a talent for working with all people, and that explains why people had so much respect for her. She was very involved in the community. She worked with a group of ladies who helped to establish the health center in our neighborhood. It is called "The Neighborhood Union Community Health Center." If you go there, you will see a plaque with the names of the charter members and my mother's name -- Freddie Grant Stephens-- is on the plaque. I guess I got my desire to be concerned about the welfare of the community from my mother.

She was her own engineer. [Laughs]. When fixtures would break down--for example, when the toilet wouldn't work—my mother would fix it. When painting needed to be done, she was the one who did the painting. If something broke while Daddy was at work, she would fix it. My daddy would often say, "I wouldn't be surprised if I come home and find our bedroom out on the front porch." [Laughs] I remember when my brother Grant, who was a student at Delaware State, brought his wife Evelyn home to meet the family. My mother began preparing for the visit and there was a room in the house that she wanted to paint, to fix up, in order to welcome them. The color she wanted the walls to be was a cocoa type color, but all she had was a large can of white paint. So, my mother told my youngest sister to go to certain neighbors and ask them if they had any cocoa. Of course that's what she did. She went to one neighbor and then another neighbor and another, and each time she would say, "My mama said please send her some cocoa." My mother took all of the cocoa neighbors gave us and poured it into that white paint and got the shade of malt she wanted. I thought it was amazing. Who ever heard of taking cocoa to tint the paint? I bet Home Depot doesn't know about the use of cocoa. My mother painted that room a beautiful malt, and we kept the room that color throughout her lifetime.

She didn't work away from home. She stayed at home and took care of the family. She did our hair. She cooked. And she sewed. She made our clothes, especially the girl's clothes. She taught me how to sew, and she taught me on that old pedal sewing machine. I grew up playing with white dolls. Actually, I don't think Black dolls were being made at that time. I will never forget the Christmas I went into my grandmother's bedroom early in the morning before everything had been put under the tree, and I saw something hanging from the mantelpiece. It was a doll my mother had painted from Caucasian to a pretty brown. The doll was not quite dry. If I'm not mistaken, I think I have that doll downstairs. Isn't that something?

I began school, in first grade, when I was only five. I think my mother sent me to school at such a young age because, with six children, she needed some freedom. The school I entered was Ashby Street Elementary, which is nowcalled E. R. Carter. Of course it was an all-Black school located in our neighborhood. Children at white schools received new books. We didn't. We received raggedy books with writing all inside. Our parents told us not to focus on the torn cover or what was written inside, but on the contents because the contents of the book would be building blocks for our lives. They did not let segregation stand in the way of our education.

After Ashby Street, I went to Washington High School, and I graduated in 1942. I was advanced. [Smile] I entered Spelman that same year, but Spelman was not really where I wanted to go to college. With my father having six children and caring for a wife and a mother-in-law, he couldn't afford to send me to school out of town. He might have tried if I had asked, but I didn't ask because I didn't want to put such a burden on him. I became interested in Spelman when my mother rented a room in our house to a young woman who had finished Spelman in 1939. She was taking piano lessons from my mother, and the two of them became very chummy and, true to character, my mother assisted her. One day, much to my surprise, whom did I see coming from the bedroom I shared with my sister? This young woman! My mother had rented our bedroom to her! Everything turned out very well because the young woman became like a big sister to me, and, of course, she always talked about Spelman. She took me to my first Christmas Carol Concert, and that was it: I wanted to go to Spelman! I applied for admission and was given a scholarship for eighty dollars. In 1942, that was a lot of money! What was happening in that year? World War II. I remember coming home many times during my freshman year and seeing my mother standing at the kitchen sink just crying. The radio would be on, and there would be news about a battle in World War II. We didn't have television, so we had to picture what was happening. My mother would be crying because she had two sons who were in active duty. One was in North Africa, and the other was in Hawaii.

My mother died in 1952 at the age of fifty-four. Her death was a shock to us. My baby sister was twelve when my mother passed, and I was twenty-five. I can say this, my daddy never married again. He passed twenty years after her death, in 1972, but he never got a second wife. I remember when my father took two ladies to an affair. We told him, "Daddy, you don't do things like that!" Daddy said, "Why not? I'm not obligated to either one." So, one sat on the front seat, and one on the back seat. My daddy was something! He dated, but he never remarried.

I grew up remembering how hard my mother cried during the War, and I was so moved by her tears that I hoped I would never have to feel that kind of mother's pain. Now isn't it interesting that I married a Navy man? His name was Oscar Marion Dansby, and we met when we were young adults. We began dating after he came to my home, unannounced, seeking information about a school catalog. We were married on August 9, 1958. Seven years later, I gave birth to our only child, a boy, whom we named him Oscar Fredric Stephens Dansby. Our son Fredric grew up listening to World War II Navy stories his father told him, and that is probably why he enrolled in the Navy ROTC training program at Auburn University. When he was offered an ROTC scholarship, I didn't want him to take it because I remembered what my mother had experienced, and I knew payback for the scholarship was service in the military. There was no war going on at the time, but if a war occurred, I didn't want my son to have to serve. I can hear myself telling him, "Do you have to take that old scholarship? Your daddy and I are managing to get you through school." He said, "Oh, Momma." So I said to him, "Forget it. Okay? Just forget it." And when I tell you to forget it, I mean, "FORGET IT." That's when I started going to a church called Mount Herron Church of God. I heard they had intercessory prayers on Saturday mornings, and I needed something within me spiritually to level the stump. I need spiritual reinforcement.

Well, my son enrolled in ROTC in order to become a pilot and take training in Pensacola. There were eleven boys in the program, but only five were chosen to go to Pensacola. My son was not one of the five. He wasassigned to take surface warfare, which meant being on a ship. When he was serving his tour of duty, Desert Storm broke out, and my son had to go to war, but the ship he was assigned was safe away from the battlefield. I said, "Thank you, Lord." I will never forget the day we went to see Fredric before his ship departed from Yorktown, Virginia for tour to the Mediterranean. We boarded the ship and we were carried to areas in which the men had been assigned. When we were led to the front of the ship, we were so proud to see Fred driving that ship to Norfolk, its designated station! The helmsman repeated the exact command that Fred gave and Fred would acknowledge by saying "Very well." We were so very proud of him. He lives in Virginia Beach with his wife Sandra and their three children: Brianna, Cathryn, and Benjamin.

Let me get back to Spelman. I entered there and I finished in 1946 at the age of nineteen. I thought about going to The School of Social Work at Atlanta University, but the Lord led me to teaching, and I loved it. I think I was influenced by the fact that my maternal grandmother taught night school. Just watching her was an inspiration. I don't ever remember saying I wanted to be a teacher, but when we finished college, most of us became teachers. It was almost expected that we would, so I became a teacher. My very first teaching job was at a school called Bush Mountain. Did I shed tears when I saw that it had only two rooms, no running water, and an outdoor privy? Out of my thirty-eight years with the Atlanta Board, the first three years at Bush Mountain were my best. In fact, Bush Mountain is where I learned to teach. One of the highlights of my teaching career was the recognition I received from the Freedom's Foundation at Valley Forge when I was teaching at Collier Heights Elementary. I was the first Black member of the Atlanta Chapter of the Foundation. The principal gave me permission to spearhead the school's participation in national competition for the Freedom Foundation award. I documented our year of celebration in a scrapbook artistically done, and I sent the scrapbook to Valley Forge, Pennsylvania as our entry into the competition. The following year, we were informed that we had won a national award: the George Washington Honor Medal. The scrapbook remained on exhibit in the museum at Valley Forge, Pennsylvania, for a designated period. Of course the Medal was placed in the trophy case at Collier Heights School. Just think. I went reluctantly into teaching, but I ended my career by sponsoring a project that resulted in my school receiving a national award. What a destiny!

Mrs. Mary Eloise Stephens Dansby

Earlier this year, I was listening to the radio and I heard about a program that wants people to go to China to teach. I sent for an application, just to see what was involved. Well, when I got the information back, I realized that you have to sponsor your own trip there. When my health gets better, I don't know what I might do because I don't know what's all in store that God wants me to do. You know, I believe in the saying, "Age is nothing but a number." I refuse to sit around and do gloom and doom.

MRS. EMMA DEGRAFFENREID

Talladega, Alabama

Nurse's Assistant

My father was a blacksmith, and his skills were very needed in the country because we did everything with horses and horses wore shoes. . . He was a relatively young man when he died. Only forty-two. At the funeral, the minister said, "Would you people that owe Mr. Birch money, please pay his widow because he's gone now." We didn't know folks hadn't been half paying my father. Some said, "I'll pay you Saturday" or " I'll pay you Friday", and they didn't get around to it. Some of them were Black people, and some of them were White people.

Mrs. Emma DeGraffenreid

My full given name is Emma Elizabeth Burt. That's on my birth certificate, but I used just my first name, Emma, from kindergarten to the fifth grade and after that I used just my middle name, Elizabeth. I liked it so much better. People call me Liz now, except for two friends from the East who came to Anderson College in Indiana. They call me Betty. I was born in Talladega, Alabama on August 10, 1920. My parents were born in Talladega, too, but my mother was born in the city and my father was born in the county. Her name was Alice Bertha Cunningham before she married my father. His name was Samuel Prophet Burt. They had eight children, but one died from whooping cough. My one and only brother was the fourth child, and I was the fifth child. You want all of the names? Florence, Tina, Helen, Sam, Elizabeth, Willie Mae and Lucille. My sister Willie Mae died from pneumonia when she was twelve. She had been sick for a long time. I was fourteen when she died. All of my siblings are dead. I'm the only one left in my family.

In those days, very few people went to the hospital to deliver their children. They had their babies at home by a midwife. My mother had all of us at home, and the midwife who delivered me was my grandmother on my father's side. She delivered a lot of the babies in Talladega. I didn't know very much about what she did because grown ups didn't talk about childbirth back then in front of kids, but my grandmother did tell me about one baby she delivered who had a broken arm. She said that happened during delivery. I didn't know my grandmother was a midwife until I was a little older. I knew she had a little black bag, but I never looked in the bag to see what was in it. Her name was Carrie Burt.

My father was one of four sons in his family. As I said, his middle name was Prophet, which is Biblical, you know. Each son in my father's family was given ten acres, so each son owned land. That's how we got to be landowners in Talladega. The land came from my father's parents, really from my Grandmother Carrie. There were forty acres of land and three houses on those forty acres. I really don't know how my grandmother got the land, but I do know that all four of her sons had land. We went to a family reunion in Talladega in 1998, and thirty-six of the original forty acres are still in the family's name. Isn't that something? We lived on the ten acres of land my father was given, but it was mostly a wooded area. It wasn't land you could farm. But there was a beautiful orchard on our land with every kind of fruit you could name. We had just gobs of fruit. But we children in the family hated that orchard because it meant work for us. When the fruit was ready to be picked, my mother would make us go up there and pick up the fruit that had fallen to the ground and give it to the pigs. When grapes, cherries, apples and pears fell to the ground, they would draw bees. So, every morning, my mother would send us out to pick the fallen fruit, which we would throw into the pig pen. The pigs were glad to get it, you know. We had plenty of fruit. Plenty of fruit! In the fall, my mother would dry apples and peaches. We would peel and slice them and put them on a canvas on top of the smoke house. And after they were dried, we would put them in white bags, and in the winter we'd have all the dried fruit we wanted.

My mother also did a lot of canning. She would buy glass jars that had lids with rubber rings. She would cook the fruit or the vegetables on the stove until they were good and done. Then she would put them into the jars while they were piping hot and she would seal them. We would put the jars on shelves in our smokehouse so that in the winter we had anything we wanted – fruits and vegetables and even jelly. We never had to worry about going to stores to buy food. Mostly we went to the store to buy sugar and flour and not even corn meal because we would take the corn we grew to the mill and they would grind it and make corn meal. Sometimes we bought lard and cooking oil, but we didn't have to do that often because we raised pigs and we would make the fat meat into lard. So, we had everything on our farm that we needed to survive, and people back then knew how to survive. It was necessary for us to know how to survive because there were no other houses close by. You see, we lived three miles from the city. We lived on Ashland Highway, Highway 44, and that was considered the country. There was a sign on the road right in front of our house that said, "Talladega 3 miles." So, you see, we were exactly three miles from the city limits, but we didn't let that stop us from leaving the country and going into the city to buy things, you know. If we wanted to do that, we would pick berries, blueberries or blackberries, and take them into the city and sell them and

Mrs. Emma DeGraffenreid

then we would buy candy and popcorn. We would always give our mother part of what we earned. So, we would go into the city because, as country kids, we didn't see three miles as a long distance. That was nothing for us. Three miles? We could walk it in little or no time. There were more Blacks in the city than there were in the country, and each one had their little field.

The house I grew up in was built on our property the year I was born. This meant we never had to move. We had two porches. One we called the front porch, and the other we called the side porch. We had four rooms and a small kitchen. We had a double fireplace that heated two rooms. We had a heater for another room, and the cooking stove was heat for the kitchen. We did our laundry by hand. All of the children had chores. When it was our turn to wash dishes, we made sure the water tank on the stove was full of water so that our dishwater would be nice and warm. Since we had our own orchard, my father kept plenty of wood for the fire. We had an outdoor toilet. All of the houses now have light, water, gas, and in-door toilets. I see that when I go to Talladega to visit. As I said, we made everything on the farm, but we went to the store for some things. The store was about two blocks from where we lived. We would go there to get milk and bread. It was owned by a White guy. Blacks and Whites shopped together at the store. I don't remember having any conflict with White children when I was in Talladega. The biggest thing we would do would be to bump White children with our book bags. But we didn't have any problems. Blacks and Whites lived together, but we didn't go to school together. I don't ever remember my parents talking against White people because we worked for them. We had a lot of fun chopping cotton and chopping corn with White people. My mother never worked in the fields. She stayed home and took care of the family, and sometimes she took in washing and ironing from other people. But she didn't work in the fields. She thought it was terrible when people kept their children out of school to do work. Kids would say, "We're not going to school today. We gotta iron." My mother said she would never keep us out of school to do things like that. We would do it after school. Black women in Talladega mostly did cooking and cleaning for whites, but my mother never did that. As I said, she took in washing and ironing, but mostly she stayed home and took care of the family.

My father was a blacksmith, and his skills were very needed in the country because we did everything with horses and horses wore shoes. He would shoe horses for everyone in the county. Black and White. People used wagons then, and wagons had iron rims on the wheels, and my father would repair the rims. He would sharpen farm instruments. Being a blacksmith was a very respectable job. My mother found out when he died that my father also used to help dig wells and clean out wells and that's how he got pneumonia. Getting wet, you see. The funny thing is that on the day he died, the Sunday School lesson was about healing. My mother took care of him for about three or four months. She had a doctor out once in a while, but in those days very few people had the doctors out, you know. The only time we'd see doctors was mostly at school when they'd come through and give shots or vaccinations or things like that. If somebody had a real rare sickness, they would seek a doctor. But most of the time, they listened to all these home cures or whatever they called it. My mother had a doctor out for my father, but the doctor couldn't save him. He was a relatively young man when he died. Only forty-two. At the funeral, the minister said, "Would you people that owe Mr. Birch money, please pay his widow because he's gone now." We didn't know folks hadn't been half paying my father. We didn't have any idea who owed my father. Some of them were Black people, and some of them were White people.

What I remember about growing up in Talladega is that I was happy there with my family and with neighbors. I also remember that Talladega was segregated. But this is the funny thing. Black kids and White kids sometimes played together. I know that to be a fact. From my own experiences, I know that to be a fact. There was a filling station down the road from us that a White family operated. We knew the kids very well, and we played with them a lot. They would help us wash our dishes and sweep our floors and make our beds, and then we would go help them. After we did our chores, we could play in the playhouses all day long. Now, my oldest sister got a job working in town for a White family named Dumas. That was after my father had died. She worked to help out, you know, financially. Mr. Dumas was president of a bank in Talladega, and he and his wife were good to my family. Mrs. Dumas

Mrs. Emma DeGraffenreid

bought all of us material for our dresses, which my mother made on a Singer Sewing Machine. And every time someone in the family had a birthday, she would buy them something just really nice. But this one thing I will never forget about Mr. Dumas. He complimented my mother for having beautiful handwriting. He said, "Alice." My mother's name was Alice. He said, "Alice, if you were White, I would hire you to be the secretary of the bank." I thought about that after I grew up. That a shame, isn't it? He said, "I'd hire you for a secretary" if she was White. And there was the White family my sister Helen worked for. They came from New York, and they were very nice people. The husband, Mr. Mulberry, put up a foundry in the city and hired a lot of Black people and paid them good money. When I went to the ninth grade and had to go to school in the city, his wife had her chauffeur take me to school every morning. They were from up North (well, from the East because they came from New York) and I don't think they were as prejudiced like Whites in the South, but I will tell you this: Mrs. Dumas took advantage of us. She had been to our house many times and this particular time, she talked about how old our furniture was. She said, "You know, your mother's beds and dressers are kind of run down. I'm gonna go get her some new things." And she did, but she didn't throw our old furniture away. She had it redone because she knew something we didn't know. The furniture was what you call antiques and very valuable. Now that was a shame, wasn't it?

I started school in Talladega. Of course the schools were segregated, and Black children didn't get the same breaks at education as White children got. First I went to a school that was a part of the Methodist Church. It was called Chapel School, and it had only one room. We started school in there, but you couldn't start school in Talladega until you were six years old then. They'd put you in the primer and then in the first grade. Chapel School was like what we call kindergarten, I guess. And later on, they would send you to two grades. There would be fourth and fifth grades and other grades all in one room. A one-room school is something! In the back of the school they had nails on the wall for your coats. Everybody would come and hang up their coat. They had a table sitting in the back of the school for your lunch bag, because everybody brought lunch, and your name or initial would be on your paper bag or lunch box, or whatever. They had a table with a big thing of water with a dipper in it and paper cups. When we'd first get to school, we ask, "Can I pass the coats this evening?" The teacher would say, "I already have a name." So, in the evening when school dismissed, two people would go back and hold the coats up, and you would hold up your hand and say, "That's mine." They passed out coats, which we called "the wraps." If kids brought lunch boxes they would pass out the lunch boxes. I went to that school until I finished the sixth grade. Then my mother found out that two teachers were driving to Mumford, in Alabama, which is about fifteen miles from Talladega, and she let me go with them. There were three of us who rode every day to go to Mumford to school. I went to seventh and eighth grade at Hillside School in Mumford. And then I went to the eighth and ninth grades at Talladega Westside City School. It was about two blocks from Talladega College. School was free until you finished the eighth grade. After then, the only school Black children could attend was Drury High, which was at Talladega College. It was expensive. Forty dollars to enter and ten dollars to pay every month. Not many Blacks in Talladega could afford that kind of money. My family couldn't afford it, but I went for one year. I was in the tenth grade at Drury High School at Talladega College and let me say that some White children went to Drury High. I don't think my family could have afforded me to send me for the other years, so it was a good thing my oldest sister called my mother and told us to come to Anderson, Indiana. She had married a plaster contractor and that's where they were living. She told my mother to send us to school there because schools were free. You didn't even have to pay for your books! So, you can say that education was the reason we left Talladega.

We moved to Anderson in 1937. I was seventeen at the time. I finished School there. I graduated from Anderson High School in 1940. When my brother got out of the service in 1942, he moved there. My oldest sister was already there. My father had already passed, and my mother said, "I see you guys are not coming back to Talladega." So, she moved there in 1940. And when she died in 1968, she was living in Anderson. That was home for us. My mother is buried in Talladega because that's where she passed. She always told us that if she

Mrs. Emma DeGraffenreid

died in Anderson, bury her there. If she died in Talladega, bury her in Talladega. She was in Talladega visiting her sister Willie when she died. My mother was a very gentle woman, and people say I take after her. They say I got my gentle spirit from her, and my sense of humor from my father. He did make us laugh.

I met my husband in Anderson. His name was Bert DeGraffenreid, so I was a Burt that married a man named Bert. [Laughs] He was from Louisiana, and he has the oldest of twelve children. We met in 1942, and this is how it happened that we met. My best girlfriend was going with a cousin of his who lived in Anderson and she told me one day that she wanted me to meet him. She said, "I hope the two of you will fall in love." What attracted me to my husband, first of all, was that he was a nice man and, second, that he was handsome. [Laughs] We went together almost two years before we married. We married in Anderson in 1944. When I met him, I was taking care of a White lady's children, Mrs. Heilman. You know, when I graduated from high school instead of me doing like the other ladies, going to the General Motors plant and getting a good job, I started living with a White family that had two boys. I loved children! Bert said that I acted as if the two boys were mine, but it was because I love children, you see.

I guess you can tell from the name that my husband was mixed. His grandfather was a White man. His grandmother was a little short Black lady. Her name was Mary, but everybody called her Mama Mae. She was a housekeeper for a White dentist in Louisiana. Well, she lived with him and she had three sons and three daughters by him. White people threatened my

husband's grandfather because he was living with Mama Mae. Folks would tell him, "We're gonna get you. We're gonna get you." They meant they were going to get him for going with a Black woman. One night, they came to his house and knocked on the door. They said, "I have a toothache." He wouldn't open the door, and they said, "You better open the door or we're gonna break in. My tooth is hurting." He was scared to open the door because he knew they didn't come for any toothache. There were three of them, I think, and they were White. So they broke in and beat him. Mama Mae said he lived for only three days. He lived long enough totell who did the beating, but the police didn't do anything to the men. That's a shame, isn't it?

So, my husband is what you would call mulatto. When my husband would visit Anderson--to see his uncle and his cousins, you know—he would go to this White barbershop and the White lady there would cut his hair. One day, he took a Black friend with him and he said, "You can come on in here and sit while she cuts my hair." When the lady finished cutting my husband's hair, his friend said, "Well, while I'm here, I'll just go on and get my hair cut.: And the White lady said, "But I don't do Black people's hair." He said, "You just got through cutting my uncle's hair!" She didn't know my husband was Black because of the texture of his hair. I guess my husband could have passed, but he didn't. He was a good husband, and he was very helpful in the house.

We were married for almost four years before I could get pregnant. So many years had passed without a child that we were going to adopt children. One night I had such a bad pain in my side that my husband had to rush me to the hospital, and it was then I learned why I didn't get pregnant all those years. It was something about my blockage affecting my ovaries. Well, the doctors removed my blockage and what a blessing! After that, the babies came. I had nine girls and two boys. I gave birth to eleven children! I heard a lot of old wives tales when I was pregnant, but I didn't believe in them. A lady was telling me the other day that when she had her first baby, her mother had heard this old wives tale that if you go to sleep while you're in labor, you'll go blind. She said her mother just about drove her crazy while she was having her baby. Her mother would slap her in the face and say, "Wake up! Don't you go to sleep!" She said, "I'm not about to go to sleep because of the pains and stuff." She said her mother had heard that if you go to sleep while you're in labor, you wouldn't wake up. And you know it's just nothing to that. But a lot of Black people believe in superstitions. Some one said that when God created mankind, he threw money and signs up in the air. The White race was busy picking up money, Black people were busy picking up signs. We have more signs in the South than I can tell you. You know like, down South, some people, if they're walking down the street

Mrs. Emma DeGraffenreid

and they see a black cat go across, they will turn around and go another way because the black cat means danger. I used to walk with three other ladies down there every morning at six o'clock. Rain, shine, sleet, or snow, we walked. It's a wooded area but it's a walking path, and one lady went around a tree. Three of us were going on and she went around the tree to make some more room. One of the ladies said, "Well, I just can't walk no more today because, did you see her split that tree? Honey, that's bad luck." And down South, some people didn't want a lady to be the first to visit them after Christmas. They would say, "Oh well, honey, I'm glad to see you, but I know my chickens won't be any good this year. They'll all be pullets." That's what we called female chickens. If a man comes, that was a sign that your chickens would be roosters. You know, all that kind of stuff. I didn't grow up believing in superstitions because of my religion. I grew up in the Church of God, and I'm still in the Church of God. It includes all people who are Christians. Instead of believing in all those superstitions, we were taught to believe in the Word of God. When it came to those signs about bad luck, my mother told us, she said, "There's not but one bad luck and that's to miss heaven and go to hell." When I was pregnant, I didn't listen to them. All I was concerned about when I had my babies was not having all that pain, and that's why I wanted the doctor to give me something for the pain, and each time, that's what happened with all of my children, and I had eleven. I had every one of them in the hospital, and General Motors, where my husband was working, paid the bill. Each time, I got good care in the hospital, and when I worked at Community Hospital on Two South, with patients that had bad hearts, I always gave them good care. I'm not bragging, but I was chosen as the first Employee of the Year the hospital ever honored. They gave me a nice big plaque and a fifty dollar defense bond. The plaque is still there. My husband was still living at the time, and he was very proud. He died from kidney failure in 1997. We were together for fifty-three happy years, and we had eleven children: nine girls and two boys. Our children gave us nineteen grandchildren, and those grandchildren gave us nineteen great grandchildren. God has blessed me all eighty-five years of my life.

I moved to Atlanta three years ago, in 2003, when my daughter Kelly moved here from New Orleans. She is a doctor and her husband David is a professor at Clark Atlanta University. I like being here because I am with my great grandchildren, but sometimes I miss being in Anderson. What makes me happy? I don't know how to word it. I am happy when I can make somebody else happy. What makes me sad? I am sad when people mistreat other folks, you know, for just little or nothing. If I could talk to anyone who has been a part of my life, I would choose a first cousin who was my same age. We did everything together. Before we got married, she would live in one half of the house and I would live in the other. Her mother died in childbirth. We were really, really close. I would ask her how she got over.

MRS. JENNIE DRAKE

Atlanta, Georgia

Realtor

I would try to get by without doing my homework, and teachers would say, "Oh well, that's all right. Jenny Weaver knows." The truth is I don't think I knew anything .There was one teacher in particular, an eighth grade teacher at Washington High School, who remembered me when she was in her late nineties. In fact, she remembered everybody who had been in her classes. She remembered me as Jenny Weaver! She would say, "Lil Ole prissy Jenny Weaver was just as smart as she could be. She was right. I was prissy.

My name is Jennie Marie Weaver. I was named Jennie after my father's mother. Her name was Jane, and don't ask me how we got from Jane to Jennie. I never liked that name. Everybody would say, "Oh, my grandmother was named Jennie," and I didn't want to be like anybody's grandmother. No indeed! When I was older, I gave myself my own name: Jacqueline. I remember once that several guys from Morehouse came to our house and asked for Jacqueline, and when they told my mother where they had met "Jacqueline," my mother said, "Oh, that must be Jennie." I didn't go to the door. I didn't want to be called Jennie. No indeed! My middle name came from my mother. Her name was Mattie Marie Taylor and, of course, after her marriage to my father, Mattie Marie Taylor Weaver. Evidently I was not born because I don't have a birth certificate! My daughter Pauline is trying to get one for me, and I know it will show that the name I was given at birth was Jennie Marie Weaver. As I said, I never liked Jennie, but that is my name.

I had two sisters, who are now deceased. One was named Pauline, and the other was named Carolyn. I was the baby in the family. I was born in Atlanta on December 20th in 1913. I will be ninety-two this coming December. When I was born, my sisters didn't get much for Christmas. I was the only doll they got. My sisters adored me because I was the baby of the family. Carolyn and Pauline were closer in age than I was to either of them. There was a difference of eight years between Carolyn and myself. My father was Paul Weaver, and he was from Fairburn, Georgia, and, as I told you, my mother's name was Mattie Marie Taylor. They met in college when my father was at Morehouse and my mother was at Spelman. That must have been in the very early 1900's because my father graduated from Morehouse in 1906. They divorced shortly after I was born. My father felt that there were no jobs good enough for him because he was a Morehouse man. When Mama suggested that he get a job at the post office, my father said that those people were beneath him. Everybody was beneath him. That's one thing about Morehouse men. They are instilled with the fact that they are somebody. Sometimes that works, but when the ego gets too big, it's not good at all. And it didn't work for

Mrs. Jennie Drake

my father because he really felt that most jobs were beneath him. I guess that is why he opened several private schools. They were located in the Pittsburgh area and, of course, there weren't many students for any of them and so he didn't make any money to speak of. He was an entrepreneur, you see, and my mother was not for that entrepreneur thing. She didn't think she was too good for a job. In fact, I can remember her taking in laundry between jobs. Times were hard, and we didn't have it easy. No, indeed. But my mother was determined to do for her three daughters and see to it that we did well. She was a very hard working woman, and she didn't think she was too good for a job. But whenever she got angry with someone on the job, she would say, "I have the same job I had when I started this job, and that is the job of looking for a job."

I admired my mother, and most people who knew her admired her, especially young people. They would come and talk to her and seek her advice about different things. When "Ein" lived with us—his name was Clifton Hubbard—h e spent a lot of time talking to my mother and he would go to her bedroom and stretch out on her bed. That's how close they were. And then there were soldiers who knew my mother from her work at Traveler's Aid and the USO. There were so many people at her funeral, so many. My mother was a wonderful woman, a wonderful woman. She saw to it that my sisters and I would visit my father on the weekends, and we would take him dinner on the holidays—Thanksgiving and Christmas, you know. My mother saw to that.

I lived for a year in Chattanooga with my Aunt Clara. I actually had two aunts who lived in Chattanooga: Clara and Pinkie. One Christmas, they came in a truck and offered to take me back with them. That was, let's see. It must have been in 1931 because I was in the fifth grade at the time. My aunt Pinkie had two step daughters who were around my same age, and my aunt Clara had five daughters, so I had many cousins to play with. In fact, the main reason for my being in Chattanooga was to spend time with girls my age rather than with my sisters Pauline and Carolyn, who were a bit older than I was. I was in Chattanooga when my sister Carolyn delivered her daughter Jean Marie. That was in 1929, and I had just gotten to Chattanooga, and

I was looking forward to a fun summer. My mother called and told me to come home because Carolyn had delivered the baby. I said, "So what?" And you know my mother told me to get my butt on the train back to Atlanta, and that's what I did. I should have been happy that Carolyn named her baby daughter after me, but I was too young to understand what that meant. I was only sixteen at the time, and I wanted to stay in Chattanooga with my cousins. When I got back to Atlanta, Carolyn was already home with the baby. We were living on Beckwith Street at the time, and that's where I first saw the baby. Well, when I saw Jean Marie, I became attached to her right away. She became like my very own child, and I took care of her as if I were the mother. Every time she did something new, like say her first words or take her first steps, I was really happy. When she was in the Spelman nursery, I would pick her up and take her home because Mama was working. I was with her so much that some of my classmates thought she was my child. But, you know, at first, it was a terrible time for me because I was only sixteen and at that age you are ready to have a good time, not ready to see after a baby. But I loved her and I even loved taking care of her. We were very close, and we are still very close. In fact, she lives around the corner, and every Monday, Wednesday and Friday she takes me to water exercise.

I spent the fifth grade in Chattanooga, but all other grades I went to school here in Atlanta. I finished elementary school at what was then Ashby Street School. It was later named E. R. Carter, but I think it is closed now. My mother was a teacher, but she taught in schools located in various small towns, like Villa Rica and Monticello and because my mother was a teacher, my teachers thought I knew everything. The truth is I don't think I knew *anything* . I would try to get by without doing my homework, and teachers would say, "Oh well, that's alright. Jennie Weaver knows." There was one teacher in particular, an eighth grade teacher at Washington High School, who still remembered me when she was in her late nineties. In fact, she remembered everybody who had been in her classes. She passed recently, and there was an article in the newspaper about an all-day party for her when she turned one hundred. Her name was Anna Lou Ware Hendricks. It was amazing that she could remember her students. She

Mrs. Jennie Drake

remembered me as Jennie Weaver! She would say, "Prissy Jennie Weaver. Lil Ole prissy Jennie Weaver." That's what she called me. She would say, "Jennie Weaver was always just as smart as she could be." She was right. I was prissy. To me prissy means being kinda fast and, well, prissy.

When I was in the eleventh grade, I had a boyfriend who was a student at Morehouse. He remained my boyfriend for about two years, and then he went back to Shreveport. I think I met him at the corner drugstore. He asked if he could come to see me and I told him yes. Well, when he came to the house, I told my oldest sister, "Oh I don't want to see that guy." So, she went to the door and told him that I was not at home. He went somewhere and used a payphone because then, you see, there were no cell phones. He called my house. I answered the telephone and I didn't recognize his voice. He said, "Oh you're just coming in?" And I said, "I haven't been anywhere." He said, "Well, I just left and I'll be right back." Another thing, my mother did not allow boys to stay past ten o'clock. This boyfriend would come at two in the afternoon when his classes were over. He remained my boyfriend for a long time, but my mother didn't particularly like him. I think it was because he was a Morehouse student. My mother thought Morehouse men were conceited, which is one of the reasons she spoke against him.

There was not much we could do in the way of dating then because there was nowhere to go. That was in the thirties, and times were difficult, and, besides, Atlanta was very segregated. We had two theatres in the Black community, and we would go there on dates. There were clubs on Auburn Avenue and there was a house on Ashby Street where we would go for parties. Our house had a large living/dining area, and we would have dances there sometimes. I don't remember there being a record player. What I remember is somebody would play the piano, and we would dance. There was no drinking, only dancing. Yes, we would have dance parties at my house, and sometimes we would charge. That was a way, like renting rooms, that helped pay my tuition. I don't remember how much we charged, but it couldn't have been more than about ten or fifteen dollars. Parties would start at about nine o'clock and they would be over no later than one minute after midnight. People would leave the party by foot. You see, we walked everywhere because few people had automobiles. I have to explain the difference between a party and a dance. Back then, going to a dance meant going to dance, and there would be no drinking. Going to a party, on the other hand, meant you would drink. I went to dances, not to parties. I loved to dance. But drinking? Oh no! That was something my mother did not approve of. She did not drink. She was a complete teetotaler! For me, dating meant going to a dance. That's all. It didn't mean sleeping around. Oh gosh, if I would tell my mother that I was going to somebody's house, to a male's house, to spend the night! That's not the kind of dating we did. Well, it's not the kind of dating I did. However, some girls did sleep around and get pregnant, so, yes, girls were having sex before marriage and, quiet as it's kept, abortions are nothing new. We knew girls who had abortions and some of them died. No, abortions are nothing new. My niece Janice, who is now in her early fifties, remembers a classmate of hers who died from having an abortion. Janice said, "Oh, I would have been dead either way. If the abortion didn't kill me, Mama would!" Sometimes girls would go out of town and come back a couple of years later with a baby. Other times, they had abortions here in the city. There were several places girls went for abortions. There was one in our community. The people who performed the abortions were called shade tree doctors. You know, just like you have a shade tree mechanic? We knew where they were and often who they were. You could ask around and find them.

I went to Washington High School, and I graduated in 1931. Then I entered Spelman, but I had to come out in my junior year, so I did not graduate. I had an appendectomy and it did not go well. The incisions burst, and I had to have a lot of tubes that did draining. I didn't graduate, but I enjoyed being at Spelman. One of the first persons I met, and you may have met her by now because she's still a favorite at Spelman, was Marguerite Simon. She's a lovely person, a very lovely person. She is really a person to be admired. And I met a young woman, from Athens I believe, and her name was Tiny Holmes and she was tiny. We would go out to play baseball and each time she would throw that ball towards me, I would dodge. To this day, I do not like anybody to throw

Mrs. Jennie Drake

anything to me. I did not like baseball and that was one of the things we did at Spelman. We played baseball, we went to the gym, and we had to spend a day at the old building. If we wanted to meet boys, we couldn't meet them at Spelman because they couldn't come on campus and we couldn't go over to Morehouse. So, we met boys at a drugstore on the corner of Fair and Chestnutt called Yates and Milton. Day students especially would meet boys there for lunch. Some of the boarding students would sneak off from campus and come to my house. You see, I lived on Beckwith, which is close to Spelman and to Morehouse. Our house had two bedrooms downstairs and two upstairs. My mother would always rent rooms. That's what people did back then, probably because hotels weren't open to Blacks and so, different Black families would rent rooms. In fact, that was how I was able to pay my tuition. My job was to prepare breakfast, lunch and dinner for the boarders. I remember the time my mother rented a room to a postal worker and I missed preparing breakfast several mornings because I had stayed out late dancing. He stopped renting with us because I had slept through breakfast too many times, and he stopped renting with us. Whenever I would cook pork n' beans for lunch, Einstein would say, "We didn't have any money this week." He was a Morehouse student who boarded with us for three years. Actually, his real name was Clifton Hubbard, but we called him Einstein because he was very smart. He had an automobile! Now that was good because when students would come to my house, he would drive them back to campus. Sometimes we would have parties at my house, and sometimes there would be music. We always had a piano, and we always had books and magazines. That was one of the sacrifices my mother made. She believed in education. I think her background had a lot to do with that. She grew up in the area of Peter and Larkin Street where there were manufacturers. She didn't talk too much about her parents, and I didn't know them. One sister did washing and ironing. That was the one who lived in Chattanooga. Mama said she never did want to do laundry for people. So, I think that's the reason why she continued to get an education. She finished Normal School at Atlanta University. That was a two-year program and, back then, with two years in normal school, you could become a teacher. I am talking about the early 1900's. You know, I have very little information about my mother's family or, for that matter, my father's family either. My mother never did talk much about her mother, and I want to know more about them. My daughter Pauline has been trying to find out something about our ancestors on my mother's side. We have been out to Southview Cemetery, you know, looking at where they were buried and things of that sort. All that we know is that my mother's name was Pinky Taylor, and her father's name was Joe Taylor.

I met my husband, Phillip Drake, on a street corner, and I married him six months later. He was going in one direction, and I was going in another. I was actually going to the Terminal Station because Mama was working at Traveler's Aid at the time, and it was located in the Terminal Station, which is now the Russell Building. It's right there at Spring Street and Mitchell. I was at Spelman at the time. I was walking to the Terminal Station, and he saw me, and he asked me if my name was Carolyn Weaver. I don't look like my sister, but he asked me if my name was Carolyn Weaver. I told him no and I kept walking. About two or three weeks later, he passed our house, and my sister Carolyn was having a little birthday party outside for her daughter Jean. She said, "Oh, there goes Philip Drake." She spoke to him and he came over and spoke to me. And that was how I met Philip. So, it was not a street corner romance. He was six or seven years older than me. I met him in June. I remember the month because Jean's birthday is in June, and we were having a party for her. That was in 1936. We married six months after I met him. I was twenty-two when we married. When we courted, we mainly went to movies close by or he visited me at my house. I think once or twice we went to a club called the Roof Garden, a dance hall on the sixth floor of a building on Bell Street and Auburn Avenue. Philip could dance, but he didn't like to dance as much as I did. I don't remember how he proposed, but I remember that we went to the Justice of Peace to be married probably because Mama didn't like Philip at first. You know, mothers don't want anybody to take their daughters. At first, we lived with her and then one day I told her we were going to get a room. She said, "That's nobody's idea but yours. Philip is perfectly satisfied here." We were going to move out because Mama would tell us what we could and could not do. Phillip didn't seem to

Mrs. Jennie Drake

have any trouble with that. I remember when she told him, "I don't want those drunken people coming into the house." You see, Phillip worked for Southern Railway. Well, he told them not to come. So, when my mother said it was nobody's idea but mine to move, what she meant was that Phillip didn't want to move because he was "perfectly satisfied" living there. The idea to move was all mine. I told Phillip, "You are here till death do you part." And sure enough, they remained close up to my mother's death. He and my mother were very close, very, very close. My mother was very fond of Phillip. Well, actually, everyone was because he was so easy going and congenial. My niece lived with us and he was just like a daddy to her. When he came home the night she died and he saw the hearse in front of the door, I had to call the doctor for him, he was so upset.

I have to give Phillip credit for being a very good father and also a very good husband. He never tried to tell me what to do or what not to do. If I wanted to buy something, I would go ahead and get it. He would give his check to me, and if I were not at home, he would give it to my mother to give to me. Whatever I did with was up to me. He put up with me with everything! But Phillip was somewhat like the men we hear about. You know, men who want their wives to stay barefoot and pregnant. Phillip felt that way. He saw cooking and seeing after the children as my responsibilities. He really didn't want me to work away from home, but I did. You see, Phillip came from Auburn, a small town in Alabama, where they did farming. I don't think his mother worked away from the home. Well, I did. I worked at downtown Rich's, and when we would go to a party, Phillip would say, "Oh, no, she's not going to work tomorrow." I would say to myself, "He'll be calling a taxi for me to get to work." Some of my friends bragged about not working, but I wanted to work. I worked at Rich's and then I worked at the Georgia Teachers' Association. That was during the forties. I worked because I liked bringing in my own money. It is to his credit that Phillip never tried to prevent me from working. Phillip died in 1989. We were married for fifty years, and we had four children: Pauline, Phillip, Jr., Michael and Millicent. We had been married for only two years when I became pregnant with our first child. My husband was excited. With my first pregnancy, I asked my mother what it was like, and she told me it was like a dream. After I delivered my first child, I told her it was like a nightmare. You would think after a woman has one child, she would not want to go through that again. You see, I didn't have epidurals because my doctor didn't believe in them. I delivered all of my babies without anything! The natural way!

The only time I didn't mind the birth pain, and actually wanted it, was when I delivered Michael, and that was because I had lost my son, Phillip, Jr. He died when he was four months-old. Today we call it infant death syndrome, but back then we called it crib death. I felt that his death was God's punishment for my not wanting to have another child when he was born. After Phillip's death, I would call my doctor almost every day, and he would come each time I would call. Our house had twelve or fourteen steps. The doctor was a short fat man, and he would run up those steps. The last morning he came to see me, my hair hadn't been done and I was not dressed. He took one look at me, went down the steps, got into his car, and then came back up the steps to tell me what he thought I needed to hear. He said, "You need to get up out of bed and clean up this nasty house and get yourself together." His outburst apparently worked because I thought about what a shame it was for me to keep calling that man away from caring for sick people. Losing Phillip, Jr. was such a terrible experience, and it took me a long time to get over my grief. And so, when I was pregnant with Michael, I wanted him! And when he was born, everybody watched Michael. He could not be in a room alone because we were afraid, you know, that something would happen to him.

All of my children were born in Black hospitals. There were several then in the City of Atlanta, but all of them are now closed. Back then, doctors would come to your house. They would have a bag with them. Also, back then, pharmacists would sometimes bring you medicine. Now you have to go to the doctor's office or to the emergency room. You have to call an ambulance, and the fee is very high. So much has changed. In the thirties, forties and fifties, it was safe for you to walk the streets at night. We did not have a lot of violence. It's not like that today. It's not as safe it is used to be. You're almost afraid to walk out of your house.

Mrs. Jennie Drake

I'm all locked in with burglar bars! But things have changed in other ways for the good because now we don't have to live with segregation, and that's what I grew up with. Segregation. My grandchildren are living in a world very different from the world in which my children grew up, and the world my children knew when they were children was very different from the world I knew when I was a child. Change happens.

I can't complain about my life. I have been blessed, and I am still being blessed. I have two grandchildren and four great-grandchildren. I guess you can say that my life has been one of fulfillment. Now there was one thing I wanted to do that I did not do. You have been talking to me these many times, so you probably know what that is. I wanted to be a dancer. I wanted to be on stage. On Broadway, maybe. I loved to dance, and I still love to dance. Even with my brace on, I love to dance. I recently danced the electric slide, and I loved it! If my daughter Pauline should read what I have been telling you, she would probably say, "Mama, surely you didn't say that!" But what comes up, comes out and so that's just me.

MRS. ANNA ENGLISH

Philadelphia, Pennsylvania

Teacher and Principal in Atlanta Public Schools

I liked to read a lot when I was growing up. To look at me now, as decrepit as I appear to be, you wouldn't believe my favorite spot was to climb way up into a tree. I would get lost up there. There was a big field across the street from where we lived and about maybe four hundred yards down there was this wonderful tree in the field. It was so relaxing to just climb the tree, open my book and read without being disturbed.

Mrs. Anna English

The given name on my birth certificate is Alma Elizabeth Edwards. I was born in Philadelphia, but I moved to Atlanta when I was nine months old. My father was Lovett Howard Edwards, and my mother was Alice Clyde Ray Edwards. She simply liked the name Clyde. [Laughs] There were six children in the family: Robert, George, Thelma, Anna, Katherine, and Lovett. I was number four. There were three girls and three boys. You see, George was the name of my oldest sister. My sister Katherine died during the influenza of World War I, and my brother Lovett was run over by a car and died from the injuries. That happened here in Atlanta in the early thirties. After he died, I just went through misery on top of misery. I was four when that happened. At first, I was overcome with guilt because we were coming out from the field and he was behind me and I didn't have his hand. My brother was only four when he died.

I had a wonderful relationship with all of my siblings, but I was closest to my sister Thelma. She was two years ahead of me in high school and in college. She went off to service in WWII. My brother Robert, the oldest child, left home at an early age and made his way to Chicago where he spent most of his life. My sister George became the mother of some wonderful children that I enjoyed being mommy to. My father was born in Troy, Alabama, and my mother was born in Newnan, Georgia. They met when they were both students at Clark College. I believe that was in the early nineteen hundreds. Mom was a beautiful person. She had long hair and she used to unwrap her hair and brush her hair one hundred strokes every night, and sometimes she would let us do it. I always enjoyed doing that. My mother never worked away from home. Even when times were hard, and they were because of the Depression, she stayed home. I will say this, however. She was noted for the beautiful way she could iron, and that was appreciated by white people. So, she did ironing for them as a way of earning money, but she did the ironing at home.

One thing I will always remember is that Mom had a thing about lightning storms. Whenever there was lightning, she would want us to be absolutely quiet. Well now, that's not easy for children to do. That's not easy to do at all! But we managed. Mom would put us under the bed and tell us to be quiet so that we would be safe. But we were devilish. I learned that if I kept treasures under the bed, I would have them there to play with when there was a lightning storm. My sister Thelma and I played Jack Straws under the bed, and that was our favorite game. Can you picture today's children doing that? But we never made the mistake of rolling the jacks over anywhere close to the wood part of the floor because we didn't want Mama to come and get on our case. She didn't know about "time out." Mama knew to spank! She spanked us with hairbrushes, with her hand, with whatever she could find. She knew how to spank! But whenever any of us got sick, she was very kind and considerate, and she did everything she could to make us feel better, so much so that my sister Thelma and I would sometimes accuse the other one of just trying to be sick so that Mama would be extra nice to us. This was in the late nineteen twenties and early thirties and at that time, when people were sick, they depended on themselves and friends and whatever memories they had of what would be good—like, whether you should be on a chest protector or when you should not grease your neck and stuff like that. The Great Depression came and money became even more harder to get than it had been. People didn't have money for doctors, so they tried home remedies.

What I remember most about growing up in Atlanta was that we would have picnics and we would pack a lunch and walk to a park or somewhere within walking distance and spread the table and enjoy ourselves. And then we would play on the equipment that was available. We played the usual game of hiding, but I liked to read a lot when I was growing up. To look at me now, as decrepit as I appear to be, you wouldn't believe my favorite spot was to climb way up into a tree, which was my favorite place to read. I would get lost up there. There was a big field across the street from where we lived –that was on Proctor about two blocks west of Simpson --and about maybe four hundred yards down there was this wonderful tree in the field. It was so relaxing to just climb the tree, open my book and read without being disturbed.

My father was what you would call a handy man, and he was the kindest man I knew. We had no misunderstanding about who was in control, but Daddy taught me about tenderness.

Mrs. Anna English

I remember the time I stepped on a splinter (I used to be a wild little barefooted girl), and he told me to sit down. He said, "I'll get it out for you." He said, "It's going to hurt. I know it's going to hurt but I'm gonna try not to make it hurt too much." So I stuck my foot up, and it hurt, but I didn't cry. My father was careful to be tender when he was removing the splinter. He built a house for us on Hunter Street. It was a beautiful house with a sleeping porch. All the children slept there. It was a large house and, for the times we were living there, it was pretty well appointed. We lived there in the late twenties, but then the Depression came and Daddy lost his job, we couldn't up the payments on the house. So we had to move to a much smaller house, and I regretted that. One of my unrealized dreams was to buy that house and give it to my daddy before he died.

I remember that Daddy always had a car, even during difficult times, and he used to take us for long drives around Atlanta. He would take us out where the Governor's Mansion was then. It wasn't where it is now, and he would take us there and we were able to see how differently white people lived from us. There were lavish houses with shrubbery in the yard, and at Christmas time there were lights, lights, lights everywhere!

I went to the Ashby Street School here in Atlanta, and it is still standing. I liked school because it gave me a chance to prove what I could do. But I learned very quickly not to always have my hands stuck up in the air trying to give answers because the kids did not like that. So I learned how to keep my hands by my chin. There was a field across the street from school that provided me so many hours of carefree play. We never had to worry about cars or anything, and I could play in that field knowing that I was safe. Atlanta was different then from the way it is now. After Ashby Street School, I went to Washington High School. That was in the thirties and at that time you could start at Washington in the fifth grade. I entered in 1934, and I finished in 1939. I graduated at the age of fifteen because I did so well in school that I skipped a grade. I didn't date in high school. Well, let me start from this end. Whenever I wanted to do something, I knew that my parents would say, "You're too young." So it did not come as too much of a shock to me when I asked Daddy if I could go to the senior prom that he said, "Go to the prom? What you gonna do at the prom? You don't know how to dance." And I didn't, and the more he talked about it, the more crazy I realized the thought of it was. But I was hoping I could go. My daddy did not change his mind, and Mama didn't intervene. I didn't go on my first date until I was a junior in college, and it was a strange experience for me because I had never been on a date before. All I wanted to do was hurry up and get home. I finally did get to go to a prom, but that was after I had finished college and was teaching at Washington High School. I was at the prom as a chaperone. Imagine that? I went to my first prom when as a chaperone for students!

At Washington High, I was what was called a mid-term graduate, and that didn't sit too well with my peers. For many years, they didn't recognize me as a member of the class of 1939, and when they did, I was not interested. I graduated from Washington on a Thursday and on the following day I entered Clark College. I was either naïve or marvelously stupid and didn't know that that you didn't wear plaits to college, but I did! So I went right straight on over with my plaits, and I started college in my plaits. I want to emphasize that I began my college years at the Old Clark, the college on the hill! It was located then where Carver High School is located now. That location is of historic significance and so I am proud to say that I studied at "the old Clark," the college on the hill. I spent my first two years there and my last two years where the college is now located, in the Atlanta University Center. I was a double major, French and Social Studies, at Clark, and I enjoyed my studies very much. Everybody treated me like their little sister because my sister Thelma was already a student at Clark when I went there. So she was looking out for her baby sister and everybody knew it. I didn't get a chance to be alone by myself anywhere without somebody saying, "That's Anna. That's Thelma's sister." Let's see what year did I graduate from Clark? Since I had my stroke, I sometimes forget the dates of things. I will have to tell you next time. I know I graduated a year after I should have graduated because I had to drop out of college for a year. Daddy simply could not afford to have my sister and me in college at the same time. Both of us had scholarships and tuition was only three hundred dollars a year, but he couldn't afford to pay for both of us.

Mrs. Anna English

Thelma was closer to graduation than I was, so there wasn't any thought in terms of what we would do. I told him, "I'll get a job," and I did. I put most of the money I earned in the bank, and that was when I started my first bank account. I thoroughly enjoyed the experience of working because it made me realize how much school meant to me. I wasn't deserving of any rah, rah, rah or anything like that, but I did have a deeper appreciation for college.

The year that I was out of school, I worked in a White lady's kitchen. The house I worked in was located in the West End area. The area is now all Black, but when I worked there, it was an all-White community. In fact, the only Blacks you saw there were Blacks who were working for White people. We were living on Parsons Street at the time, and I rode the street cars to work. I did whatever was asked of me on my job. It was assumed then that Black women could do anything and do it well. I'm not sure that was the case, but we would try to do whatever we had to do in order to assist our families. That work experience made an indelible impression on me. It made me say to myself, "I'll not do this again."

I was in college when the War was still going on, and I remember that many of my classmates were called up. In fact, many of the students were called up and had to leave immediately. According to what kind of record they had established, some of them had already accumulated hours sufficient to complete, and others had to finish in the years after they came back from the War. You were picked for the War by number. We had a strong suspicion that everybody knew what color the people were whose name had been put in. I knew a lot of Black persons who went to War. In fact, my first husband, Clarence Jackson, went. I met him when I was at Clark College. We had a very strange courtship because he liked to drink and I didn't. The way he handled that was that he and I would go out and have our fun and he would bring me home and then he would pick up another girl and they would go out, and that's when he had fun. That's why I said the courtship was strange. I sat myself in the corner one day and said, "Now either it's gonna be one of us or the other." I told him I didn't like what was happening. He said, "Well, what do you want me to do?" I said, "I don't know what you are going to do, but what I want you to do is just be satisfied with the fact that I'm not going to drink. You can drink if you want to, I don't mind." So he said, "Okay." And that took care of that! We married when I was in my junior year. I was short of turning eighteen. He went to war shortly after we married.

He wrote at least once a week. Many times it turned out to be two or three times a week, but at least once a week. Mail was at such a particular point that I never was sure when he would get the mail. If the soldiers had moved out, the mail would be waiting for them when they came back. When he returned from the War, he came back with a very changed attitude, and I saw a side of him I had never seen. It was hard waiting for him all those three years, but I thought he was worth waiting for. It turned out he was not worth the wait at all. We separated and later divorced. He went back to Columbus and he opened a drugstore there.

While he was in the War, I continued my studies at Clark. I was determined to graduate, and I did. The date was 1943. My graduation was very, very lonely because my parents had split up, and neither one was living in Atlanta. The night before my graduation, my sister Thelma was commissioned a lieutenant in the Women's Auxiliary Corps, so she was not able to be there because she was taking care of business for the government. My older sister George was the only person in my family at my graduation. I have to thank a friend of mine for saving the day somewhat for me. He had gotten a job coaching at Clark, and he asked me what was I going to do after the graduation. I told him, "I guess I'm gonna go home and take off my clothes." And he said, "Would you like to play tennis?" So I ended up rushing home, changing into my tennis clothes, grabbing my tennis racket, and rushing back two blocks to the tennis courts. That's how I spent my graduation day from Clark College. I graduated in 1943.

I met my second husband, Lewis Edward English, at Central Methodist Church. I was twenty-one at the time and since I had already been bitten once, I wasn't going to be bitten a second time. I waited for ten years, TEN YEARS, before I said yes. We would go to sports events because I have always been interested in sports. We'd do movies every now and then,

Mrs. Anna English

but we didn't live in the movies. I started playing bridge with some girlfriends, and we would do that once a month. We had enough different things so when we got back together we could each make a contribution to the conversation. I went with him ten years before I agreed to marry him. We married on February 18, 1955. He was such a sweet person. When we realized we couldn't have children, we adopted our daughter Barbara. That was in 1959. She was thirteen years old. She made such a difference in our lives. She brought us immense joy. I remember one day when we were washing the windows and the phone rang and I had to go to another room to answer the phone. When I came back, there she was wiping the window, just wiping it down. I just wanted to hug her and kiss her. Instead, I took that picture of her. I caught her in action. I have looked at that picture so much, and it's meant so much to me. She's the joy of my life. If anybody had told me that such happiness could result from adopting her, I would have been shocked and very surprised, but I have just been overwhelmed with it. She has just been fabulous. Even when she went away to college, she did it in such a manner that Let me explain.

I went to Clark and my husband Lou went to Morris Brown, so Barbara went to football games for both schools. Clark and Morris Brown used to play on Thanksgiving Day every year, and we would have people over to the house after the game. We never knew how many people we were going to see at the game, and we never knew how many we saw would be free to accept an invitation to come to our house after the game. We had so much fun at the parties. We just enjoyed ourselves very, very much. So when Barbara got ready to send out her information to colleges, she surprised me. She sent it right straight on out, got a response, ended up with a full scholarship, and neither of us knew a thing about it! And to Bennett! To Bennett yet! So we said, "Oh, how in the world did we let that happen!" It was the best decision that we could have made.

Barbara has two sons, Christopher and Gregory, and both of them look as if her husband Jerry brought them right out of his mouth. He is tall and slim. They are tall and slim. Oh, I love my grandsons to death! I love them. When they were younger, I would get down on the floor and play games with them. It was just like, "All right. All things are cancelled. Nothing's important but you two!" They are now in their thirties, so that was during the seventies when I was romping with them on the floor. My nephew Lovett, the oldest child of my sister George, lived with us most of his life. He now lives in East Point. He knows that I was very disappointed that he didn't go into teaching. [Laughs]

You asked me about all of the elephant paraphernalia in my house? Well, I am a Delta and proud to be a Delta. Barbara is Delta. My sister Thelma was a Delta. In fact, her being a Delta at Clark is one of the reasons, but not the only one, I pledged Delta. I was just impressed with the girls in the sorority. They had lots of activities for girls who lived on campus and those who lived in the city in their own homes. I observed the Deltas and saw what an impact being a member of the sorority could have on your life. Members of the sorority were the best of friends, and I just liked the camaraderie that they had. But the pledging process was too long. It seemed to go on and on and on and on. Back then, the members were much more secretive than they are today about when a line was going to come out. The girls on my line would have meetings and we started trying to outsmart the "big sisters." We were going to figure it out. It didn't work! I learned that that there are some things in life that are worth waiting for. I enjoyed the pledge process, even though I did think that sometimes we were asked to do some ridiculous things like wearing dresses that made us look like we were pregnant. I won't ever forget it! People don't even look around at folks now when they are wearing maternity clothes, but back then they looked! Yes, they did! And we had to wear those dresses every day for a week! I made Delta in 1941 at Clark College. There were seven girls on my line. I'm a Delta through and through!

I worked in the Atlanta Public School System for forty-one years. When I retired, APS had the number of years as forty because they didn't count the one year I worked as a substitute teacher. I worked as a teacher for fourteen years and as a principal for sixteen years. I decided to be a teacher when I was in my sophomore year at Clark. Then our choices for careers were limited. So, I settled on teaching. Most of the girls who were in college with me became

Mrs. Anna English

teachers. That was a major career option for Black women, that or librarian. I was never disappointed that I made that career choice because I really enjoyed my work with students. I loved my work! There is nothing as wonderful as seeing a light come on in the faces of students. Each time I saw that light, I felt that I had made a contribution to a student's life.

When I started teaching, I was doing supply teaching at Washington High School and then I was assigned to David T. Howard because they were badly in need of teachers. I stayed at Howard ten years, ten wonderful, beautiful, never-to-be-repeated years. From 1944 to 1954. I was teaching at Howard when the Brown Decision was being argued before the Supreme Court. I loved the school and I was deeply saddened when it closed. Deeply saddened. Howard was a school of achieving students and dedicated teachers. Vernon Jordan writes about the impact Howard had on his life, but having worked at Howard, I can tell you that students like Vernon Jordan were the rule, not the exception. As I said, Howard was a school of achievers.

When Price High School opened in 1955, I was selected for a staff position, and I stayed at Price for five years 1954 to 1958. By then, people above the local school level had noticed what kind of work I did, and so I went to the area office and from there I was moved to West Fulton as an assistant principal. From there I moved up to principal ship of Peyton Forest Elementary School. I spent sixteen wonderful, beautiful never-to-be-repeated years at Peyton. It was a school of achievement during my years there. Oh, wait a minute. I skipped over seven years. Somewhere between all that I have told you about, I was assigned to the area office as a resource teacher. Now that was an eye-opening experience. I didn't know, until I actually was in the classroom with some of the teachers, how difficult teaching was for some people. A resource teacher is a person who has enough knowledge about different approaches to doing things so that she can come in and make suggestions about what might work and so forth.

When I became a principal, I knew that things would be different. For one, there would not be as much comradeship. But I also knew that there would be an opportunity for me to try things. I discovered that sometimes people want to do things and they want to do it now. They want to have finished it now, when they're talking to you. Getting them to slow down and take a look around and anticipate things that might go wrong so that they are better prepared to handle problems that come up – that is a major challenge. You know, they are sitting on "ready" eighty days a month. Sometimes from the little bits of information that they learn from honing, they're able to anticipate problems and when they really get ready to fly, they're really ready. Every good thought isn't a guaranteed thing, but it can lead to something. And you must remember that while all thoughts don't bear fruit, many of them will lead you to something.

I have been guided in my work, and in my life, by this belief: "Don't ever let your dreams die. Whatever it is you have been dreaming of, work on it." I think I have accomplished enough of them to say that if I were called home today, I would do so without too many regrets.

I have enjoyed talking with you. I feel that you have added to my growth. You know, it's amazing, you're around people who are in school all your life, all your working life, but after you quit work you suddenly are shut off from them. You've been a real blessing to me!

MRS. ELIZABETH GROSS

Bradley County, Tennessee

Community Activist and Aquatics Teacher

I grew up in the church. I sang in the choir at our church, and I even directed the young people's choir. Much of that to me was like preserving the art of your people. When I would hear the people sing, I would say that makes more sense than singing about going to heaven. The people in the church would clap as they sang and, later on, they used the piano. One of my favorite songs was "Blessed quietness. Holy quietness." [Singing] "On the stormy seas, the spirit speaks to me and the billows cease to roll." It was a beautiful song.

I was born in Bradley County, Tennessee, which is a small and beautiful community located in the foothills of the Smoky Mountains between Chattanooga and Knoxville. My father was born in Lowden, Tennessee, which is in the mountains of East Tennessee. His name was William Mack Kline, and he was a molder in an iron factory in Bradley. My mother was born in the city of Pulaski. Her name was Alice Smith and, of course, after marriage to my father, she was Alice Smith Kline. Her father was a stone mason, and his sons were stone masons. According to the oldest uncle in the family, he came to this country from North Africa, so my maternal grandfather was Moorish. You might find this surprising, but, back then (and we are talking about the late eighteen hundreds), there were a lot of people of African descent who came to live and work in this country. The only way I can explain the last name of Smith is to say that my mother's father took that name as did many people who came to this country from other places. It's an easy name: Smith.

I remember when my mother took us to visit her community in Pulaski. I believe I was twelve at the time and, of course, too young to understand the economics of the fact that my mother's family had a home in town and a summer home in another location. Her father built both homes, and I remember that there were horses at both places. So, really, my mother's family was fortunate to be doing so well at a time when many colored people were, you know, not doing well. I think that being a molder was somewhat of a privilege in those days, which would explain why, even during the Depression, my father had a decent job. There was never a time when I felt poor, though by many standards, we were. We were rich with family love. When I think about my childhood, I reflect on four neighborhoods in Tennessee that are important to me: Bradley County, Lowden County, Pulaski, and a little community in Lowden called Paint Rock. I associate Paint Rock with my father's Indian heritage. My father never said he was Indian, but we knew that his mother, whom we called Grandma Jinny, was Indian, and she lived in Paint Rock. We learned that from older people in the community. My father's father was German and Cherokee, but Granma Jinny was all Cherokee.

My father was not formally educated, but he was quite well read, and I attribute that to

Mrs. Elizabeth Gross

the education he received in missionary schools. I think the schools might have been in homes. You probably learned in some of your classes that missionaries would go to the mountains and establish schools for people in the communities. That certainly happened in my father's community. He was educated in schools that missionaries established in Lowden, and apparently they were good schools because my father was so well read. They were one-room schools with one teacher and as many as thirteen students.

When I think about how my parents met, I visualize my mother riding in a carriage or in one of the earliest model cars and she is working in the community between Giles County and Bradley County. I can see her working with others to set up tents for a worship service, and I can hear her singing. [Smiles] In her own way, my mother was a missionary, and she was doing this kind of work when she met my father. They married on April 30, 1913 somewhere in East Tennessee. They had eight children, but only six survived. During that time, it was not uncommon for children to die at a very young age of illnesses—like whooping cough, for example—that we don't hear about today, largely because of vaccinations. The children my mother lost, a boy and a girl, died in infancy. The first child to survive was my sister Loreta. Mom heard the phrase "a little reader" and she named my sister, Loreta. After Loreta, there was my oldest brother James Albert, who was named after my father's brother, and after James Albert, there was my brother Jones David. We called him J.D. He carried the names Jones from my mother's father. After J.D., my mother lost her second child in infancy, and then came the second set of children, all of whom were girls. I was the first born in this set, and I was named Mamie Elizabeth for my father's aunt and Mamie for my oldest sister. The other girls, in this order, were Eloise Alice and Irma Ethel. I am called Beth from Elizabeth.

My oldest sister Loreta is still alive. She's ninety-two, nine years my senior, and she lives in Kentucky with one of her two daughters in a home passed down through the generations. Loreta is just a marvelous person, truly a marvelous person! She was the model for the rest of us. I recently found a letter I wrote to her on one of her birthdays, telling her how grateful we were because she had been such a model. I know it was hard for her because my father wanted all of us to be perfect, and he was stricter with her because she was the oldest. She was alone, but we had one another, and I guess that was why Dad was not as strict with us as he was with her. She was alone, but the three of us went as a group. Daddy would take Loreta here and take her there. He didn't do that with us because, as I said, we went as a group. But even with the second group of girls, my father made it a point to get to know the boys who came to see us. He would take them hunting, you see, and spend time with them in that way. My father was an elder in the Church of God, and I knew that he taught Sunday school classes or Bible classes, but I didn't know that he taught young boys in the church about sex and morals. Isn't that something? He taught them that they should be pure just as women should be pure.

I have fond memories of going hunting and fishing with my father and going swimming in Mouse Creek. You seem surprised that a girl would do those things, but, you see, my father, probably because of his Indian heritage, didn't make gender differences. I hunted and fished just as my brothers did. I shot against the sheriff in Bradley County, and I made the highest score. My father was very proud of me. He was proud of all of us, and he praised all of us when we did well and when we did the right thing. But my father would tell us that a haughty spirit comes before a fall. He was a proud man, but he didn't have the kind of race pride I have experienced among friends. This was probably due to the fact that my father and his parents and his grandparents did not have the plantation experience and, as a result, he wasn't socialized to think in racial terms. If you ask me about my father's identity, I will say to you that he was a child of God. It would not have made sense for him to have a single racial identity because his family, and my mother's family as well, were so racially mixed. His paternal grandfather was German, and his paternal grandmother was Cherokee. My grandfather's sister on my father's side had a family by a man who was a big dairy farmer in the community of Paint Rock and in Lowden, and he was White. My mother was about my complexion, but her other sisters were very fair. They looked alike, but they were different in color. My mother's younger sister was exceedingly fair with blue eyes and that perhaps explains why she was called Pinkie. I didn't

Mrs. Elizabeth Gross

know her name was Mattie until much later in life. Where I came from, there were so many racially mixed families that we just didn't think in racial terms the way people might have in other parts of the South, or even the way people think in racial terms today, not only in the South, but all across the nation. With our families being so very mixed, how could we be more proud of one heritage than of the other?

My mother was a very special woman--loving and gentle and very caring. In fact, both of my parents were special people, and I often say that the world would be a better place if there were more people like my parents. My mother was orphaned at an early age. She was thirteen when her father died and even younger when her mother died. She was a tiny woman and, really, we didn't see how she did all that she did because she was so tiny. We would say, "How do you manage to do that?" She would say, "Oh, it's not I. I'm just a conduit. God works through me. She would say to us, "Don't give me any credit." She was always helping someone in the community. I remember her taking care of a man who had been shot. I don't know the circumstances under which he was shot or how my mother came to take care of him, but I remember that she did, and I remember because she would take us with her to his house. I remember being in the room. The shades were drawn, and the room was dark. My mother would wash the man and bathe him and, you know, take care of him. I also remember her helping an insurance man who was taking care of his mother. The other thing I remember my mother doing is turning a mattress. You probably don't know anything about that, and I doubt that you've seen anyone turn a mattress. Seeing my mother do that stands out in my memory. She was so little, but she turned the mattress. And she never weighed more than one hundred and five pounds in her life!

Both of my parents were very religious, but religious in a sense that was very broad and that involved spirituality, ethics and morality. I remember the care my mother took to keep us from being narrow in our thinking. She would often go to a publishing house in Bradley County and get books for us about different religions because she wanted us to know that there's a big world out there and, as a result, our world included people from different religions: Seventh

Day Adventists and Jehovah Witnesses. She didn't want us to get stuck in one way of thinking or in one denomination. As I told you, my father was an elder in the Church of God, and that is where we worshipped as a family because my mother believed we should worship together, but we knew there were different denominations and ways of worshipping that were different from ours. Is there any wonder that I became a Unitarian, and my sister became a Bahai? My sister Eloise sent her children to Quaker campus and some of her children became Quaker. I grew up in the church. I sang in the choir at our church, and I even directed the young people's choir. At that time, we used our hands as instruments. We would clap as we sang and later on we used the piano. One of my favorite songs was "Blessed Quietness. Holy Quietness." I can't remember all the words, but it was a beautiful song. [Singing] "On the stormy seas, the spirit speaks to me and the billows cease to roll." It was a beautiful song. In our community, there were Scotch on one side of the mountains, and Irish on the other side of the mountains. The Scotch sang shape notes, and they invited people in the community into their homes to learn those notes. People in my church learned to sing shape notes (do, re, mi, fa, so, la, ti, do), and I am sure they learned that from the Scotch. Of course, the younger people picked up on the gospel songs, and we did that by listening to the group, *Wings Over Jordan*. There was no television at the time, so we listened to them over the radio, and we began to pattern much of our singing after their songs. We also sang the hill gospels, and they had four-part harmony and the choir had four-part harmony. This was peculiar to East Tennessee. I still have one or two song books of the gospels that came out of the hills. We had a quartet, the Kline and Merideth Cousins, that was often invited to sing in White mountain churches. I remember a few White people attending our church.

I went to a public school in Bradley County called College Hill High, and it was not far from where I lived. It went all the way from kindergarten to the twelfth grade, and it served not just students who lived in my community, but students who lived in other communities as well. The school bus would go twelve miles away to Charleston, Tennessee. Students from North Georgia also attended the school, and they boarded with teachers and families in the community. The principal of the school was a man named Professor Knox, a graduate of Tuskegee, and I remember that he would bring in science and math teachers from Tuskegee. There were no White children in our school, but there were White children in our community, and we played with them all the time. But we didn't go to school with them. Yes, that was a bit confusing to me, but I guess that was one thing I blanked out. I guess I thought, as a child, that their churches were different and so their schools would be different. On some level, you knew they thought they were superior, but on some level you thought they were inferior. Because you felt that you were on the right side, a little bit closer to whatever good there is. It's interesting that we had daily and close contact with Whites, but we lived with Jim Crow, with all the signs all the time. You know that was one of the reasons we didn't go to movies. In fact, I didn't see my first movie until I was a big girl. We didn't go to the movies because my father did not want us going to the top and sitting in the balcony. Also, he didn't think movies were morally good for us. He just didn't want us to have the experience of climbing steps and sitting in the balcony. Neither one of my parents wanted us to experience the indignities of Jim Crow. Really, segregation is one of the reasons we didn't do lots of things. That is one of the reasons we didn't travel very often. I do remember traveling by train to Kentucky and, of course, the train was segregated. There were sections for Colored and sections for Whites. I must say, though, that I don't ever remember drinking from a colored water fountain. I think my parents just avoided those things as much as possible. Either my parents did what they could to keep us from those indignities or they found a way around them. I think about this when I think about my mother reading books to us. That was a ritual in our family. I am seeing my sisters and me bathed, with our panties on, and we are lying on the bed and my mother is reading to us. But how could she get so many books if only Whites could use the library. Later, unashamed about it, she told us a White friend got the books for her. We experienced discrimination, but we never developed hatred for White people. My family's philosophy of love kept us from absorbing that kind of thinking. We never felt inferior or superior. We knew we were considered Black, but we also knew about our White ancestors. Race was not what mattered, you see. That is how we were reared. In fact, when I was married my husband and someone described my marriage by saying I was marrying a White man, my mother's response was "She's marrying a man who **happens** to be White." My husband was of Russian, German and Rumanian descent.

I finished Cottage Hill school in 1943, and I finished at the head of the class. There were only twenty-three students in the class, but my father was very proud that I was valedictorian. He would have been proud if there were only five students in the class. Professor Knox' wife, who taught at College Hill, thought I should go to Fisk rather than to Tennessee A & I. In the fall of 1944, I entered Fisk University. I was ready for Fisk, and I was full of anticipation about going there. Fisk was nationally regarded as an excellent institution, and I can say that during my four years there, I had the opportunity to meet so many famous and brilliant people. Scholars and artists were always coming to speak at Fisk. Dr. DuBois, Langston Hughes, J. A. Rogers, Paul Robeson--these were only a few of the people I heard speak at Fisk. The student body was Black, but the faculty, for the most part, was white and the president, Dr. Thomas Jones, was White. I believe he was the last White president of the University.

I was at Fisk during the historic decades of the forties, the War decade, and that was the first time women were given jobs in the munitions industry. You know, when men went off to war, women got the jobs the men had once held. That was a first for women. Black women and White women worked side by side in war plants. In fact, in my first summer home after entering Fisk, I worked in a TNT plant in Chattanooga where they made ammunition for the army. I majored in biology and minored in chemistry at Fisk, and I finished in 1947. Actually, I finished early, ahead of my class. I wanted to go on to medical school, but there was no money for me to do so. You see, I was the oldest girl in the second set of children in my family. I continued my education after Fisk by studying gross anatomy at Meharry. I was one of two women in the class. You have to keep in mind that this was during the forties and doors were not open to women until much later, not just in medicine but in all most areas. I remember that

Mrs. Elizabeth Gross

there were many veterans studying at Meharry and, of course, they were men.

After a year at Meharry, I went to New York. That was in 1947. I got a job working in the toy department at Macy's, and while I was working there, I heard that an employment agency on behalf of Mount Sinai was looking for someone to work in a project on the effect of measles on pregnant mothers. That was good news for me because, at Fisk, I had done research incubating chicks and studying the internal anatomy of the chicks in different stages of embryonic development. So, I applied for the job because I knew I was very qualified, and the agency hired me because of my resume. I was very qualified. But when I showed up at Mt. Sinai for the job and they saw me, they decided not to hire me. There was nothing on my resume about my race. Well, when they tried to deny me the job after offering it to me, I wasn't going to stand for it. I had already quit my job as a cashier at Macy's and now I'm left with no job at all! I told the manager that I was going to call the NAACP and whomever else I could think of. Of course I was bluffing because we did not even have a NAACP chapter in my town at that time! Later, when I married my husband, he and I would be involved in many civil rights activities, among them founding the first NAACP, but at the time there wasn't one. The man at Mt. Sinai didn't know that. So, I threatened to bring in the NAACP, and that's how I got the job!

I worked at Mt. Sinai for about four years. I was working there when I met my husband, Robert B. Gross. He was studying at Julliard at the time, and both of us were living in a resident hotel that was next door to Columbia University. In 1948, he accompanied me to my sister's wedding in Chicago and that's where he met my mother and my father. We married in 1950. When I became pregnant with our first child in 1951, I was ecstatic, absolutely ecstatic. I was twenty-seven, and, by notions then, that was "old" for starting a family. My husband and I had four children: three girls and one boy. Pamela, Rachel and Gail Klein were born two years apart. My husband and I planned everything. Robert, our only son, was born four years after Gail. The baby, Nina Shaun, was born two years after Robert. I had no problems with the pregnancies or the deliveries with the exception of Nina, who came early. All of the children came fast, and all were born in New York and, this will surprise you. They were born at the same hospital and delivered by the same doctor: Clementine Paolone. I lived in New York for forty plus years and I still go back and forth because my son has the family house.

I moved to Atlanta in 1986 to be caretaker for my first two grandchildren, the children of my daughter Gail. I now have eight grandchildren, and they are the joy of my life: Gail's Terry and Toni Diane. Nina's Ahanu and Mahala. Robert's Justin and Ryan. Pamela's Anna Rose. I moved to East Point, to this home, in 1990. I have been as busy here in Atlanta as I was in New York. For ten years, I worked with the Fulton County Commission on Elderly Affairs. I have also worked with Mrs. Lowery in SCLC, with our Neighborhood Association, with the Georgia Council on Child Abuse, and with the AARP. I'm committed to the age movement, which is relatively young. I think we talked about this in an earlier conversation. Did I share this little poem with you? *King Solomon and King David led very merry lives/With many, many lady friends and many, many wives/But when old age crept over them—/With many, many qualms/King Solomon wrote the Proverbs/ And King David wrote the Psalms.* The point is that they did some of their greatest work when they were older. As you know, I teach water aerobics at the YWCA, and I was quite thrilled when the Y recognized me for fifteen years of service to the community. The director asked me some weeks ago to collect stories from some of the students on what the experience means to them. I am so delighted when I hear some of them say, "My medication has been cut in half, and my doctor tells me to keep on doing what you're doing." I love working with seniors at the Y and, you know, I can't think about quitting. At eighty-three, I'm going strong and loving it because, you know, if I quit, I think that maybe I'll start falling apart. [Laughs] But if I quit, I'll do other things, for example get involved with my gardening.

You ask me so many questions, so many good questions. You ask me what makes me happy, and I would have to say that I am happy when my children are happy. Beyond that, I'm happy being in the world and feeling it and appreciating it. It's a beautiful world. It's a great place to be. What makes me sad? It makes me very sad that the world solves problems—or

Mrs. Elizabeth Gross

tries to solve problems—by fighting. War is the beginning of so much evil. It creates orphans and widows. It destroys minds. War makes me sad, very sad. And narrow thinking makes me sad, especially when it's about religion. Only Matthew and John walked with Jesus and Luke never knew anyone who knew Jesus, but he's the one who heard the angels. All of us can hear the angels. Regardless of our religious faiths or our racial identity, we are all connected.

Yes, I believe in miracles. You can't be a gardener without believing in miracles and, as you know, gardening is my passion. When you see your plants growing and you see the trees growing, you are moved to realize that life is such a fascinating thing. A marvelous wonder! Why are we here? I think we are to serve. Everyone can serve. I think we are here to appreciate the good in people.

MRS. LILLIE HARRIS

Chattanooga, Tennessee

Resident Director at Spelman College

We'd be sleeping and her machine would just be going. First, she had a foot pedal, and then when the electric machines came, she got an electric one. My mother told me once that when I was a baby, one of the hospitals asked her to come and do some sewing for them all day. She said the only way she would do the sewing is that I had to be there, too. So, she put me in a carriage, took me with her, and put me by her sewing machine. Everything I wore and everything she wore, my mother made. And it had to be detailed. Sewing was her way of making a living.

Mrs. Lillie Harris

The name on my birth certificate is Lillie Mae Hughley. H-u-g-h-l-e-y. I was born in Chattanooga, Tennessee in 1918, and I was born at home. Very few people went to a hospital during that time. The doctor would come to your house. Yes, the doctor would come to *you*. I know the name of the doctor who delivered me because I have my birth certificate. He was a Black physician named T. E. Taylor. My father was Will Hughley, and he was born in West Point, Georgia, and he had four brothers and two sisters. Everyone in the family left West Point and moved to Chicago except my father. They probably moved because they could find jobs there. You know the way people did during that time. When one person went somewhere and found jobs, the others followed. That's what Black people would do, you see. They would leave the South and go up to Chicago and Detroit and other cities up in the North. That's what my father's family did. They moved to Chicago. Everyone, that is, except my father. I didn't know very much about my father's father because he died before I was born and by me growing up in Chattanooga, away from them, I was not around my father's family enough to ask questions. So, a lot of things about his family I don't really know. But I knew my father's mother. She died two years after my father died. I wasn't around her very much, but I did know her.

My mother was Ozella Hughley. Her maiden name was Jones, and she was born in Waverly Hall, Georgia, and she was an only child. Her father was Sam McGhee, and he was White. He supported her as long as he lived although he couldn't claim her. I don't know all the details about how he met my grandmother because my mother didn't talk to me about it too much. I know this happened in a small country town out from Columbus. She did have a picture of him and everything, but I don't know under what circumstances Sam McGhee met my grandmother. My mother, for some reason, didn't discuss him very much with us. The main thing she said was that he arranged for my grandmother to bring her to Columbus because he didn't want her to grow up illiterate, and that's where she went to school and it was a school for Blacks. My mother didn't "pass" for White. Actually, she wasn't fair enough to "pass." That's my mother right there (showing framed picture). She was fair-skinned, but she wasn't white-skinned, and she had hair that was very pretty, but it wasn't straight hair. She had long, curly hair. Now, my grandmother was brown-skinned, but my mother had more of the features of her father. I don't know whether or not what happened with Sam McGhee and my grandmother was consensual. Her name was Lillie Jones, and I'm named Lillie after her. She had that one child, my mother, and she never married. She died from complications after a hysterectomy when I was five months old. My father died when I was eight and my father's mother died after him. And so, after that, all of the older relatives were dead.

My father worked for the railroad, and my mother stayed at home because there were five children to care for. I had one sister, whose name was Cora, and three brothers. William was the oldest and then there was Judge Neal and Edward was the youngest. Two of my brothers and my sister were older than me. My sister Cora was eight years older, William was fourteen years older, and Judge Neal was ten years older. My brother Neal went to Morehouse when he was eighteen and I was eight and my brother William married when I was somewhere around seven years-old, but he and his wife lived with us. So, it wasn't like we all grew up together sharing in things, you see. It wasn't that kind of thing because the last two of us, my brother Edward and I, we were kind of a good distance in age from the others. He was the one I played with, and I always wanted a little girl as a playmate. They said that I would slip off and go and play with somebody's little girl.

My sister Cora died when she was nineteen, and I was twelve. She had the flu and then had a set back that went into tuberculosis. That was in 1929. Back then, people didn't know too much about tuberculosis, so they didn't know how to treat it. She died a year after she took sick, and she was buried three days before Christmas. My father died during the Christmas Holidays in 1926. He was killed in a train wreck the day before Christmas Eve. It was really a horrible time for us. My father was a dining car waiter, and the train he was working on had come from Florida and was stopping in Atlanta and going to Chattanooga. My brother Neal was a student at Morehouse at the time, and he was coming home to Chattanooga for Christmas. His name was Judge Neal Hughley, but he always signed his name J. Neal Hughley because he didn't like his first name. He was on the same train with my father, but he didn't get hurt because of where

Mrs. Lillie Harris

he was sitting. Dad was in the dining car and my brother was in the day coach, because during that time if Blacks ate in the dining hall, there was only one table for Blacks. And when they sat down to eat, the curtains would be pulled so that you wouldn't be sitting in the same space with White people. My brother said the curtain took his appetite, so he wouldn't eat in there. That's why he was sitting in the day coach when the two trains ran together. Everybody in the dining car died. My brother was thrown from his seat, but he didn't get any injuries. My father was in the dining car, and that's why he was killed. That accident happened at six o'clock the day before Christmas Eve. My brother Neal went all through the wreckage looking for my father, but couldn't find him. He called my mother, and she told him to take the rescue train home. The next morning, we got the newspaper off the porch and read about the train wreck. The newspaper had the names of White people killed and injured, but my father's name was nowhere in the paper. **Nowhere** in the paper, you know. It wasn't until ten o'clock in the evening that the railroad authorities called and told my mother. They said that my father was killed instantly and that he never knew what hit him. It was terrible. I dearly missed him, and for years I would dream he was somewhere and had amnesia or something and he was going to show up one day. The years went on and I realized I could forget that dream, you know? My mother took care of our needs, but there was nothing she could do to replace my father. You know what I'm saying? For four straight years we had death in our family during the holidays. Four straight years! So when Christmas comes, I feel blessed if everyone is all right.

My father died in 1926, and the Depression came soon after then, so it was very hard, but my mother saw us through. She took in sewing so that she could stay home and take care of all of us. We'd be sleeping and her machine would just be going. First, she had a foot pedal, and then when the electric machines came, she got an electric one. So, that's how she made a living so that she could take care of the family. Her talent as a seamstress made money for her without her having to leave home. More White people came to the house than Black people for my mother to make things, you know. My mother told me once that when I was a baby, one of the hospitals asked her to come and do some sewing for them all day. She said the only way she would do the sewing is that I had to be there, too. So, she put me in a carriage, took me with her, and put me by her sewing machine. Everything I wore and everything she wore, my mother made. And it had to be detailed. Sewing was her way of making a living. And Mama had real estate. She and my father bought their first home when I was two and then they bought other property, so we were not poor. Mama had three houses besides the one we lived in; that was after my father died. We were not wealthy people, but as far as the average Black was concerned, we lived pretty good. We were what you would call middle class. But when the Depression came and the banks failed, it hit us hard and my mother lost a lot of money. I don't think she ever recovered the money she lost. Even so, we were blessed. During the Depression, Mama's sewing kept us from the soup line and from being really destitute. The Depression was a terrible time, I tell you. It was a terrible time to go through. So many people were in the soup lines. I was young, but I was old enough to remember how it was devastating for so many people. It really was. Franklin Roosevelt came in (he was President then) and he opened up jobs for people and pulled the country out of the Depression. I remember when he started Social Security, and it has been a blessing to people. And I don't understand our current President because Social Security has been a Godsend. Can you imagine Black people saving their money to go into stocks? They know nothing about stocks. There will be a lot of poor people who will not be able to live when they get older.

I went to public schools in Chattanooga, and they were segregated schools. Most of the teachers were women, and they were all Black. As I said, back then, neighborhoods were mixed with people who did different kinds of work. So, our teachers lived in the same neighborhoods as we did. I did have one or two male teachers, you know, but most of the teachers were women. Most Blacks went into the teaching field because there was actually not much they could do to make a good living. But, in spite of that, some of them were very good teachers. **Very** good. Everything was segregated, and we didn't have much in the way of what there was to be taught about Black people. There were no Black pictures in our school books. We didn't do a lot in the way of celebrating Black history, not the way people go all out now. A whole

Mrs. Lillie Harris

month dedicated to Black history? That didn't happen when I came along. It was just something you would discuss in the classroom. There was a lot of segregation, a lot of segregation. I didn't witness any racial violence, but I knew it was happening. Our parents didn't let us out that much and really there wasn't that much we could do as teenagers except be involved in church activities. Besides church, there wasn't too much for us to do. In order to go to a park, you had to go to Lincoln Park where it was all Black. I'm sure there were places that I would like to have gone but couldn't go due to segregation. No Blacks lived on Lookout Mountain during that time, but they worked there as housekeepers and waiters at the White clubs. What parents did for my generation was to talk about getting an education. They didn't talk about race and segregation, you see. "Get an education!" That is what we always heard. They believed it was the most important thing in life. We were told to move forward and the only way to move forward was with an education.

When I think about those years, I wonder why someone did not step up to do something about the way Black people were treated. I wonder why there was no one like Tubman, you know, and people like her, people who could move things forward for Black people. And I say that, because, during the time that I came along, people were apathetic. They could have probably encouraged us to do more about segregation, but they accepted it. I think they could have done a little more about segregation. I really do.

Your generation doesn't understand what it was like to live with segregation, but my generation grew up with it. We lived with it and through it. I accepted it when I was growing up because it was the law, you know. I sat in the back of the bus and I went to places from the back door and things like that that we had to do. But when I got to be a young lady, I didn't accept it so easy. Once when I got on the bus in Chattanooga, the bus moved before I could sit down and I grabbed the overhead strap in order to keep from falling. This White man said to me, "Get in the back where you belong." And my answer was that I was trying, but I couldn't move because the bus had pulled off suddenly. So, when I got home I told my mother about it because it really hurt my feelings. She told me not to let that situation make me feel bad or feel that I was any less of a person because of that experience. As far as the fountains were concerned, I never drank from public fountains. I didn't like that, so they never had to worry about me drinking from their fountains. Segregation was awful, and I didn't know if it would ever end, but I always hoped it would. I hoped one day things would be different.

I left Chattanooga in 1948 and moved to Atlanta. My oldest child Alfred was in high school, in the tenth grade, at the time. When we moved here, I didn't like it at all, because Atlanta was a big city. Chattanooga was a small city and I was used to that. But I grew to like it because of the opportunities here, you know, and I've been here so long now that Atlanta is home for me and home for my children. When we moved here I joined Jackson Memorial Baptist Church and, later, I moved my membership to Greater New Light Baptist Church, where I am currently the oldest member.

We moved to Atlanta because my husband was given a job here. That was three years after my husband was honorably discharged from the Army on November 27, 1945 for his service during World War II. My husband's name was Edward Harris, and he was born in Buckhead, Georgia, which is in Morgan County near Madison. I met my husband in grammar school at Main Street School in Chattanooga, and we started dating when we were at Howard High School. We married at an early age. My mother didn't want me to marry because she thought we were both too young, but sometimes you can't tell young people anything. I didn't listen to my mother, and I regret that because getting married did away with a lot of my youth. When you marry, you settle down and you take on responsibilities you wouldn't have to if you weren't married. You know, you miss the carefree part of your life when you marry. My husband and I had four children: Alfred, Yvonne, Gwendolyn and Edward. All of them, except Edward, were born at home and born in Chattanooga. They were born at home, but a doctor delivered them. I didn't have a midwife; I had a medical doctor. That's how it was done then. By the time Edward was born, the trend had changed. When my first child was born, the doctor was there, but the other two were born before the doctor arrived. We had **nothing** for pain.

I took motherhood very seriously, *very seriously*, but I did not raise my children the way

Mrs. Lillie Harris

my mother raised us. She was very, very strict. I was a little more lenient with my children. For example, she didn't talk to us about a lot of things. That's the way it was with older people when I came along. They wouldn't tell you things. For example, they never discussed what coming into womanhood meant. But when my girls came along, or when my children came along, I would explain everything. I always told them, "You can't say 'I didn't know'." I felt it was my responsibility to keep them clean and fed and to teach them about life. They never left home without a full breakfast in the morning. My life just centered around them. To me, my children came first. When they got to be teenagers, I'd tell them, "If you want to go to college, I am behind you one hundred percent; if you don't, you must get trained in something. You will have to work in order to make a living." And another thing, I didn't allow my children to "hang out". All four of my children chose to go to college. At one point, both of my girls were at Spelman, and my oldest daughter said, "Mama it's hard on you for both of us to be in college at the same time. Maybe I'll stay out a year to help out." I said, "Okay, if that's what you want to do, but now, understand, when you stay out, you have to go to work. You have to work every day because you're either working or you're in school." She went back to school. I explained to all of them what the consequences were if they didn't go to college: They would be somebody's maid or something, you know. There's no harm in being a maid, but you just don't make much money. If you want a good living, you've got to prepare for it.

I stayed at home with my children, and I made clothes for the girls. I didn't like to make boys' clothes, but I'd make the girls' dresses. They *always* looked pretty. I just wanted them to have what they needed, you know. Now keep in mind that my children were growing up in Atlanta when the city was segregated. We came here in 1948 and the city wasn't integrated until some twenty years later, so I had the same challenge my mother had when we were growing up in Chattanooga. I had to let my children know there were places they couldn't go, you know, because of segregation. I would have loved to have taken them to cultural affairs and things like that, but we were not accepted in places like that. You know, it's hard to teach your children that they "can't do this" and they "can't do that" because of their race. It's hard. It was hard for my children to understand that, and it was harder for me to teach them that. That's one thing we haven't thought that much about--how hard it was for Black parents to teach their children to accept segregation, but you had to teach them that in order to protect them, you know. But I never told my children, "You have to drink out of this fountain." They were not allowed to drink from "colored fountains." They had to wait until they got home to get water. It was really something to live with segregation.

I spent some of the happiest years of my life working as a resident director at Spelman. How I came to get that job is that my brother Neal was college minister at North Carolina College, and he and President Albert Manley were good friends because Dr. Manley also worked at North Carolina College. When my mother died, Dr. Manley asked my brother if I would be going back to help the King family, and my brother told him that he didn't know. Dr. Manley said, "Well, tell her I have something I want to offer her." And that's how I came to Spelman as a resident director. I worked there for nineteen years. I started in 1966 after Mama died, I retired in 1983, and then they called me back. I worked for two more years. [Laughs]

When the young people started the Civil Rights Movement, I was proud that somebody was finally standing up and making an effort to bring equality to our race. I was very happy for that, and I admired the people who sacrificed their lives and went forward to do so. I felt that I was right in the middle of the Civil Rights Movement because I helped Dr. Martin Luther King's wife, Coretta, with the children when she would go out and do freedom concerts to raise money for the Movement. Bernice was six weeks old when I started to keep the children, and she was almost three when I left. My service to the King family was only a small part, but Mr. Harry Belafonte's contribution to the Civil Rights Movement was a big thing. My daughter Gwen was one of the original young people who were arrested during the Movement. The other two older ones had already gone to work, so they were not free to march, but Gwen was a student at Spelman at the time. She sat-in and marched and demonstrated. I was always scared to death because, you know, during that time, every now and then somebody would get killed. They *did* kill people during that time. So, quite naturally, I was afraid, but I was also very

Mrs. Lillie Harris

proud. I think I can say my family was active in the Movement because of my work with the King family and my daughter Gwen's participation in sit-ins and my brother Neal was in the Movement when he was working at a college in North Carolina. I was proud of Black people when the Movement started, *real* proud. We finally had the courage to move forward.

My oldest son Alfred was Captain A. A. Harris and he was a part of the second group of Blacks to join the police force in Atlanta. You wouldn't believe it, but, when he first joined the squad, he wasn't allowed to arrest White people. *No* Black officers were allowed to arrest White people at that time. They were ordered to hold them until White officers came. But we saw all that change. I was proud of my son. I'm proud of all my children, but he was my first-born child. I lost Alfred four years ago, and that was devastating for me. He was in the hospital I know for about three months, and I was there *every* day. Even though my health was not good, I was there. My doctor and everybody told me I did not need to be there, but I *had* to be. It was terrible losing him. It's terrible to bury your child. It really is. I feel sorry for anybody who loses a child, no matter how old or how young the child is. It's a heartbreaking thing. My son had six children and his oldest daughter died a month after he did. I've had so much death in my life. So much death.

I was really devastated when Dr. King was assassinated. I wasn't with the King children when that happened because my mother had become ill and I had to take care of her, but I helped the family as they were preparing for the funeral services. It was really heartbreaking because I felt like he had sacrificed his life so that things would be better for us. He wasn't like the average father coming home every day. There were days he would be traveling, and when he would come through the city, somebody would take him a change of clothes and he was on his way to somewhere else. So, they were deprived of a lot of attention a father gives his children and that's why my heart went out to them when he was assassinated. I know about the pain of losing a father, so my heart went out to the King children.

I've had so much death in my family, but I am a blessed woman. I have thirteen grands and about twenty-three or twenty-four great-grands and five great-greats. I have an army.

[Laughs] See that sign there? (Points to magnetic sign on the refrigerator). It reads: *WELCOME TO DO DROP-INN.* My grandson put it there. He said, "Somebody's always in and out of here." I always keep all kinds of junk here. I got popsicles, I got cookies, I got. . . . Would you like a soda or something? I have so many grand-kids, I don't have time to be lonely! They keep me busy, so my life is always full. You will be surprised to know I always wanted to be a missionary. Yes, isn't that something? I wanted to be a missionary. But after I had a family, I just knew I couldn't do that, but that's what I always wanted to be. People tell me that's what I am because I'm always doing things for people. When I could really get around, I was always trying to help somebody. That was what I wanted to be: a missionary. Isn't that something?

DR. CARRIE JOHNSON

Atlanta, Georgia

Teacher and Community Activist

I don't know that any of my great grandparents ever experienced slavery, but I do know that my grandmother Hattie was born during the third year of freedom, and she would talk a little about how hard it was during slavery. But, you know, life was so treacherous; they just didn't want to talk about it. We would get bits and pieces about how hard it was during the eighteen seventies. I think that is true of most Black families, and that is one of the reasons stories about slavery weren't passed down through the generations. It was just something they didn't want to talk about.

My name is Carrie Lucile Clements Johnson. I was named "Carrie" for a paternal aunt who, by the way, was a 1913 graduate of Spelman Seminary. She always told us that she led the class. She was my father's second oldest sister. I was named Lucile for my mother, whose name was Lucile Clements. That's spelled C-L-E-M-E-N-T-S. I was born here in Atlanta, and I was born at home. My family lived on Delbridge Street right off Vine Street, which was then a thriving area, but shortly after I was born, we moved to Griffin Street, where we lived for twenty-five years. I'm the seventh child of nine children, eight of whom survived. Yes, there were eight of us. You have to bear in mind that we didn't have Roe vs. Wade back then, so, for a family to have six, seven or eight children was just the norm. All of us were named for someone in the family. My oldest brother, who is deceased now, was named Emanuel for my father. My oldest sister Hattie was named for my father's mother. Then, let's see who was next? Anna, my second sister, was named for my mother's mother. And then there was Nathaniel. No, I think Simon came before him, but I never knew Simon because he died when he was nine months old. I was named Carrie for my paternal aunt, but I don't know where the name Vivian cam from; she was the eighth child. I think that was just a name my father liked. Dorothy Olivia was the ninth child, and she was named for my father's sister. I think my father's side of the family dominated in the names of my siblings.

My mother had a child born in every month from June to January and two in September, so you know we didn't have a lot of money. Nobody had a lot of money in those days. There were eight children, and none of us were spoiled. My mother had to give a lot of attention to my brother Walter because he had asthma. Some days we thought he would take his last breath. We sometimes thought Mama was closer to him, but she wasn't. She didn't have any favorites. She had a way of making all of us feel loved and very special.

My father, Emanuel Clements, was born in Jasper County, which is in Monticello, Georgia. I used to tell him that he made two good decisions in his life: one was to marry my mother and the other was to move from Jasper County to Atlanta. He married my mother in Jasper County in 1917, and they moved to Atlanta around 1920. My father's father, Simon

Dr. Carrie Johnson

Columbus Clements, had lots of land in Jasper County and he hired many people to work the land. He was what you would call "country rich." How he came to acquire money and land, I don't know. Now that you are asking me about me, I have a desire to do some research and get some answers, but all I can tell you now is that I have no idea how he acquired money and land at a time when most Black people in the South were having such a difficult time. My grandfather even bought houses here in Atlanta on Lee Street, and this was during the nineteen forties. He and my grandmother Hattie had nine children, and my father was the only one of the children to have a large family. I don't know that any of my great grandparents ever experienced slavery, but I do know that my grandmother Hattie was born during the third year of freedom, and she would talk a little about how hard it was during slavery. But, you know, life was so treacherous; they just didn't want to talk about it. We would get bits and pieces about how hard it was during the 1870s and on up to the twentieth century, but we didn't get a lot of stories. I think that is true of most Black families, and that is one of the reasons stories about slavery weren't passed down through the generations. It was just something they didn't want to talk about.

My mother's parents were Anna and Willie Clemons, and they were from Jasper County, also. They had nine children, but they were not as well off as my father's parents. They were farmers. Up until 1920, the family spelled the name C-L-E-M-O-N-S. The reason they changed the spelling was that a teacher in a one-room schoolhouse in Jasper County told my grandparents on my father's side that the correct spelling was C-L-E-M-E-N-T-S. Some relatives spelled it both ways. Now we spell it C-L-E-M-E-N-T-S. When my parents were growing up in Jasper County—and I'm talking about the early nineteen hundreds—Blacks were considered less than second class. My father's mother was never Mrs. Clements. She was always Aunt Hattie. My father saw racial disrespect and experienced indignities and, as a result, he didn't like White people. In fact, he had disdain for them. That was evident in all of my father's dealings with White people and in the way he parented us. White insurance men who came to families in the Black community to collect for nickel-and-dime policies never came to our house on Griffin Street. Never! We lived on a hill across from Beulah Baptist Church and there were high steps to our house. If White people came up those steps, my father would chase them away. In the nineteen forties, that was a rather bold action on the part of a Black man in the South. My father began preaching in 1932 and when he would travel to small churches in small towns, he knew that he could encounter White policemen (and they were all rednecks at the time), and, if you were Black, they would stop you for driving slowly. All of the many negative experiences he had with White people fed his disdain for them and affected the way he parented us.

My father didn't let us go downtown, away from the Black community, because that was where you came face to face with White racism. You have to understand that we lived in an all-Black neighborhood and, in a real sense; we lived in an insular environment. Movies, churches, schools—everything we needed was in our communities. We had our own theaters: the Ashby Theater, the Lincoln Theater, and the Eighty-One Theater. We lived in a world of Black culture and most of that culture centered around the colleges. That's where we would go to see plays. If there was an art show at Atlanta University, we would attend, and we took music over at Spelman. The colleges were just kind of our focal point for entertainment. And we went to different programs and activities at Booker T. Washington, which was located in our neighborhood. Adults went to clubs over on Auburn Avenue. The Peacock and the Top Hat are two that come to mind. But I don't have to tell you that I couldn't go to clubs. [Laughs] My point is that my parents tried to protect us from having encounters with racism. You know, we just didn't go downtown unless we had to because that meant riding the bus. The Jim Crow bus was the most disgusting form of segregation I experienced. I mean, it was awful! There was a sign on the bus that read "Colored passengers will seat from rear to front. White passengers will seat from front to rear." At Magnolia and Griffin, Magnolia and Vine, we would be okay, but when the bus reached Mitchell and Five Points downtown, we had to move to the back as White people boarded the bus. We were constantly moving back. And we faced segregation when we traveled by train. I can't remember the name of the train we rode out of Atlanta for our trip to

Dr. Carrie Johnson

Detroit, but it was a segregated train and we were always so very happy when we reached Cincinnati, Ohio. That's where we would change to the New York Central, and on that part of the trip we could ride in integrated coaches and go into the dining room. I remember those trips so very well. I remember how we felt when we could move from hot segregated coaches to cool integrated coaches. I have to tell you that the main reason I rushed to buy a car when I started teaching was to avoid traveling in segregated buses. Because you are White and I am Black—Colored is what they said then—I have to move back? It doesn't matter how poor you are. If you are White, are you better than I am because I am Black?

When we shopped downtown, we had to sit in a certain section, and if we wanted to buy a hat, we had to put on a veil. I can understand that [Laughs] because back then we wore a lot of grease in our hair. If we tried on clothes, we had to do so in a special section for Blacks. And when we went to the Fox Theatre, we would have to climb steps and sit up in the buzzard's roost. We would sit there in all our finery. Those were gross and very painful indignities, but we just accepted them. Segregation was nothing easy. Nothing easy at all, so I can understand my father's feelings about White people. I don't think I inherited his disdain, and I say this because when we were growing up, we had contact with Whites through our participation in various activities at the YWCA. I took music at Spelman, and the teachers were White. My parents didn't teach me to hate White people. What they taught me—taught all eight of us— was that we were as beautiful as anyone else and that our role was to be the best we could be. "You are not less than anyone. You are as good as the best." That's what they taught us.

Atlanta was a tough city when I was growing up here, and it was certainly a tough city for a Black man and a Black woman who were rearing eight children. Unfortunately, my parents moved to Detroit before Atlanta changed. They moved in 1956, and the Movement here began in the sixties. You won't find this in "Eyes on the Prize" or other documentaries on the Movement here in Atlanta, but a social club called Club Coterie, was instrumental in bringing about some changes at Rich's. Club members decided to stop patronizing Rich's until "Colored" and "White" signs were removed. You see, there was the White ladies' restroom, and there was the Colored women's restroom. Whites could eat in the Magnolia Room on the sixth floor. Blacks could eat only in the restaurant in the basement. Our boycott started in 1959, and it lasted for seven or eight months, ending in 1961, I think. We boycotted Rich's because, you see, Rich's was the largest retailer in the city. Most Black people in Atlanta participated in the boycott. Let me say this. Stores, like W.T. Grant and S.H. Kress, which was forerunner of Kmart, had separate fountains—one for Blacks and one for Whites. Ridiculous, isn't it? Rich's had only one fountain—people used paper cups—but like the other stores, it had separate restrooms and separate eating areas. Our boycott was a major Civil Rights coup. I wish my parents had been here to see the changes.

I have to admit that we had more than our share of color problems and hair problems in the Black community. All of the school queens and their attendants were usually fair skinned with long hair. At Laboratory High School, a private school run by Atlanta University, most of the students were fair skinned with long hair. When I would talk to my mother about a young man, her question was "Well, is he in the coal business?" I said, "Mama, what are you talking about?" Her asking about "coal business" was a reference to skin color. We always told my mother that she was color struck even though my father is probably about my color or darker than I am. My great grandfather was Irish. My family ran the gamut of complexion. In fact, there were two Matties in the family. One was dark and one was fair. One was called "Black Mat" and the other, "Yellow Mat." Nobody took offense to that. I guess the reason is that we were so very mixed as a family. Most Black families were. I had a very dear friend who lived one block from me, named Sandra Shepherd Reed, and her father was the chief engineer over at Atlanta University. People called her "Red" because of her complexion and, as you can see, I'm very brown skinned. Sandra and I would go downtown sometimes and Whites would look at her. This was in the nineteen forties. So, of course, if we walked up to a counter, let's say in Rich's, the attention would be on Sandra rather than on me. Salespersons would say to her, "May I help you?" They'd kind of ignore me, but it was okay because I knew that I was okay. That's what my parents stressed: knowing that I was okay, that I was as good as the best. Race and color didn't take anything away from us.

My father was a very, very strong and domineering man. I mean, he ruled his house. My mother was up at four o'clock every morning because Daddy had to be at work at five. He was a postman, and he delivered mail in the Atlanta University area. Whatever we were doing before, we had to bring it to an end before Daddy came home. Everything stopped. I mean, my father ruled the house. You know, I didn't understand him when I was growing up, but now that I am grown, I do. When I was young, I would wonder why he kept us at home and why he made us do this and that. He gave my brothers more freedom than he gave me, and he made my male visitors leave at nine o'clock. We didn't go out during the week. Sunday was courting night. We went to church, maybe to a play or a movie. If we wanted to go to a movie at night, we had to ask my father. If I went somewhere at night, I had to be with somebody they knew or I had to be with my brother. Would you believe my brother took me to my junior/senior prom? Black parents were very protective of their children. Very protective! And girls had a much harder time than boys. God forbid a girl would get pregnant! Girls who became pregnant out of wedlock kind of stayed in, stayed at home. They were essentially ostracized. If a young woman—say, sixteen or seventeen—died, many people believed that she committed suicide because she was pregnant or that she had complications from an abortion. You see, abortions weren't legal at the time and they weren't safe, so women sometimes did die from abortions. It was rough for a girl who became pregnant. She wasn't stoned or anything like that, but she certainly was not accepted by the community.

We were taught to believe in family and to do things together as a family. In the wintertime, we would sit in the middle room where there was a fireplace and sometimes Daddy would tell Brer Rabbit stories, and we'd parch peanuts and throw them into the fire. On Saturday, we cleaned house. We mopped, waxed, and dusted. On Sunday morning, we went to Sunday school and church and on Sunday afternoon, we usually went to choir practice or to what we called "ACE League," a youth organization. We spent Saturday evening getting ready for Sunday. We all ate breakfast together on Sunday morning. Many times, Mama would fry chicken and we'd have grits and eggs and biscuits. We had to recite Bible verses, and Daddy would call on one of us to pray. That must have occurred between seventy-thirty and eight in the morning, and after that we left for Sunday school. Most of the day was spent in church. We couldn't go to the movies on Sunday because Daddy saw Sunday as the Lord's Day.

My father was a very bright man. He attended Clark College in the early nineteen hundreds and he became a minister in the AME Church in 1935 or 1936. I think becoming a minister was one of the ways he dealt with his racial frustrations. He was an excellent minister, and he built several churches. He retired from the post office in Atlanta in 1956, and he and my mother moved to Detroit, where his family had relocated in the 1940s. I said to him, "Well, Daddy, I've never seen old folks move north." It just so happened that his mother was still living at the time (she was ninety-nine) and his brothers and sisters were living there, so he wanted to go to Detroit. My parents bought a house in an area they called "Indian Village," and he built a church on the east side of Detroit, Mt. Calvary A.M.E. Church. It is going well today.

My mother did not work. She did a little day work from time to time just to have her own money, but she was in the fullest sense of the word a housewife and a mother. I know you are not surprised to hear that. After all, she had eight children and a husband who worked two jobs, so what time could she have had to take a job away from home? So, my mother did not work. She was a very strong woman, very resourceful, very sweet, very warm, and always pleasant. She was like that with my father all the time. We didn't have a lot of money, but we always looked good because she made our dresses. As we said in the Black community then, my mother "did" our hair, and she cut our brothers' hair. So, you can understand why I say that she was resourceful. In spite of responsibilities of caring for eight children, she made each one of us feel very special. She believed that you did what you were supposed to do and when you were supposed to do it, and you didn't spend time complaining. If there were something she had to do, she did it, and no hurdle of any kind could stop her. I think I have my mother's perseverance. I don't know how she did it, but she made us believe that we could do whatever

Dr. Carrie Johnson

we wanted to do. My mother was the most influential person in my life.

I went to E. A. Ware School, which was located where Jordan Hall at Morris Brown College is now located. The school was named for Edmund Asa Ware, who was the first President, I believe, of Atlanta University. I walked to school. Actually, during that time, you walked everywhere. You walked to church, to school, to the theatre. EVERYWHERE. And you never had any fear of anybody snatching you or sexually abusing you. I would like to write a book about the community of Griffin Street or Vine City of my childhood because it was such a special place and so very different from the Vine City we know today. Everybody knew everybody. Every time you went down the street, you had to go from side-to-side speaking. As children, we played hide-and-seek. We skated. We rode bicycles. We played hopscotch, and we played marbles. When you walked down the street, you could always hear someone playing the piano or the violin. We always had to be our very best. We always had to bring those "A's" home. I think you can say that segregation made us come together in a way that made us clear hurdles. We developed confidence in ourselves and a sense of purpose because we had role models in our families, in our neighborhood, and in our schools. We had great teachers, and we knew they cared about us. Yes, our schools were segregated and yes, we had double sessions and, yes, we used old beat-up, raggedy books from White schools, but none of that kept us from achieving. We had marked-up desks, but that didn't have anything to do with our learning to read and write and think because we had excellent teachers at Ware and also at Booker T. Washington High School. In fact, I would say that we had the brightest and the best because Blacks couldn't get jobs in corporations or in government, and very few of us owned our businesses. As a result, many of our brightest minds went into teaching.

I finished Washington High School in 1947, and I was two years younger than my peers because I had been skipped twice. All of my friends and I got scholarships to Spelman, Clark, Morris Brown, or Morehouse. I chose Morris Brown College because I was given a one-year scholarship and was told that I could keep the scholarship all four years if I made the honor roll. I graduated from Morris Brown College in 1951 with a B.S. in Business and Education. In

1951, I began teaching at South Fulton High School. It no longer exists, but it was located in East Point. I went to Columbia University in New York for my Master's and let me explain that I went out of state because White institutions in Georgia did not admit Black students. University of Georgia didn't integrate until 1961 and Georgia State didn't integrate until 1964 or 1965. So before integration, the State of Georgia paid Blacks to go to other institutions, prestigious and expensive ones, to keep us from going to White schools in the State. That's how I came to earn my Master's at Columbia in 1954. I earned my Ed.D. at the State University of New York at Buffalo in 1978. I met my husband, Alfred Johnson, here in Atlanta and we moved to Buffalo, New York. We married in 1967 and we have a daughter named Alfia. We returned to Atlanta in 1986.

When women in my generation finished college, we looked forward to teaching three, four or five years, getting married, having a family, and living happily ever after. We were encouraged to get an education because our parents didn't want us to be exploited by White men. Without an education, we would be in jobs that would make us vulnerable to the painful experiences that were a part of our mothers' and our grandmothers' reality. Also, we always knew that we had to work because Black men did not have the kinds of opportunities that they have now. We were taught to see the Black man as provider and protector, but we would have to work in order to supplement his earnings. Your generation has so many, many, many, many more opportunities than a young woman of my generation and perhaps that explains why, in my opinion, young women of your generation are materialistic. So, your world is different from the world my generation experienced. I mean, it's just so very different! It's different because Black women are pursuing the professions, and it's different also because they think of achieving for themselves rather than being identified by their husband's achievements. I think what we see in your generation is that Black women have come into their own. They are not as dependent on their husbands as my generation was or my mother's or my grandmother's. And that's a good thing!

I am really pleased that Spelman has an oral history project that focuses on Black

Dr. Carrie Johnson

women of the South and I am really honored to be included. It has been a wonderful experience for me, a very nurturing experience and, you know, it has caused me to think about who I am and why I am. It has given me a new perspective on life, and that perspective helps me relate to young people of your generation, and I hope it helps young women of your generation understand your mothers and your grandmothers. It has also given me an opportunity to do some introspection because there are many questions about my family I need to be able to answer. For example, you asked me how my grandfather was able to acquire land and money, and I have no idea how to answer you. We don't take time to pull the pieces of our family history together, and we should.

And you ask me philosophical questions that cause me to think. What makes me happy? What makes me sad? Those are very important questions, and how I answer them helps me understand who I am. I am sad when anyone in my family is sad. I am happy when they are happy. That is the immediate answer I give to that question, but I know I will go into deeper thought when you leave. That is always what happens. Hours after one of our interviews, I return to a question in order to give it more thought. In that sense, this experience has caused me to really think about who I am, and that's a gift that I will always cherish.

MISS ANNIE JEWELL MOORE

Daytona Beach, Florida

Entrepreneur and Fashion Designer

[My grandmother] was a professional midwife, and she delivered babies to Black women and White women as well. Most of the people would pay for my grandmother's services with chickens and eggs. My sister would ask about the little black bag and Grandma would say, "When you're old enough, I'll tell you what's in that bag." One day, she took out all the instruments and showed them to us. I don't remember much about them because I was not as interested in what was in the leather bag as my sister was. My grandmother delivered me at our home in Daytona Beach, Florida.

Miss Annie Jewell Moore

I was born in Daytona Beach, Florida, but I grew up in Griffin and in Atlanta. .My father died when I was three years old and my sister Minerva was several months. After his death, my mother decided to move to Griffin, where her parents lived. That was in 1922. My mother's name was Orah Sims, and she was born in a little village called Vaughn, Georgia, just a few miles up the highway from Griffin. Her parents were farmers. Their names were Tom Sims and Anna Sims. I called them Grandfather and Grandmother. Their farm was four miles outside of Griffin and close enough for them to walk downtown. When they lived a little farther up the highway in Vaughn, Georgia, they would travel by buggy or by wagon. My grandmother had her own horse, and she would connect the horse to her buggy, which she used on a regular basis because she was a professional midwife. She was also a caterer. She was a very enterprising woman. She was a professional midwife, and she delivered babies to Black women and White women as well. Most of the people would pay for my grandmother's services with chickens and eggs. She took whatever they could give her, and she never turned anyone down. I remember her little black bag, but my sister was more curious about the bag than I was. She would ask, "Grandma, what's in that bag?" And Grandma would say, "When you're old enough I'll tell you what's in that bag." One day she did. She took out all the instruments and showed them to us. I don't remember much about them because I was not as interested in what was in the leather bag as my sister was. My grandmother delivered me at our home in Daytona Beach, Florida.

My father was born in Zebulon, Georgia, which is really not too far from Atlanta. His name was James Moore, and he was the second oldest child in a family or twelve children. His mother (her name was Phoebe) had silver-white hair and black heavy eyebrows. She was a ruddy color. She and my grandfather met in either in Georgia or in South Carolina. His name was Albert, and he was the offspring of a slave woman and her master. So, my great-grandfather on my father's side was White. This same slave woman, who would be my great-great grandmother, had another son but that one was by a slave. Of course, the master favored my great-grandfather because that was his child, and he put my great-grandfather in charge of a lot of his affairs. When they were freed, the two brothers separated from each other. You know about "forty acres and a mule." Well, the master gave my great grandfather forty acres and a mule, but my great grandmother's other child got nothing.

My mother met my father in Griffin through a man who was a friend they had in common. My father would write my mother letters, and my grandparents would intercept them. My mother used to say, "Your grandparents courted your father for me." My parents married in 1917. They had two children: myself and my sister Minerva. He was thirty, and she was twenty or twenty-one, which was considered kind of old because, during that time, girls married at seventeen. When they married, my father was working for Southern Railroad as a chief wagman, which means that he and his group were responsible for getting the luggage on and off the train. He was chief of that group of workers. He was a handsome man, tall with a clear olive complexion. My father died in 1922 of food poisoning. By the time the doctors discovered what was wrong with him, there was nothing they could do. After his death, we moved to Griffin to stay with my grandparents. Seven years later, my mother remarried and what is interesting is that the man who introduced her to my father also introduced her to my stepfather. His name was Felix Hall, and he came from Molena, Georgia. His father migrated from Cuba, but he passed before my stepfather married my mother. My stepfather was very good looking and always wore a smile. I was very close to him. In fact, he was like a father to me. He would tell us stories about World War I and his time in France. Of course you know there was segregation in the Armed Forces, so Black soldiers were all in one regiment. He was inducted at nineteen and, because of injuries he incurred during the War, he had seventy per cent disability. He passed in April of 1970 from complications from the groin injury he incurred in the War. My mother passed six years later, in 1976, from a cerebral accident, which means bursting of the vessel. Both my father and my mother got their wish. Neither one of them wanted to linger in a long suffering condition. Within a week after their sickness, each one passed. So, we said we were thankful for that because they didn't want to linger. They didn't want to be considered a burden on someone.

 I had a very happy childhood. Very happy! One of my fondest memories is of my visits to my grandparents on my father's side. On Sunday morning, we'd always have milk-fried chicken. That's chicken grown on milk. During the week, we'd have mostly cereal, eggs, and maybe some salmon, but on Sunday morning we always had fried chicken. That was good. I enjoyed going to the county fair, and I also enjoyed going on school picnics because my mother would always go with the class. She would be one of the parents to chaperone. I must tell you that my mother was my very first teacher, and that was at Esmond School in Griffin. She taught different grades, and the grades would be stationed at different places in the church. The school my sister and I later attended was the Ashby Street School located right across from the Marta Station on what is now named Lowery Boulevard. I went to Griffin Vocational High for one year. That was in 1933, the year my mother moved back to Griffin. The school had a regular curriculum plus some vocational courses like sewing, cooking and millinery. I took all three plus math, English and science. I entered Washington High School here in Atlanta in 1933, and I graduated in the class of 1938. I graduated at the top of the class and was given a Loving Cup that was inscribed with "Highest Honors" for my achievements. I gave the cup, my yearbook with autographs, and my class ring to the Washington High archives. You should know about Washington High because it was the first high school in the State of Georgia for Blacks. In some of the counties and cities, Blacks couldn't go higher than the tenth or eleventh grade. That's how racism was then. If you were Black and wanted to finish high school here in

Georgia, you had to come to Washington. As a result, the school was flooded with students from the different parts of Georgia. They roomed with relatives or with people in Atlanta who gave them room and board for a fee. The teachers at Washington High were top-notch, and they were all Black. Some of them had master's degrees and they were being paid less than White teachers who didn't even have a bachelor's degree. Mr. C. L. Harper, principal at the time, took up the cause of Black teachers and fought for them all the way to the court. He wouldn't permit any teachers or anybody else to get involved in the struggle for equal salary for Blacks because he knew they would lose their jobs. Mr. Harper won the battle, and so salaries were equalized. The State "punished" him, so to speak, by retiring him prematurely, but he won the case. There is a statue of him at the Ashby Street MARTA Station, but that isn't where the stature should be. It should be at Washington High School. That is where it should be! White people played a dirty trick on us by not permitting the statue of Mr. Harper to be at the school he served. The excuse was that there was a law requiring so many feet between statues and since the Booker T. Washington statue was already in place, there was, legally, no room for a statue of Mr. Harper. Now, have you looked at all those statues around the Capitol?

Being top of the class entitled me to a freshman year at Spelman free of charge. So, my mother only had to pay forty dollars and buy my books. I went to Spelman from 1938 to 1941. My mother was between jobs for a year. This necessitated my dropping out of Spelman from one year, from 1941 to 1942, in order to work and save for my senior year tuition and other college needs. I graduated in 1943. There were sixty seven graduates in my class. I lived at home with my parents over on Sunset Avenue, and I would walk everyday from Sunset to the campus. Everyday! If it rained, my mother would want me to get on the trolley, but I didn't want to do that because I had to transfer to the Fair Street bus. It was a long and drawn-out process. Walking was easier and quicker. Another reason I hated to take the trolley was that you would run into friction. You see, Atlanta was a very segregated city. My parents and grandparents had to live in the system and they learned, you know, to work and survive in the system. I was blessed that they shielded us from it as much as possible. What we were told about racism was not to be subservient or cower down. We were told, "You're who you are, and you're as good as anybody. You just happened to be born the color that you are. You are to respect and be respected, and you are to be aware of racism because it's like a snake." I can remember my mother saying, "Like a snake. You know, snakes are in the grass and you have to be aware that they are there in order to avoid being bitten, but there was just so much staying away from "the snake" Black people could do because they had no rights to speak of on the job situation. Take my mother's experience as an example. She was able to get a job with the Department of Public Welfare because my father was a veteran, and veterans' wives have a priority on certain government jobs. She went from there to the Department of Recreation. As a matter of fact, she was on the ground floor of that department. When she was at the Department of Public Welfare, she would have to train Whites who hardly finished high school, and they would then become her boss. I guess she must have dealt with it all right because we didn't know about it or hear about it until we were grown up. She had her goals and objectives, and that was to care for her family and see that her daughters were educated. So, she put up with it, as most Black parents did. And although my father fought in the War, he still had to deal with racism. Black service men were treated awful, just awful. The only hospital they could go to was a substandard hospital in Tuskegee. As I told you earlier, my father had a seventy per cent disability discharge because he was injured in the groin area, but if he didn't tell you he had an injury, you would not know because the limp was slight. So, the first five years of my parents' marriage were struggling years, and that was right in the heart of the Depression. My parents went through a lot because of racism, but we didn't know much of anything about racism until we were older in part because our parents shielded us from racism as much as they could and also in part because we went to all-Black schools and lived in all-Black neighborhoods, so the only direct contact with Whites would be public transportation and downtown shopping. In spite of all that we experienced, we were never taught to believe that Whites were superior to us. Our parents taught us to believe that all of us are God's masterful creations.

As a child, I was considered old and ahead of my time. People would say, "Well, you act like a grandma." I didn't quite understand it, and I felt very uncomfortable whenever people would say that about me. My sister was an outgoing person. She engaged in games and so forth. I guess I was more into puzzles and drawing, freehand drawing. I was also into reading. I read a lot, but what I liked doing most of all was working with drawing pencils and crayons and sewing clothes for my dolls. I guess that was the first indication of my talent for design. And maybe what led me to go into fashion was that we always had dolls, and my grandmother did a lot of embroidery and crocheting. That fascinated me, as did my mother's ability to make doll clothes by hand. I remember my grandmother had a friend whose daughter, because of a handicap, was sent to a special school where she learned to sew by hand. The first time she came home from that special school and I saw all the gorgeous doll clothes she had made, I wanted to learn to sew like that. I was six or seven at the time. And then when I went to the vocational high school in Griffin, I made my first dress, and I thought it was perfect. So, that's how it started. At a very early age, I was preparing myself to be a fashion designer.

I went into fashion design in a serious way when I was living in Detroit. I went there in 1948 because my sister was living there and, as you know, we are very close. I stayed there for thirty-four years, from 1948 to 1982. So, Detroit was the natural place I would have my salon. The name of my salon shop was Ann Moore, Couturiere. Couturiere is a French word that means sewing, or suture. In the case of fashion, it has reference to dressmaking, high dressmaking. The salon was located on West Grand Boulevard in Detroit. It opened in 1963 in the fall. I closed the salon in 1970. After then, I spent ten years in Detroit Education. I returned to Atlanta in 1982. I have been back to Detroit for a visit two times since 1982.

There were three haute couture houses in Detroit when I opened my salon. Two of them were White-owned. Mine was the only one Black-owned ahaute couture salon in the city. The White salons were located in Grosse Pointe, an area with old wealth. It would be comparable to Buckhead here in Atlanta. My salon was located at 2621 West Grand Boulevard, and it was diagonally across the street from Motown, five minutes from Saks Fifth Avenue, the General

Miss Annie Jewell Moore

Motors building, and the Fischer building. I saw the building in which my salon was located eight years before I moved in. I would pass the building and think to myself how excellent it would be for my salon with a built-in boutique, and I would send up a prayer because I knew the building was just ideal. This went on for approximately eight years before I actually found myself in there. I had eight hundred dollars for the building. The realtor was able to get the owner of the building to lease it to me for a year, with a conditional lease for the next year at one hundred and fifty dollars a month. I had the whole lower floor and one-half of the lower floor beneath me, which was my workroom, and the full parking lot in back. I lived on the premises and, of course, I decorated my living space with special care. The upper level of the building housed two plastic surgeon interns who worked at the plastic surgery hospital, Straith Memorial Hospital, located two buildings over from me. It was a famous hospital, and celebrities would go there to get things done. I remember that Dean Martin and Loretta Young used to go there. The head nurse would come to shop and visit us from time to time. We called her "The Straight Gazette" because she would tell us who was over there getting what done! [Laughs] In the building next door to mine, there was a two-story building that housed an insurance agency owned by a Black man. His office was on the first floor; he rented the upstairs space to a dentist and to a psychologist. When I closed my shop in 1970, he bought my building and connected it to his.

During the years I had my salon, I did designing for wealthy Whites in Grosse Pointe. In fact, I made the 1960 opera gown for Mrs. Glancy, who was what you would call very, very old money. She was a social contemporary of Mrs. Ann Ford, who was the first wife of Henry Ford II. In 1960, Mrs. Ann Ford was the chairperson for the Metropolitan Opera concert. The Met coming to Detroit! That was the highlight of the social season. In that year, my agent, who was a young Swedish girl, made contact with Mrs. Glancy. When I met her, I thought at first I was looking at a Black woman. Mrs. Glancy had just returned from Florida where she had gotten a deep, deep suntan. It was very disarming, very disarming. I showed her the rough sketch of an opera gown that I had made on a white sheet of paper, and she accepted the sketch as it was. I had less than two weeks to do that dress. When we delivered the gown, we had been up for seventy-two hours! Mrs. Glancy said she had never been fitted so well or so easily. And that wasn't the only gown I made for her. I made the dress that she wore to the art luncheon and the dress that she wore, a short dress, to the Hunt Club Ball. Mrs. Glancy said, "I like to hit all the highlights of the social season in an Ann Moore." She said that. When her friends learned that I was Black, they put pressure on her not to let me do any more designs for her. So, I didn't get any more calls from her, and if you don't get a call, you don't get commissions, you know. That was all about race, all about race. I encountered that all the time. And I got it in a different way from my own people. You see, there were two social groups in Detroit -- the barristers' wives and the doctors' wives guild. They were considered the apex of the Black society. I wasn't in either one. I was not a native of Detroit. I was from Atlanta, and I was a graduate of Spelman College. You don't have to have bachelor's degree to be a dressmaker, so my being a Spelman graduate was of little weight. I mean, this was the mentality. There was a male group called "Cotillion" that sponsored young girls making their debut, and I was not included in that either. It was a strange thing. It was a strange experience. I thought we Blacks would embrace each other and we'd stick together. This is the way I was brought up. This is what I did. My parents emphasized to go to a Black first if you can get the service there. Go to a White only when you can't get the service from the Blacks, and we were brought up that way. Black people have some very deep, deep psychic scars. As a friend of mine said, 'Unfortunately, Black people are still letting the great White father think for them."

My path to fashion designing was anything but easy because I was a pioneer. At first, I went to Traphagen School of Design, which is located in New York. It's one of the oldest designs school in the nation, and it's still in existence. I went there in the summer of 1946. I also went to Fashion Academy that located in New York, but it's no longer in existence. I was there from 1949 to 1950. It took me two years to get in there. And I went to Ecole Guerre Lavigna in Paris during the summer of 1954. I think my experience at Fashion Academy was the most challenging of all because only two Black persons before me had studied there, and I had

Miss Annie Jewell Moore

to wait for two years, for two years, before they would admit me. When I was finally admitted, I signed on to live in the Three Arts Club in New York, which was comparable to the YWCA. Supposedly, it was open only to girls who were studying the three arts: music, ballet, and fashion design. But there were White girls living at the Club who were **not** in the arts. You see, what I mean about racism? When I went to check in, a little white-haired woman was at the desk and I said, "I'm Ann Moore." She was surprised that I was Black and she tried to cover herself by saying, "Oh, you weren't due here until tomorrow." But I couldn't be denied a room because they had already admitted me. What happened at breakfast the first morning was interesting: I walked into the dining area and started at the beginning of the steam tables and by the time I got to the end, the whole kitchen force was out there gawking at me. There had never been a Black woman at Three Arts. This was in 1949. I was later put in contact with a lawyer who reprimanded me for moving out of Three Arts Club. He said they had been trying to integrate the Club for years because it received public funds. He took my case, but the court date was delayed until 1950 after my enrollment at Fashion Academy was finished. By then, I had returned to Detroit and did not have the funds to return to New York. I was in the fashion industry for twenty years and during that time I created more than a thousand designs.

When I was younger, I wanted to produce a family. Well, that didn't happen. I lived through WWII and also through the Korean War and the Vietnam War. In the peak of my youth and the peak of the youth of my male contemporaries, Uncle Sam was sure to get hold of them and send them off to war. I believed that if there are two people the Lord wants to put together, nothing will keep them apart. I also believe that everyone is not destined to marry. I believe there's a certain amount of predestination in all of our lives. By that I mean that certain things are destined to happen, regardless what we do or try. Then I looked back at my life and said, "Well now, it didn't go the way I had envisioned, dreamed, or wanted necessarily." I wanted to be in business, and it was a long, hard struggle to get into business. I think to myself that if I had had a family, I wouldn't have been as free to move around as I have been able to do. Maybe that was destiny. I know it was my destiny to be a fashion designer, to be a pioneer. I was a woman, I was Black, I was single, I was educated, I was moral, I was a pioneer. I wasn't able to pay myself a salary because I had to pay others a salary to keep everything else going. All pioneers pay a price, and I was a pioneer in fashion design. I am thankful to have survived and I am thankful and very happy about my achievement. I'm thankful for being alive.

DR. ZELMA PAYNE

Montgomery, Alabma

College Professor and Nutrionist

Rosa [Parks] got on at one corner, and I would get on at the other. The bus driver would say, "Pack on back! Get on back!" I remember two bus drivers on that line who were humane. . . The bus ride was behind me once I got to school because I would be with my friends. My teachers were lovely, the school was small, we had programs, and we had each other. At the end of the day, we would catch the bus with our friends, and it would fill up with school kids. We'd go across town, get off at our stops, and walk into our houses. Riding segregated buses was only a small part of our day. It didn't keep us from being together and enjoying each other.

My full name is Zelma Allegra. That's a musical term meaning 'merry': Zelma Allegra Payne. My mother's friend, Ella Bell Williams, gave me my middle name. I was born in Montgomery, Alabama, at Memorial Hospital. My mother, Thelma Price Payne, was also born in Montgomery and, like me, she was an only child. My father, Esco Payne, was born in a small town outside of Montgomery called Millbrook, but he and my mother met in Montgomery. He was a bicycle rider and, if I recall correctly, he passed my mother on the bike one day, turned around and came back to talk to her. She was nineteen at the time, and he was twenty-two. They were married in 1929 shortly after that first meeting. My father was one of seven children, and all of them except my father lived in cities away from Montgomery.

I never wanted for love when I was growing up because, being an only child, I had my parents all to myself and my maternal grandparents as well. Their names were Ardella Price and Frank Price. I was very close to them. Very close. The first house my parents and I lived in was my grandparents' house. It was truly an intergenerational house—three generations under the same roof—because all of us lived there together: my parents, my grandparents, and me. I couldn't have been happier. Every place inside the house and outside was like my own special playground. I would ride my tricycle round and round the large round table located in our dining room, and I would swing from one of the chinaberry trees that were so lovely in our backyard. My grandfather made the swings for me, and my grandmother, who was homemaker, made all of my school uniforms. You see, when I grew up, we had to wear school uniforms. I remember that they were blue and they had a white collar.

I knew only joy in my grandparents' house. Unfortunately, when my grandfather died, and that was in 1939, we had to relocate because the government bought the property in our area. We lost out to what is called eminent domain, which we are hearing so much about in Atlanta and, actually, elsewhere in the nation. If the government feels that a given piece of property or a given area can benefit a larger number of people than the residents, then the government, because of what is called eminent domain, can buy the property, and you, as homeowner, can't refuse to sell. **That's** "eminent domain." Well, that's what happened to my

Dr. Zelma Payne

grandparents' house. The government bought the property to build Cleveland Courts, one of the first housing projects in Montgomery and, needless to say, my grandfather was not paid the full value of the house. But that's how it can go, and often does go, with eminent domain. We moved to a house located on Holt Street, which is historic because the first mass meetings in the Montgomery Movement were held at a church on our street: The Holt Street Baptist Church.

When I was in the first grade, I went to a Lutheran school down the street from where I lived and after the first grade, I went to a laboratory school at Alabama State College, which is now called Alabama State University. I rode to school with a lady who would pick up children at their individual houses and drive them to school. You could call that early carpooling, I guess. When I entered the sixth grade, my parents thought I was old enough to ride the city bus to school, especially since the bus stopped a block and a half from our house. I was so very proud of myself! I would drop my bus tokens in the little slot and ride across town to the laboratory school. Would you believe tokens cost only a nickel? [Laughs] By the way, the bus we rode was the same one Rosa Parks rode. She lived in Cleveland Court projects in back of me, and all the people who lived there rode that same bus, or rode that line, which was called the Washington Park/South Jackson line. Rosa Parks would get off downtown to go to work, and we would keep going across through town to get to school.

The laboratory school went from the second grade through twelfth, and students who went to the school were a pretty selective group. You had to get good grades in order to be a student at the laboratory school, and you had to be serious about your schoolwork. We never went home from school without homework to do. We had homework everyday. Everyday! My mother was a second grade school teacher, so I imagine I was very disciplined around my schoolwork. She taught first in the county, which was called Pineapple, Alabama, and when I was in about the ninth grade, she taught at a school that was closer to where we lived. By the time I was finishing high school, she had been transferred to Carver Elementary, a big school located in the heart of the City of Montgomery. After Carver, she went to Dannelly Elementary School. The fact that my mother was a teacher and also the fact that the laboratory school was serious about learning meant that I had to be a serious student. And I was.

People are so impressed when I tell them I grew up in Dexter Avenue Baptist Church. That's where Dr. King pastored. I'm always asked what it was like growing up in Montgomery and, sometimes, it's as if people think Montgomery was the only city with Jim Crow buses. They ask, "How did you deal with that?" I tell them the same thing I will say to you: it was difficult. When I rode the bus to school, after I got old enough to ride the city bus, the first four seats in the front were reserved for Whites. You might recall I told you that I rode the Washington Park/South Jackson line, the same bus that Rosa Parks rode. I got on at Holt St., and Rosa got on at Adeline, which was the next block up. More Blacks rode that bus than Whites did because Blacks were going to work in the stores downtown. The bus driver would say, "Pack on back! Get on back!" We had to go the side door and pack in. The bus ride was behind me once I got to school because I would be with my friends. My teachers were lovely, the school was small, we had programs, and we had each other. Riding segregated buses was only a small part of our day. It didn't keep us from being together and enjoying each other. When I'd get home, I would go to my piano lessons. Learning to play piano was a part of my upbringing—actually, a part of southern Black culture for girls. There were many programs at our churches and, of course, in our schools. What I'm trying to say is that the bus ride was only one part of our day.

When we were in town—that is, away from the Black community—we knew that we had to deal with segregation, but we knew how to take care of ourselves and how to protect ourselves. For example, we made certain that we parked our cars in the right place and that the parking meter did not run out so that we wouldn't get a ticket. Before we went shopping, my mother made sure that we had a snack or a meal, including water, prior to leaving home. You see, the lunch counters were for Whites only, and so we always had something in the car if we became hungry. Segregation didn't prevent us from being proud people. If anything, it intensified our pride. My grandmother, Ardella Price, would tell me, "Hold your head up and walk like you know where you are going." She emphasized how important it was for me not to look down. To this day, I don't look down. You know, I think that growing up in the days of surviving the insults of segregation gave my generation role models who represented the "Blackness" of quality. In my case, those role models included my parents and grandparents, my teachers, my Sunday School teachers, and people in the community. I remember how much I learned about integrity and being a lady at meetings of the "Sunbeam Band" and in my classes at the laboratory school. Adults always focused, as my mom did, on what she called the uniqueness of being "black."

Would you believe I learned how to drive when I was thirteen? My daddy would let me shift the gears in the car while he was behind the wheel. One day, when we were at a picnic, I told Daddy to move over and let me drive. He said, "Oh Pudding', you can't drive." That's what he called me. "Pudding." I said, "Oh, yes I can." Once my daddy knew I could drive, he gave me the responsibility of backing my mother's car out of the garage and putting it on the front so that my mother could drive it out of the driveway when she went to work. I was driving at thirteen, but I didn't get my license until I was sixteen because that entailed saying, "Yes Sir" to the White man, and I didn't want to do that. The first time I went to get my license, I simply refused to say, "Yes sir." The next time, my mama and my daddy said, "When you go back down there, say 'yes sir'." I did, but only because I wanted to get my license.

I was seventeen when I entered Tuskegee, and I was really excited not so much about going away from home, as many college students are, but about going to Tuskegee! I fell in love with the school when my eighth grade home economics teacher, Ms. Linnie Hall, took us on a field trip to Tuskegee. I majored in home economics, but I should tell you that home economics is not about sewing and baking. It is about much more than that. It involves learning about nutrition and the importance of nutrition to health. That was my area of concentration when I was at Tuskegee. I had no interest in sewing although I did some tailoring of my clothes. I was interested in nutrition, and so that's what I studied. It was a privilege studying at Tuskegee! You really can't talk about the history of black colleges without underscoring Tuskegee, its distinctive achievements and its rich tradition. When I was there, the President was Dr. Frederick Patterson, who would later be the founder of the United Negro College Fund. Every aspect of our lives at Tuskegee was infused with ritual. I'm a uniform child. [Laughs]. I wore uniforms in lab high, in high school and at Tuskegee. This is the cape we had to wear at Tuskegee. My mom kept it all these years. We would march to the chapel wearing our capes and our navy blue skirts and white blouses and black shoes and, of course, stockings. See these initials. Z.P. Those initials stand for my name—Zelma Payne. If I took my cape off and put it down somewhere, maybe in the dining hall, I would know which cape among the many capes was mine because my mother sewed in my initials. This was made in 1948, my freshman year at Tuskegee.

There was no guessing what it meant to be a Tuskegee woman. We heard the definition all the time and in a special way from the Dean of Women, who held meetings for women students twice a month after our Wednesday evening worship service. And, you know, we didn't see the rules and regulations—the restrictions—as a burden because being a Tuskegee woman was a privilege. There was a big recreation center on campus and, in that day, not too many Black colleges had the kind of recreation center Tuskegee had. It was in the center of the campus, on the lower level, and it was off limits to girls. That's where boys went to play music and cards and pool. In my day, the poolroom was a no-no for girls. In fact, if a girl were caught playing pool, she would get demerits! And we didn't wear shorts, and we didn't go to meals with pants on because in that day women weren't wearing pants. Oh, no, women didn't wear pants. Some of the girls would get up and want to go to breakfast in their nightclothes. There was an older lady named Mother Watkins, who sat by the door, and if you had on a long coat, she would say, "Come here, daughter." If you were wearing pajamas under your coat, she'd send you right back to the dorm.

We had daily room inspections in the dorms, and the housemothers would come around and check to see, you know, if we had made up our beds. Housemothers would check to see if we were out of the dorm and gone to chapel. Of course, we had special seating in chapel, so we were marked absent if we were not in our assigned seat and we would get demerits. If we got a

Dr. Zelma Payne

certain number of demerits, we were sent home. I never got any demerits my freshman year, but my junior year was a different story altogether. I got demerits, but this is why. I liked candy and Booker T. Washington's great-granddaughter and mother had a candy kitchen across campus. I got caught two minutes after seven buying candy at the candy kitchen. The problem was not the candy. The problem was the time. We had to be back on campus at seven. When my friends and I were coming back on campus, the Assistant Dean of Women saw us. We were late, so we got three demerits.

I became an AKA at Tuskegee, and Booker T. Washington's granddaughter was my advisor. In my day, becoming an AKA meant two things: finer womanhood and scholarship. It pushed you to be a scholar and to make good grades. It also grounded you in the principles of lady hood, of womanhood. You had to be a lady in order to be an AKA. In that day, because of Jim Crow, you could not check into hotels and being a member of the sorority was a bonus because if you needed assistance when you were traveling, you could always call on a soror. Today, the young women don't seem to know what joining the sorority is all about. Scholarship has been lowered, standards have been lowered, and dressing is lowered. Everything has changed. And this "skee-wee" sound you hear from AKAs today? We didn't have that back then. Absolutely not!

I graduated from Tuskegee in 1952 and accepted a job teaching at Alcorn State University. That was my very first job ever! I had four classes. One was a class on food study and preparation and another was a class on meal planning and table service. Now that is something we need to put back into the curriculum because people don't know how to plan a meal or how to sit down and eat with appointments, and that's what this particular class taught: how to set a table, how to plan meals, and how to plan for special occasions. A third class was a class on basic nutrition—that is, what happens to the food we eat and what takes place in the body during digestion. I also taught advanced courses in food and nutrition. I loved teaching, but I didn't like living in the country, and Alcorn is definitely in the country. The switchboard cut off at eleven thirty. Imagine that? We couldn't get a taxi because there were no taxis where we lived. When we went to a grocery store or to a drug store, we had to go to Port Gibson, which was the closest town to campus, and it was seventeen miles away. Port Gibson is in Mississippi. It was a very prejudiced town, very prejudiced. It is an understatement to say that I didn't want to remain at Alcorn State, so I went home. That was in 1955, the year the Montgomery Bus Boycott started.

I wasn't surprised that the boycott took place in Montgomery. You see, Black people in Montgomery were very proud. Very proud. We had Alabama State University and churches that had strong leaders and very active and involved members. Also, people in different communities in Montgomery were in communication with one another. So, Blacks were ready for the boycott. At the mass meeting the night before the boycott began, they were excited and they were organized. The next morning, no one was surprised that the busses were empty. People were walking! If you were going to town, people would pick up strangers, perfect strangers. That's what my parents did. They would stop and the person might say, "I'm just going down the hill." And my parents would say, "Oh, fine," and they would give the person a lift down the hill. Somebody else would be going all the way downtown. "You want a lift?" my parents would ask. The person would say, "Yeah." The door opened, and we had a passenger. That just shows how trusting we were of one another and how ready the people were for change. We gave people we didn't even know a ride. We wouldn't dare do that today. But that's just how close people were in that time. We had each other as a race, and we felt good when the boycott began. Of course, you know about Martin Luther King, but there is another man you should know about in reference to the Montgomery Movement. His name was Ed Nixon, and he had worked with the NAACP for many years. He was a recognized and respected leader, but he was not as articulate as Dr. King, which is probably why he was not chosen as spokesman for the boycott. He was a Pullman car porter and had not had the privilege of a good education. You know, being pastor at Dexter Avenue Baptist Church and spokesman for the Montgomery Movement propelled Dr. King to national prominence.

I left Montgomery before the boycott ended to take a job at South Carolina State

Dr. Zelma Payne

College in Orangeburg, and that's where I taught for five years. Orangeburg was a small town, but there was a train in the city that ran through town right to campus and there were buses, so Orangeburg was not like Alcorn. It was a small town, but it had major transportation, including an airport! [Laughs] The airport was only forty miles from campus and I would fly in and out of Orangeburg while I was teaching at the college. The city was predominantly Black at the time, but it's now integrated. I had some good students at South Carolina State, but I also had good students at Alcorn State. Students are students. It's how you relate to them and how they relate to you that counts. I left South Carolina State to take a teaching position at Spelman. That was in 1956. The job was available, I wanted to live in a city larger than Orangeburg, and Atlanta was an exciting city that offered cultural activities. I enjoyed teaching at Spelman very much. I found the students to be emerging leaders who didn't accept the cookbook kind of education. They were intellectually curious and they made you, as a teacher, want to do excellent work.

In l967, I left Spelman and moved to East Lansing, Michigan, where I worked on my doctorate at Michigan State University. While I was there, I had a part-time job as an admissions counselor. I was one of the first Blacks to integrate the Office of Admissions and Scholarships at the University. I was at Michigan State when Dr. King was assassinated. I couldn't believe that he had been killed. I just couldn't believe it. Students in the evening class I was scheduled to teach that night were shocked, and I was shocked in a special way because I was Black and because Dr. King was a part of my
Montgomery memories.

I left Michigan State with my doctorate in l971, and I was contacted
by the Dean of Allied Health at Emory University, where I taught for four years and served as Director of the Graduate Dietetics Program. I was the first Black to do so. Doctors were among some of my students. You see, as I was explaining to you earlier, nutrition is a combination of chemistry, biochemistry, and biology. It deals with life and with what happens to the food that we eat when it goes into our body. It's biology. It's biochemistry. It's anatomy. In order to be

a nutritionist, you have to take courses in chemistry and, really, in order to be a doctor, you have to know about the biochemical and physiological processes we study in nutrition.

I enjoyed my work at Emory, but when Dr. Audrey Manley asked me to come back to Spelman, I accepted her offer. I returned to the College in 1974. I remained at Spelman until 1980. I saw one of my former colleagues yesterday and we laughed about the fact that when we first met each other and were teaching at Spelman, there were only forty faculty members and we met in the science building, which was called Tapley Hall. Now, the number of faculty has increased so much and the campus is so much larger that faculty don't get to know one another. Then, all students were required to go to chapel. That is no longer the case. And students had to adhere to certain dress codes. I don't think that is the case today. These are different times, very different times.

I have been fortunate to do a great deal of traveling out of the States and, of all of my trips, the one to Recife Pernambuco, Brazil, was perhaps the most exciting. What inspired me to make the trip was reading "The Diary of Carolina Maria de Jesus" for a course at Michigan State University. The book was written by a Black woman who lived in the slums of Sao Paulo, Brazil. A *New York Times* reporter discovered her diary, and that's how it came to be published. Carolina's experiences in the slums (called favela) just touched my heart. When I was visiting Recife Pernambuco, I found the poverty to be just as Carolina describes it in her diary. Sometimes I say that I'm done with traveling because of the threat of terrorism and all the restrictions imposed on us when we travel, but I am game and should the opportunity arise for travel to a country of interest, I'll be on that airplane!

A typical day for me? Let's talk about today. I walked the track, as I always do, at six this morning. I came back, took my shower, had my breakfast, and I've gotten telephone calls for my birthday, but I was ready for you. [Laughs] I have my club meeting at five. I'm a member of The Utopian Literary Club , one of the oldest literary clubs in Atlanta. It is now eighty-eight years old. Our oldest member, Mrs. Ann Cooper, will be one hundred and three in January. I stay busy. I serve on the Genesis Board for the homeless shelter, Advisory Board of

Dr. Zelma Payne

Foods and Nutrition at Tuskegee University and the International Board for Home Economics, and I do some consulting work in fundraising, but the work that makes me happiest is doing the shopping for the elderly who are no longer able to drive.

What makes me happy? Oh so much, so very much makes me happy. I've had a good life. I had a good education. I had good parents. I've traveled widely to places all around the globe. I have good friends. I am involved in some very meaningful activities. I have retired, but I am engaged in so many activities. In fact, I seem to be busier now than I was before I retired. I am happy with my life and pleased with my achievements. My many blessings make me happy.

What makes me sad? You know, young women of today's generation find it difficult to believe that women of my generation have a good feeling about our lives in spite of Jim Crow. They wonder how we did it, and I wonder why they are not taking advantage of the many opportunities they have, opportunities segregation denied us. When you ask me what makes me sad, I would have to say that is what makes me sad.

MRS. LAURA LYNEM RATES

Cynthiana, Kentucky

Degree Auditor at Spelman College

[My mother] would pass when there was something she wanted for her family or something she wanted to do that racism denied Black people. For example, she would go to stores and try on hats. Now, when she did that, she wouldn't take me with her because Whites would be able to see that I was Black or African American. She would take my oldest sister Marie, who looked Oriental, or my sister Lillie, who looked White. My mother wouldn't go to the back of the bus. She would sit where she wanted to sit and if they asked her to move she would say, "I'm not going to move." I honestly believe my mother would have been outspoken about race even if she had not been fair enough to pass.

Mrs. Laura Lynem Rates

Everyone knows me as Laura Rates, but I want you to know me as Laura **Lynem** Rates. My maiden name is very important to me: L-Y-N-E-M. It's such an unusual name that I always say that anyone with the last name LYNEM, whether that person is in prison or on drugs, is probably related to me. My family is originally from Kentucky, but there are a lot of LYNEMS in Detroit, Indianapolis, Dayton and Kentucky. If I did some research, I believe I would discover that **Lynem** families in Detroit and Dayton have roots in Kentucky. Blacks in the South and in border states like Kentucky migrated to different cities in the North. My father was Sheley Lynem and he was born in Cynthiana, Kentucky as the sixth child in a family of fifteen. [Laughs] You might find this interesting: My great grandfather, my grandfather, my father and my brother--all of them were named Sheley. So, it's a very special family name. Unfortunately, my deceased brother Sheley didn't have any children, so the Sheley name is gone, and I'd like it to stay in the family for generations to come. That's why, at a recent family reunion, I suggested that someone name one of their children Sheley.

My mother was Marie Hayes and she was a native of Kentucky, but she was born in Lexington. She met my father when she would come to Cynthiana with her aunt to visit the Davis family who owned a funeral home there. My father went to Wilberforce University after he finished high school and they met when he came to Cynthiana. My mother had not entered high school but a cousin told me years later that my mother was supposed to have gone away to school somewhere in Ohio. If she did, that might have been where she learned to do all the crocheting, embroidering, sewing and quilting that I remember her doing. She probably didn't finish high school. They would visit each other and my father came back to Kentucky to marry her. They married in 1914. He was twenty-one, and she was fifteen. In those days people married at younger ages than they do today.

My parents had five children: Carl Irving, Marie Elizabeth, Sheley Floyd, Lillie Mae and me, Laura Etta. I was the youngest in the family, and I have to confess that I was a bit spoiled. I should stress **youngest** because I was nine years younger than the oldest child. I was born in the same town where my father was born: Cynthiana, Kentucky. When you ask me to tell you about Cynthiana, the first thing that comes to mind is that it was a small town and that it was predominantly White. It was also essentially rural, but not in the sense of deprivation and unpaved roads and weather-worn houses. You see, I was fortunate that my father's parents, Grandfather Sheley and Grandmother Laura, owned land and one of their daughters, my aunt Mary, married into the David family in Cynthiana, and the David family owned land. They also owned race horses that they would breed and sell. So, my grandparents were landowners in Kentucky at a time when not that many Blacks owned land. Their house was located on a highway that was paved. I mention this because when we think about the South, especially about Black people in the South, we tend to think of unpaved roads. Well, the road that led to my grandparents' house was paved. The house had a big porch with a swing on both ends and two rocking chairs in the middle. When you entered the front door you came into a foyer and you could see steps leading to the upstairs. There was a living room downstairs but it was used mainly for guests. The downstairs also had a dining room, a kitchen and one bedroom. Upstairs there were dormitory-type rooms where the children slept. Four or five slept in one room, and they kept their clothes in trunks. The boys slept in one room, and the girls slept in another room. There were eight boys and seven girls.

I've done a lot or research on the history of the Lynem family, going back as far as 1818. When you see records dating back to the nineteenth century that have your family's name on them, that's really something. What I discovered in my research is that my great grandfather, Sheley Lynem, owned and sold property or land. That was before Emancipation. All of the records I've checked say that the Lynems were free people. I have some of the deeds to land that my great grandfather owned. He didn't know how to write, so he signed deeds and other documents with an X. Isn't that something? What really surprised me is that my great grandmother also signed documents. Now for a woman, especially a Black woman, to have that kind of recognition surprises me. My great grandmother signed X, but her name was Sarah, and it was spelled Sally (S-A-L-L-Y) on some of the documents. I guess there was a lot of misspelling back then because so many of the people working with documents were not that

Mrs. Laura Lynem Rates

educated. I lived on the family farm with my parents and my siblings for about six years. We lived in a house that was up the hill from my grandparents' house. We would walk down the hill to see them and up the hill to return home. And I say "walk" because there were no cars at that time and, besides, the road to the house was impassable except by tractor or wagon. I have vivid memories of bath time when we lived in Cynthiana. We took baths, not showers, because we had only bathtubs. We took baths in a tin tub and only once a week. You were required to take a bath once a week. And you took your bath in the kitchen because that's where the stove was and on the stove was where you would heat the water. Also, the kitchen was the warmest room in the house. Mama and Papa took a bath there also. We had to wash up everyday in the morning and before going to bed.

Grandfather Sheley loved the land, and he believed that owning land was all his children needed. He didn't stress education, but my grandmother did and that was a good thing because my father didn't like the farm. He didn't leave it, but he became an AME minister. I think I was four at the time. But when my grandfather died in 1918, my father stayed on the farm to help my grandmother with the records. There were other siblings, of course, but my father had been to Wilberforce, and it stood to reason that he would be the one to keep the records of the farm. He was the minister at two churches – one in Falmouth, Kentucky and the other in Erlanger, Kentucky – and he would go there on Sundays. During the week, he was on the farm helping my grandmother take care of the farm.

My mother kept a garden where she grew all of our vegetables, and she would can them. If freezing had been possible then, she would have done that. But at the time, people grew vegetables and then canned them. She also sold eggs and butter to people in the town. That was her own money. My mother was a very good cook and fixed fancy things. She enjoyed having guests for dinner. She used to bake bread (salt-rising bread it was called), but it would be in a loaf and we would slice it, heat it up and butter it. The bread was delicious! My mother cooked mustards, kale and turnip, but not collards. And we didn't eat grits. I didn't have grits until I married and came South. We did eat beef because we had cows for milk and sold the milk. We had pigs on the farm, so we ate pork. They would slaughter the pigs and cut up the meat for the family. We also ate veal and lamb. We had a lot of sheep, and they would shear the sheep and sell the wool. You probably don't know about Rhode Island Red chickens. They're sorta rustic in color. Well, I got them when I was very young and I raised them. They were my pets, you see, "my chickens", and they would come up to the back porch for me to give them food and for me to talk to them. I could hold them and pet them. One Rhode Island Red had a black tail and the other one had a white tail and that's why I named them "Black Tail" and "White Tail".

I grew up around flowers because my mother always had a beautiful flower garden in the summer. She decorated the churches at Christmas and at Easter with flowers she made out of crepe paper. She was very creative. She liked to write poetry and she could use a typewriter. She drove a car and she also drove the buggy. Yes, there was a buggy on the farm. It was horse-drawn buggy with a hard top. For a woman living in Kentucky in the twenties, my mother was very progressive.

I never worked on the farm, probably because I was so young when we lived there, but my brothers might have. As a matter of fact, I know they did. They would pick tobacco and sell it. That's the way they would make money to buy their school clothes. My father didn't like the farm I guess because he was very intelligent and read a lot and always wanted to learn new things and wanted to do something else. So, that's why I'm sure he went into the ministry. He would go to Wilberforce University during the summer and Kentucky State College in the summer. He didn't finish college, but he was chosen as a member of the Board of Trustees at Wilberforce University. He was the first in his family to go to college. This was around 1912. He was a good pastor. He was not an emotional minister. He didn't "whoop" and "holler" and jump around or anything like that, but everybody loved him. People might not have liked his preaching because they were used to something different but he always looked after his congregation. He would always visit them. He would always counsel them. That was the type of person he was. He had a good rapport with people and was able to talk to anyone in a quiet

Mrs. Laura Lynem Rates

way. He rose to the position of Presiding Elder in the church. My sisters and I always said that if we married we wanted our husbands to be like our father—you know, protective and caring and yet wanting you to be your own person. Both of my parents protected us girls, but they wanted us to be prepared to take care of ourselves if we were not married and also if we were married and the marriage didn't succeed. That is one of the reasons they stressed education. Another reason is that they didn't want us to have to do certain kinds of jobs in order to make money.

Both of them had strong feelings about race, but my mother was more outspoken. When it came to White people and Jim Crow, she spoke her mind. She just wouldn't take anything from White people. My mother was fair enough to pass, and she would pass when there was something she wanted for her family or something she wanted to do that racism denied Black people. For example, she would go to stores and try on hats. That was something Black women were not allowed to do in the South. Now when she did that, she wouldn't take me with her because Whites would be able to see that I was Black or African American. She would take my oldest sister Marie, who looked Oriental or my sister Lillie, who looked White. They would go to movies and enter through the front door that was for Whites only. My mother wouldn't go to the back of the bus. She would sit where she wanted to sit and if they asked her to move she would say, "I'm not going to move." And she never put us in a situation where we would experience Jim Crow. She didn't want us to be denied anything and be hurt in any way because we were Black. She just wouldn't take anything from White people. I honestly believe my mother would have been outspoken about race even if she had not been fair enough to pass.

You see, my mother's mother was raped at the age of fourteen by a White fireman in Lexington. Her name was Lillie, and that's what my mother called her: Lillie. My mother was raised by her aunt and uncle. They say her father was Italian, but we don't know this to be the case. My mother didn't like being biracial, and I think that's why she was so outspoken, especially with White people. She really didn't talk about being biracial. I don't remember any particular incidents, but I do know that there were times when our fair complexion made a difference. I'm sure that the way we looked was one of the reasons Whites had a lot of respect for our family. I hate to say that, but its true. And I believe that one of the reasons my aunt and my uncle were so good to my mother was because she was fair. My mother never talked about her complexion, but you could tell that was the reason she was so outspoken.

We lived in different cities because my father was given different church assignments. He began preaching when I was four years of age. When I was six, he was given a church in Harrodsburg, Kentucky and so we moved there. From Harrodsburg, we moved to Ashland. I was eight years old at the time. And when I entered the sixth grade, we moved to Midway. So, my parents lived in four Kentucky towns: Cynthiana, Harrodsburg, Ashland and Midway. In each place, they lived in the church parsonage. I know my mother had friendship with other women, but I don't believe she had close friends. Back in those days, a minister's wife had to keep friendships on an even keel. You couldn't single out one person for a close friendship. Women would come to the house for quilting bees and for taffy parties, something that only women did, but my mother didn't have a woman she could just sit down with and tell some of her problems to, you know? And I often think about that now. I'm sure my father gave her advice. I know that they talked a great deal and they were very close and enjoyed each other. They showed affection to each other that was unusual in those days. I was a minister's child and that meant living with restrictions and living a somewhat sheltered life. Something as harmless and natural as dancing I didn't do because my father was a minister. I had friends, but I didn't spend the night at their houses. Maybe that was one of the reasons I had close relationship with older women--Miss Suzie, Miss Edna, Miss Wilma. I would go to visit them, and we would sit on the porch in the swing and just talk. They would give me candy or cookies or cake. They'd tell me about their childhood and what they had been doing that day. Spending time with them was very important to me.

I think I was seventeen when Pearl Harbor was attacked. I remember it was on a Sunday and it really bothered me. My older brother Carl was drafted. He had finished college and had gone to Officer's Training School at Fort Still in Oklahoma to become a Second

Mrs. Laura Lynem Rates

Lieutenant. He was the only Black in his class, but he served in a segregated Army. The Army was segregated then! My sister Marie was in the WAC, and my brother Sheley was in the Army. My brother won the Purple Heart and the Bronze Star for injuries he incurred in battle. So, the War affected my family in a personal way. Actually, everybody was affected by the War because of the rationing. You see, people had to make changes in their lives because of the War. It's not like that today. There is a war going on in Iraq and thousands are being killed, but we haven't had to ration the way we did during World War II. Then, you couldn't buy certain things and you were limited to the amount of food you could buy. You were given a little booklet with stamps in it. When you bought food, you'd tear out the stamps and that way you would know how much you had left that you could buy. Even children were aware of the War. When I gave my senior class speech I talked about the War. You see I was class president. I don't know why they chose me because I led a sheltered life as the daughter of a minister and there were many girls more popular than I was. Besides, they'd been in the school longer than I had. I had been there only one year because we had just moved from Midway to Lexington when my father became Presiding Elder of the Lexington District. So I was surprised when I was chosen class president and, as class president, I had to give the class day speech. And I still have that speech. I wish my mother could have been present to hear me. I know she would have been proud. She was killed in a car accident seven months before I graduated from high school.

I had already moved to Lexington to go to school, and I was living with a family in the city. My parents were still in Midway, but they were making arrangements to move to Lexington. My father was presiding elder at the time and had to attend a quarterly meeting. My mother had picked me up in Lexington so that I could go with her to get my father and take him to catch the bus to the city where the meeting was being held. So, there was nothing unusual about this trip. After we dropped my father off, I didn't get out of the car and get up front, which is what I usually did. My mother said, "You're not going to get up front?" I said, "No, I'll stay back here." Because, you see, back in those days, they didn't have heaters in the car and I had a blanket over me. I don't know why, but that night I didn't move up front. I stayed in the back. I still don't think that I would have been hurt as badly as she was. A car came from out of nowhere, it seemed, and hit us on the driver side of the car. My mother was thrown against the steering wheel and her chest was crushed. There were no seatbelts in those days. We weren't driving fast and the roads weren't wet. The man who hit us had been drinking. He was White. After he hit us, he ran into the woods.

After the car hit us, my mother tried to talk but she really couldn't. A man who lived in a house near where the accident took place took my mother from our car and put her into his car. My mother was still alive when my father came to the hospital. She couldn't talk, but she knew my father was with her because someone asked her, "Do you know who this is?" She mumbled "Yes, my husband." I was taken from the hospital to the dentist because my mouth was injured in the accident. When I returned to the hospital, my mother had already died.

On the day my mother died, I wrote in my diary about it being the saddest day of my life. A year later I wrote, "Mama has been dead for a year. I still miss her. I wish she could be here." After my mother's death, my sister Lillie came home to live with us, my father and me, and she was really a lifesaver. I became a different person. I talked back to my teachers and to other people because I was grieving. I don't know how I got through the class day address.

My mother died in 1942. I entered Kentucky State in 1943. I didn't do too well in college my first two years and everyone was concerned about me. I had a chip on my shoulder. I was angry. I was in pain because I missed my mother so very much. Every year, I would beg my father to let me quit. He always said no but, at the end of my sophomore year, he gave in. He told me that I didn't have to return to college if I didn't want to. That was good medicine for me because I didn't have any idea what I was going to do if I stopped, you know. So, I returned to Kentucky State, and that's when I met my husband, Norman Rates. I was still grieving, and he helped me so much. For a long time, I couldn't even talk about my mother. Even now I have a difficult time talking about her death. It's a wonder I don't start crying. I've healed, but not having her is still very painful for me. Nothing--not my husband or my

Mrs. Laura Lynem Rates

children--can make me forget her death.

I met Norman in 1943 in my freshman year at Kentucky State College and at the end of my junior year he gave me an engagement ring. Two weeks after graduation, in 1947, we married. Norm and I have been married for fifty-eight years. We have lived in a number of cities and we have traveled to countries around the globe. After graduating from Kentucky State, we moved to Lincoln University in Pennsylvania because Norm was studying religion there. Horace Mann Bond was President at the time and we babysat the two Bond children, Jane and Julian. We also ran the college bookstore and post office as a way to make income while Norm was a student with a full scholarship for three years. During the summer of 1948, while we were at Lincoln, we moved to New York State to work with agricultural migrants in a program sponsored by the National Council of Churches in the State of New York. We left Lincoln in 1950 after my husband earned the bachelor of divinity degree, and we moved to Pompano Beach, Florida to work with migrants there in a similar program, also sponsored by the National Council of Churches. In 1951, we moved to Oberlin, Ohio, where my husband studied for his divinity degree from the Oberlin Graduate School of Theology. From Oberlin, we went to Morris College in Sumter, South Carolina. That was in 1953, and Norm taught at the college and served as dean of men. I worked in the library.

In 1954, my father died. He wrote a letter to me telling me how proud he was of me. I still have that letter. In 1954, I became pregnant with our first child, a daughter named Sondra. It was also in 1954 that we received a letter from President Albert E. Manley inviting Norm to come for a job interview. Who wouldn't want to work at Spelman! Norm came for the interview, got the job, and we moved to Atlanta in August of that year. We have been at Spelman for forty-seven years. We were away from Spelman from 1960-1961 when my husband was studying at Yale Divinity School. Our second child, a daughter named Shari, was born while we were in New Haven. We were away from Spelman again from 1968-1969 while my husband studied at the Harvard Divinity School. He retired three years ago and is now Dean Emerita of the College.

I served as a degree auditor at Spelman for thirty-five years, and I retired ten years ago.

I consider myself to be a blessed woman. I have a wonderful husband, two wonderful daughters, a wonderful grandson named Jordan and many friends. You ask me what makes me happy? Being with my husband makes me happy and having my family together for the holidays makes me happy. And participating in this project has made me happy. I have looked forward to your visits and to the special time we spend together when the interviews end. You turn off the tape, and we continue talking. That has been wonderful. This experience has helped me journey into my family's history, and I needed to do that. All of us do. Just talking to you about my life has made me feel good about being an African American woman and being raised the way I was raised and in such a loving family. I know the description of the project says that we are giving our mentees a gift, but you have given me a gift.

MRS. RUTH SCOTT SIMMONS

Jackson, Mississippi

Teacher

Whenever Esther would get ready to go down Farris Street for ice cream, she and her girl friends wouldn't want me to go with them. I would tell Mama, "Esther and them don't want me to go with them to get ice cream. She said my hair wasn't fixed right and I don't have a ribbon on." Mama would say, "You go back and tell Esther the ribbons don't have to match if your hair looks nice and it's plaited up and your hands are clean. Tell her I said they are to take you along with them." That went on all of my life because Esther always wanted me to always match.

My full name is Ruth Emmeline Scott Simmons, and I was born October 30th in 1916 in Jackson, Mississippi. On my next birthday, I will be ninety. I imagine I was born at home. We had a big house on Farris Street. We went back to Jackson to visit about twelve years ago, and the house was still there. Can you imagine that? Also still standing was a two-story office building that my father built in 1910. After all this time, the house and office building was still there. The house was adjacent to an oil mill and we didn't know until many years later that the mill had created my father's asthma or at least contributed to it. The doctor said there was nothing that could be done to help my father because there were no medicines then for asthma. The doctor said we should probably move to another city where the air was better. My father chose Johnson City, Tennessee.

When we were in Jackson, my mother had a buggy that she rode in and she would drive it herself. She had a surrey to hold the family because there were nine children and a mother and father so I guess we probably used both of them. I had six brothers and two sisters. There were nine children. [Smiles] The eldest girl was Vashti, and she was the first one to finish Spelman. Esther was the next elder daughter. I was the youngest daughter and the youngest of the whole family. I was the baby. My six brothers were Aurielus, William Alexander, Cornelius, Daniel, David Augustus, and Emel. The oldest brother was Aurielus and the youngest was Emel.

My brother got sick with typhoid fever. We were in Tennessee at the time, and I was about seven or eight. That would have been in 1924 or 25. He was the only one in the family that had it. I remember how faithful my mother was. She would tell us, "You don't just pick up a glass and drink from it." She would boil everything. It took a lot of work caring for my brother and people from church would come and assist my mother. It was a fine church that we were members of. That's where I was baptized, and I remember they wrapped me in a robe like a bear robe. I kept that robe on after I was baptized. It was cold in the basement and I thought I was going to freeze. [Laughs]

My sister Esther was three years older than I am, and she always felt that she should tell

Mrs. Ruth Scott Simmons

me what to do and how to do it. She was the kind of person somebody would call prissy because she loved to dress and she loved to match things. If you had on a blue dress you had to have on a blue ribbon and you if you had on a blue ribbon, of course you had to have on blue socks. I was different. If I had on nice clean socks, that would be all I'd want. Whenever Esther would get ready to down Farris Street with her friends, she wouldn't want me to go. I would tell Mama. I would say "Esther and them don't want me to go with them to get ice cream. Esther said my hair wasn't fixed right and I don't have a ribbon on, but we just going down the street. I don't have to dress up to go down the street." She would say, "You go back and tell Esther the ribbons don't have to match if your hair looks nice and it's plaited up and your hands are clean. Tell her I said that if the girls are going down the street to get ice cream, they are to take you along with them." [Laughs] That went on all of my life because Esther always wanted me to always match.

Being the baby, I started school early. I started school when I was three. You see, my mother worked at my father's Progress Printing House office and everybody else was already in school. I guess my mother thought she had had been mother long enough, so she sent me to school, and the principal was so impressed with me that first day because I knew my address, my sisters' names, my brothers' names, where my mother was working and I knew our phone number. He carried me around the school and told all the children, "Look at this little girl. This is the first time she has been to school and she knows her telephone number and she knows her address". He would ask me, "What is your telephone?" I would recite my telephone number. [Laughs] I finished high school when I was only sixteen and I never skipped a grade. I enjoyed that, but I never had any desire when I was in school to make this honor roll or that honor roll.

Oh, yes, I remember the games we played in Mississippi and particularly in Tennessee. We did more skating and bicycle riding than anything, and I remember the way I learned to ride a bicycle. Of course, my sister Esther was too prissy to ride a bicycle. [Laughs] I don't remember anything but a tricycle and that wasn't too much fun. You couldn't get any speed out of a little thing like that. [Laughs] My brother Augustus worked at a grocery store and he would ride a bicycle to work. As soon as he would get off his bicycle at home, I would get on the bicycle, and he would ride me. That was so much fun. He would say, "I can't keep riding you. I got to get back to work!" [Laughs] So he decided to teach me how to ride by myself. I remember our house was such that it was on level ground with a vacant lot in the back and a hill that led to it. My brother said, "I'm going to ride you up here to this hill so you can learn." The hill was more like a slant in the driveway but to me it looked like a big hill! The garage was straight ahead. So, he put me on the bicycle, and I was headed straight for the garage and the door was open and I could see myself going through there and hitting the back wall, but I turned and I made it. [Laughs] I was in about fourth or fifth grade. I figured I was big enough and I wanted to learn, but girls didn't have bicycles. Only boys had bicycles. They also did skating and they played baseball. Really, I didn't do anything physical until high school level at Langston. I played basketball when I was in the eighth or ninth grade, and I joined because I thought it would be fun plus the fact that the teams would go to Bristol, Tennessee and other places.

I think we must have moved to Johnson City, Tennessee, when I was in the fourth grade. I started high school there at Langston High School. We moved to Atlanta in 1928, and I went to Booker T. Washington High. It's being remodeled now, and I don't think any students are at the school now. But that's where I went to high school. I finished there in 1930 and, many years later, I taught there. That was after I had finished Spelman. The school is up the street from this house. When I was there, the street was called Hunter Street, but it is Martin Luther King Drive now, so this house is on Martin Luther King, but when we moved here, the street was called Hunter Street.

My father's full name was William Alexander Scott, I, and he was from Mississippi. My mother's full name was Nancy Emmeline Southall, and she was born in East Liverpool, Ohio. My mother was quite graceful, and she grew up in high school as the only colored in her class. She was close to her father. His name was Daniel R. Southall, Jr. He would carry her to church all the time. They would go to a White church and to a Colored church. She met my father at a

Mrs. Ruth Scott Simmons

church. You see, churches in Liverpool would host students from Hiram College in Hiram, Ohio. I don't think it was all that far from Liverpool. The students would come to the churches and sell books and bibles, you see. And so, this time, when the students were coming, the minister told my mother, "There is a young man with them, I would like you to meet." And she said, "I would like to meet him." That young man was my father. He was the only colored person in the class, and being a girl my mother didn't have any social relations. She was an outstanding student of Latin. She led her class in Latin and was the only Black student in her class. The teacher would say, "Who's going to translate today," and nobody would translate. Mama would stay up late at night studying. The teacher would say, "I guess we have to let Miss Emmaline translate today." Latin was her favorite subject.

My mother was very fair and she had brown hair. She always wore a switch. She was the oldest of eight children and she had only one sister. As I said, she was born in East Liverpool, Ohio. Oh, no, my father was not born in Ohio. He was from Mississippi and the way he got to Ohio, where he met my mother, is an interesting story. It has to do with my grandfather on my father's side. He and other slaves helped Union soldiers at the Battle of Vicksburg. What they did was to show the Union army a way through the swamps. The soldiers would not have known because they were from the North. That's what my grandfather and other slaves did. When the War ended, one of the Union generals said to the coloreds who helped them: "You all have been such a help to us. What can we do for you?" My grandfather said, "There's nothing you can do for me, but I have a son who I would like to get educated." That son was my father, and that is how it was arranged for my father to attend and graduate from Hiram College.

My mother's father owned property in Liverpool, but he wasn't born there. He was from Virginia where he was a slave. His name was Daniel Southall. He was the black son of the owner of the Southall Plantation. My grandfather had the job of managing the stables, which he did very well. During the Civil War, the "White son went to the front and was shot off his horse and killed. My mother's father kept taking care of the stables while the master was at the front fighting. He did what he was taught to do and he carried on just as if he were White. When the war was over, he had done so well and since he had stayed with the stable and the "real" son had been killed, the master, his father, gave him land. I don't know how my mother's father ended up in Ohio. I have a picture of him; he looks just like one of my oldest brothers. I think he must have gone from Virginia to Canada and from Canada to Ohio. He must have married a White woman named Amanda. They had eight children, and my mother was the oldest in the family. She had six brothers and one sister. I remember that my mother's mother would come to visit us, and my older brothers would go to meet her at the train station and they would tease her: "Grandma, they're going to get you about riding with those White people in the car. Why would you come down in the White car?" She would say, "Well, I don't run the trains. I give them my bags and I sit where they place me." She had red hair, and she was whiter than most White people. I remember that. You know, my mother said that her father actually got sick when she told him she and my father were going to move South. He was a wealthy man, and he would give each of his children land when they married, and just the thought of his oldest daughter moving to Mississippi made him sick. One daughter of one of the brothers came here, and she went to Clark. She's still living here. I don't know how old my parents were when they married. I would like to go to Louisville and get a copy of their marriage license. That's where they married. In Louisville, under the sponsorship of a Rev. Singleton.

They came to Jackson in 1910, and my father started a printing business. Actually, he had four jobs. He was always busy. He had the printing business. He was a minister. He was head of the Grand Worthy Counselor of the Court of Calanthe Lodge. So, my father was very busy. He worked so hard and that's probably why he died at such a young age. He was not yet sixty when he died. And that was the year I went to Washington High School. That was in 1928. I remember when he would come home from one of his trips, and I would be so happy to see him. I would hug him and kiss him, and then I would tell him, "You got those stickers on your face." I could feel those stickers. [Laughs] One time, he went out West, and that was a

Mrs. Ruth Scott Simmons

long trip, and when he got back, he had these stickers. I didn't know that was a thing for men.

I adored my father. I adored my mother. And I loved growing up in my family. I can never remember being alone. Some people say I was spoiled, and maybe I was. [Laughs] My brother Aurelius loved rocking me more than I loved being rocked. I grew up around a lot of people. All of them were bigger and older than I was. [Laughs] I can never remember being afraid of anything. I can never remember being alone.I was close to my sister Esther because we were the closest in age. We shared the same bedroom in all of our houses until we moved into the house that was down the street from this one. That was our family home and I was nineteen when it was built. Then Esther had her bedroom and I had mine. There were three other bedrooms upstairs and a bath. I've never had any trouble sharing.

The first time I saw Atlanta was when my sister Vashti graduated from the laboratory school at Spelman, and that was also the year my brother Aurelius graduated from Morehouse. That was in 1925. I was born in l916, so you can figure out the math and know old I was. My mother and my father and Esther and I were in the car. Gus was driving the car. I remember when my father would tell Gus to pull over to the side and stop the car. My father would go into a gas station and talk to the White man. He would tell the man that he was Rev. Scott from Jackson, Mississippi, and he was going to Atlanta to see two of his children graduate from school. The White man would tell one of his workers, "This is Rev. Scott and he wants you to check his tires and his oil and show the ladies to the restroom." And we would go and continue on our trip.That was our first car. It was a Ford Model A. I was amazed that we could roll the windows up and down. If it rained, we didn't have to worry. We could just roll the window up. And that was amazing because colored people didn't have cars and we had been riding in surreys. They had blinds that you could pull up if it rained, but the car had windows, and I appreciated that.

When we came to Atlanta, we stayed with a lady called Ma Hadley. She had a house right across the street from Spelman. I couldn't imagine my sister Vashti had lived here for two years going to high school. I was just delighted. Atlanta was such a beautiful place. The houses and the flowers and the beautiful places colored people lived in. Of course, Atlanta was segregated when we came here, but I never had any racial confrontations. I remember, though, when I was in the car with W.A., and the car broke down and we had to get on the bus to come back into town. My brother had to get off the bus before I got off the bus, so he went up and told the conductor I was his sister and be sure that she gets off at such and such street so that she can catch the bus that goes down to Auburn Avenue. The man said okay. He would do that. So while W.A. was up there talking, he just got off the bus at the front, and the man said, "Wait you can't do that!" W. A. said, "Well, I am already on the ground now." He just walked on and nothing happened, but something could have happened if the bus driver had been a racist and an idiot. He could have called the police and it would have been a scene.

We could never drink from the fountains. Mama would say, "Before you ever leave home, the first thing you do is to go to bathroom and wash your hands and know that you're not going to be sitting on these seats in public places. You didn't tell us there they have any seats for Colored people?? That's the way she did it for us. Whenever we were going any place, we always go to the bathroom first and wash our hands and we didn't drink out of public fountains. It was a long time before I knew the difference between White and Colored because there were so many light-skinned Colored people in my family and all around me. I don't remember when I realized there were differences. And my parents never told me anything about how to approach White people. I remember I was in grade school in Tennessee and the grade school was about three blocks down the street and my mother taught at the school. I also remember across the street from us some White people lived and they were so old and at night they would sit on the porch and smoke pipes. The lady would smoke a pipe and the man would smoke the pipe. What was very interesting about it was that they had a grandson and this grandson was in grade school and the old people didn't know how to teach him. They would ask my mother to let the little grandson come over and do his homework with us and he would come over and we would all do homework together but we never played together. I can't ever remember playing with any White children. You see, some of the Colored people were as light as the White people and so growing up, White and Black, we just never discussed it.

Now, in Atlanta, I didn't have any problems with race and what not, you see, because I never went anywhere by myself. Somebody was always with me. I guess I was sheltered or something. And we always lived near the heart of the White businesses because, you see, Auburn Avenue leads right up to Peachtree Street. You could walk right into the heart of the city and just come back to Auburn. I never sat behind White people on the bus. The only bus I used was the one in the Colored neighborhood, and I wouldn't go beyond Auburn Avenue. When we shopped at stores downtown, they wouldn't let us try on hats unless they gave us something to put on your head before you tried on the hat. And *Davison's* didn't want us to try on shoes. But they would love for you to put stuff in the layaway.

My brothers started the first paper in 1928, and that was here in Atlanta and it was called *The Atlanta World.* W.A. went home to Johnson City, Tennessee to talk with our parents about starting a newspaper in Atlanta because he wanted Negroes to have inspiring news, you know, about what Negroes were doing. He wanted to prove to White people that Colored people could have an important business and could give jobs to other Colored people, you know? So, our parents said okay and they gave W.A. money to start the paper and he came back to Atlanta and started working on the newspaper. The first one came out in 1928, but my father never lived to see the paper. He died in 1928 several weeks before the first one was published. I don't remember when the paper changed from *Atlanta World* to *Atlanta Daily World*, but that's what it was named. *The Atlanta Daily World.* I think my brother W.A. was a genius, and it was so tragic that he died at the age of 31. He was murdered here in Atlanta, and the man who murdered him was acquitted. That had to do with what W.A. was doing for the Black community. Would you believe the attorney who was defending the man who killed W.A. actually used the word "nigger" in the trial? He called W.A. a "nigger" that the White people were fortunate not to have to deal with anymore. That was very tragic and that was very hard on my family, especially my mother, but we didn't stop the paper.

The newspaper made for a lot of excitement in the family and because of the newspaper we met many famous people. My mother and my father met the first President Bush and Mrs. Barbara Bush, and so I met them. I met President Nixon and President Ford. I've been to the White House many times. In the early 1950's Emperor Haile Salasie of Ethiopia visited the U.S. and President Eisenhower invited my family down to Fort Benning, and Emperor Salasie brought two of his granddaughters on his visit. We spent the weekend as guests of the President with the Emperor and his granddaughters. One was tall, and the other one was short. Both were extremely beautiful young women.

Mrs. Bethune stayed with us in our house down the street whenever she came to Atlanta. She came to Atlanta to see her grandson graduate from the School of Social Work at Atlanta University. Mrs. Bethune was something! My son and I were her guests at her home at Bethune-Cookman College on several occasions in Daytona Beach. My mother was a very close friend of Mrs. Bethune and she and Mrs. Bethune often vacationed together in Cuba during the late 1940s. My mother was also a founding member of the National Council of Negro Women, and that's how I met Dorothy Height. Oh, I've met so many wonderful people! And my mother believed in community service. That's where I got involved in different organizations. I helped established the Southwest Community Hospital and Senior Social Services. I was also the first Colored woman invited to join the Downtown Atlanta YMCA Board of Trustees.

I started at Spelman in 1933, and graduated in 1937. I thought Spelman was the most beautiful place I had ever seen. We did a lot of courting around the fountain. [Smiles] I lived in Morgan Hall on the other side of the campus. After Spelman, I went to Atlanta University for one year. I guess it was just one year. I was so through with school when I finished at Atlanta University with a Masters in Business Administration. After AU, I taught at Washington High School for a short time and I earned $80.00 a month. Laughs]. I quit teaching and in 1942 I had my first and only child, a son named James Russell Simmons, Jr. after his father. I started working at the newspaper in 1943. I stayed there a long time. I didn't leave until 1998. I left then to care for my husband.

Mrs. Ruth Scott Simmons

I have five grandchildren and five great-grandchildren with a sixth on the way. They keep me happy, but I was happy before I had grandchildren. I have always been happy. Even when I was growing up with my sisters and my brothers, I was happy. I guess I am happy because I have never been alone and I have always felt loved.

Do I see myself as a southern lady? Yes. I like that. I like being called a southern lady.

Mrs. Nell Simms

MRS. NELL SIMMS

Henry County, Georgia

Entrepreneur and Director of Day Care Center

*My grandfather on my father's side owned a plantation in Henry County,
and he gave each of his children a farm, and that's how my father came to
have a farm in Henry County, and that's where I was born and reared. In
nineteen something, the boll weevils got bad and the farm wasn't paying off,
and my father decided to sell. He gave it away for like seven hundred
dollars. He owned sixty-five acres. Seven hundred dollars! Can you picture
that? I can't buy one acre for sixty-five dollars. I've wished many a time
we had stayed on the farm.*

Mrs. Nell Simms

I was born in Henry County, Georgia in 1910, but I have lived in Atlanta most of my life. We moved here in 1924 from Henry County, and that's a hop, jump and a skip just right down the road, about eighteen miles. That's in South Georgia. My mother, my father, my brother and myself moved here. My name is Nellie Mae Arnold. Mama had a friend named Nellie. I don't know if her name was Nellie Mae, but I know it was Nellie, and that's where the Nellie for my name came from. My brother called me Sister and I called him 'Bro." His name was Eddie Leroy Williams. I was his protection, and I liked that, but being a boy, he wouldn't be too protective of me. When I'd get into something, he'd tell on me. He'd say, "Sister ought not to have been there."

My mother's name was Tommie Lee Williams, and my father's name was Eugene Arnold. I knew my mother's father and mother. Their names were Riley Williams and Prosthenia Williams. I don't know how to spell my grandmother's first name, but that's the way it was pronounced. They lived in Henry County, and I guess they were born there. Grandma and Grandpa. That's what we called them. I think they had thirteen children. My grandfather had been married before he married my grandmother. He had one daughter and a son by his first wife. I didn't know the son, but I knew the daughter. I grew up with her children when we were living down in Henry County. Mama was next to her. Mama was his oldest daughter with Grandma.

Papa was a farmer, and Mama was a farmer's wife. I thought they were the greatest folk in the world. I didn't know too much about their background except that Mama had a lot of sisters, and she was next to the oldest one. I knew my grandfather and grandmother on Mama's side, but I didn't know my grandfather and grandmother on my father's side. They were dead before I was born. But my grandfather on my father's side owned a plantation in Henry County, and can you believe that I didn't ever ask or didn't ever think to ask how he came about having a plantation. He gave us of his children a farm, and that's how my father came to have a farm in Henry County, and that's where I was born and reared, on my grandfather's plantation in Henry County and on my father's farm. I didn't think to find out how we came to own land.

We had everything we needed. We had apple orchards and peach orchards. Mama canned and dried fruit, you know? We had cows, so we had milk and butter, but we had to buy our cheese. We had cotton and, of course, we had cotton seed. We would store the apples in the cotton seed and keep them until spring. It was something growing up in the country. I'd like to be there now. On the farm. In nineteen something, the boll weevils got bad and the farm wasn't paying off, and my father decided to sell. He gave it away for like seven hundred dollars. He owned sixty five acres. Seven hundred dollars! Can you picture that? I can't buy one acre for sixty five dollars. I've wished many a time we had stayed on the farm.

I was born at home with a midwife. Don't know who the midwife was. Don't even know anything about it, but I know I was born at home on the plantation. I was the oldest child. I don't know anything about my mother's pregnancy or how it was when she had me because, you know, they didn't talk then about things like that with children. Where babies came from? They just told you, "Don't." That's all. "Don't." My grandfather's land was divided up between the children and so my aunts and uncles, they were my neighbors. I don't know in what direction, but joining our farm was a White family, and I grew up not knowing (and this is funny) that I was Black or not caring, you know? We would go to their house and eat, and they came to our house and ate. We didn't have to go to the backdoor, so I grew up thinking I was good as anybody. I guess most Black people in Henry County didn't have that kind of experience, but we were on our own land. We didn't work for anybody. Matter of fact, my father had people working for him.

So, I didn't learn all that mess about Blacks and Whites until we came to Atlanta. It was different here. Where you had to sit on the streetcars and what you had to do when you went into the dime stores. I remember signs. "Colored and White." This was in the early twenties. It didn't make sense to me. I didn't worry about eating in the lunchrooms because I didn't have but about fifteen or twenty cents for a hotdog, and that suited me, you know? But when the students couldn't do it, that bothered me. I didn't really know people hated people or disliked people that much until I came to Atlanta. You know, I just didn't know. When King was

Mrs. Nell Simms

marching, I just knew that wasn't for me, you know? I saw the picture about Montgomery, and I couldn't stay in the theatre. I had to come out because I wanted to crush the screen. I wanted to throw something at the screen with them treating folks like that. This Bull Connor in Alabama and the Fire Department and how they let the water take the people up in the air and then they'd snatch the water back, and let the people fall to the ground? Me? Put up with that? You wouldn't catch me marching with King because somebody would have had to kill me before they got started. Let somebody spit on me? Not me. The young people could do that and I'm real proud they were able to carry on. I was proud of them and Dr. King. I guess I can say I knew him before he was born. [Laughs] His grandparents and parents came from Henry County. Rev. King, Senior grew up with my mother. When my mother's sister passed, he was at the funeral and he said to Mama, "Tommie Lee, you're about one hundred, ain't you?" Just asking my mama how old she was! I never shall forget that. [Laughs]

Me and my brother were pretty obedient children. If Mama said to do something, we did it. I learned how to clean because Mama taught me. If you didn't do it right, she'd say, "Well, you got to lick that calf over." When we got sick, she did the caring for us. She gave us castor oil. Any cold or anything you had, they gave you castor oil. I would say, "Mama, it made me sick!" She'd say, "That's because you needed it so badly." They gave us castor oil every springtime. And you know what? I don't have any problems with my bowels, and I believe it was because of Mama's home remedies, especially the castor oil!

Mama taught me how to be grateful and respectful, you know. She had older friends and sometimes they'd give us something. We'd say, "I don't want it." Mama would tell us, "If it's a dirty dishrag, you take it and bring it home. You don't have to keep it. You just thank them for it and bring it home and forget it." Isn't that something? We didn't get a lot of things like children get now. We made our dolls, you know. We'd take corn cobs and take the shucks and make the hair. We didn't have too many toys. I remember me and Brother had a wagon. The both of us played with it. We had one tricycle, and we had it together. We had toys that we made. Children don't do that now.

Of course, we went to church. It was about six miles away in Stockbridge, and most times we walked. I liked going to church. I really did because that's where I could play with my friends, you know. I joined church when I was eight years old because, you know, we grew up in church. I can't sing a lick now but I used could sing. My father played piano in the church and he wanted me to learn to play it, but the piano just wasn't fast enough. [Laughs] We had a school in the community named for my grandfather. It was called Arnold Grove. That's where we went to school. That's the first school I can Remember was Arnold Grove. It had one room and one teacher for twenty-five or thirty students. Most of them were our family because I had lots of cousins because, you know, Grandpa Arnold gave land to all of his children. I went to McDonough to go to the first grade, and I lived with my uncle and aunt. I had a teacher named Miss Daisy Brown, and the first letter I got through the mail came from her. It's in there on the table. When school closed, I wrote her and she wrote me back. She said she had showed my letter to several people and they did not believe I was that young and could write letters. I still have her letter with a two-cent stamp on it because that's how much you spent to mail a letter.

November 5, 1918. My dear little Nellie Mae: You did write me and I waited so long to answer you. I have shown your letter to lots of people, and everybody thinks you have been going to school four or five years. You are smart and sweet as can be. Well, I have been very sick. I had influenza. Have you all had it? That's why school hasn't opened. We will begin now next Monday. I hope you will be here to enter too. I am going to do my best for you this term so your mom and pop can see how smart you are. Did you help them pick cotton? I picked a whole lot myself. You must be smart. Wash dishes, sweep the floor,

Mrs. Nell Simms

and try to do everything your parents tell you, but I know you do that anyway. I wanted to come to see you all this fall, but I've been so busy getting ready for school. Tell little brother I hope he's going to be smart like you. I hope he can come to our school too. I am almost well now with the flu. Much love to all. I'm expecting you in school Monday. Be a sweet little girl and don't forget your teacher. Daisy E. Brown

I didn't go back to that school. I went to Arnold Grove. Miss Brown died. She had the flu. That was in 1920 when the flu was so bad. The next three, four and five years, I was at the Arnold School. When I went to the sixth grade, I went to live with my uncle in Birmingham. He didn't have any children. He was one of my favorite uncles. So, my parents let me spend a term with him and then I came back home. We still lived in Henry County, but I came to Atlanta to school. I lived with another uncle and his wife when I came to school here. I graduated from the seventh grade in Fulton County schools and then I went to the school at Clark College in the eighth grade. When I finished the eighth grade, I went to Washington High, and then I married. I was seventeen and in the ninth grade. That was in 1929. My husband was from Jackson, Georgia and he was living in South Atlanta. I met him at church because we would go to church all the time to get out, you know? That's where I met him. His name was Willie Leonard Sims. You know, I was still a child. We were born in the same year, and so we were about the same age, but I was a little bit older than him because I was born in March and he was born in May. We just slipped away and got married. I was doing day work. I worked cleaning houses, helping a lady take care of her house. She had a daughter that was my age and we worked together cleaning up like children do. I mean, whatever. Well, this day, when I got through, I went over to Summer Hill and Willie had the preacher there, so we got married. I wasn't gonna tell my mama and my dad, and he wasn't supposed to tell anybody, but he did.

Someone told my father, and my father cried. He said, "You didn't have to get married like that. Not like that. I wanted you to have wedding." My dad just cried when I got married. I said, "Well, I'm not gone anyplace. I'm here. I'm still here!"

They loved Willie. I believe they loved him more than they did me. He was just that kind of person. I don't know how we came to live with my parents, but I know this: I never get grown. My husband would tell me what to do and they would tell me what to do and I had to obey both. I wanted to a place of my own, you know? I wanted to be the woman of my home, so we decided to get us an apartment. The first apartment was in University Homes. My husband was not as bossy as he was when I was at home because I did what I wanted to do. I went when I wanted to. I had my friends, you know. I could go around with them as I wanted to. We moved there in the mid to late thirties and we lived there for six years. I think we lived at home with my parents for six years.

And then I heard about houses going up on Fair Street being built by a Black man named Mr. Atkins. I put two hundred and fifty dollars down on a house and a lot. That was a whole lot of money back then. That was in the nineteen forties. Atkins wanted one hundred down, but if you gave him two hundred and fifty, you could pay twelve dollars every month on what you owed. So, that's what I did. My husband said, "I don't think I'm gonna buy." I said, "Why not?" He said, "Well, everybody's saying that they gonna lose it." I said, "Lose it? For two hundred and fifty down and twelve dollars a month you gonna lose something? You make more than that in tips!" I said, "Well, I'll tell you what. I'm not gonna ask for it back. You go get it if you want to." When he came home from a trip, I had moved. My husband was happy. He was a good husband. So, we had a six-room house for ten thousand dollars. It was on a hill, and I thought it was just beautiful. The house is still there on Fair Street. That was my first home. We lived there for some time and then we bought a house on Bolton Road and there was a house across the street and that's where my parents lived. I sold the other house. We weren't hurting for money because my husband worked on the railroad and I waited tables for a while and I did a little sewing. I would charge two dollars for a dress. My mother taught me how to sew. She used to make all my clothes. I could sew without the pattern. If you gave me a piece of newspaper, I'd get right down there on the floor and cut out a pattern. I sewed for anybody that wanted me to make a dress for two dollars, and a lot of people would come to me. And I used to make all my clothes, too. I would go to Davidson's when Macy's was Davidson's and I would see a dress that I liked and I would go home and make it. I would buy a remnant piece of material and I would make the dress. I can't use my hands now like I could. I get vexed when I can't thread a needle and when I can't hold it and feel it. I can pick it up and then I lose the grip, so I don't do any sewing. But being able to sew back then was why I never did get a job doing anything.

I loved children, but I just didn't get pregnant. I was a foster parent, and I loved all of my children. I wish I could remember all of it, about being a foster parent, but I can't. I never thought I'd need to remember. Sometimes the children would go back to their parents and sometimes they would be adopted or what have you, you know. And it was hard, real hard, letting them leave. I remember the last children. One of them called me just last week. See that group in the picture up there? That big picture in the middle? They were the last, and there were five of them. That was about nine years ago, I think. Fulton County had five children that needed a home. They were sisters and brothers. I told the social worker, "I'll take them." And they were just as happy as they could be that I would take five of them and keep them together. They've been gone about nine years, I think. They were the last ones that I had. When they came, they were from two years to six. There were six of them. I would have taken the sixth one, but I took five. I kept them for about six years I guess, or seven, something like that.

I adopted my first girl when I was about twenty four. Nobody knew that we adopted her. Her name was Nancy Jean. I added Beverly because I liked that name. I can't remember where I went to pick her up. I think the people at the place where I went were White, but I don't remember. The only qualification was that you have a home. Of course they wanted to know about your background, but mainly you had to have a home. You would fill out papers, you know, and when they found a child that they thought would suit the family, they would let you know. I wanted a girl. Yes, I wanted a little girl. We both wanted a girl. I don't know. I prefer little girls anyway. You can dress them up like dolls. And then we adopted a second girl. Her name is Vanessa Gayles. I love both of them. Oh I just love both of them so much. I don't know how I learned to be a mama. It came natural, I guess, from me being reared up like I was with my mother and father who loved children and with relatives and all. It was natural for me to take care of my daughters. I never think about I didn't birth them. And if I hadn't had them, I don't know what I would have done. I just love them, and that's it.

I started keeping children for Fulton County when we bought our first home on Fair Street. That was in the forties. With my husband being gone most of the time, I just needed something to do and, of course, I loved children. I started keeping my neighbors' children, and my husband backed me. Anything I wanted to do, he backed me. Anything. Somebody reported that I was keeping children and the City sent inspectors, so that's really how I got my license to have a nursery. The first thing that happened was a Dr. _____, who was over Fulton County, sent a nurse out to check my place and the nurse reported that children were sleeping on the floor. I had a basement in the house, and that's where the children took naps, on the floor. This man, Dr. _____, told me that my nursery didn't come up to his nurse's expectations. I said, "Your nurse didn't come up to my expectations either. She looked like a tramp!" I told him that I sleep down there with the children when they take naps. He said, "What would you do if rats got in? I said, "What would you do?" He didn't say anything. I said, "I'd do the same thing you'd do. There are no rats in there. They sleep on the floor at school. Kindergarten children sleep on the floor, so what's the difference? But I'll tell you what. I keep children because I love them. I don't have to keep children. My husband works for me. I mean, this is the way I've been all my life, and maybe I shouldn't have been like that but I don't have to keep children. I can close today if you say so." He said, "No, no. We don't want you to close. We need more nurseries." And that's how it started. I was the first Black to be licensed in Fulton County for a private nursery. That was in the early nineteen forties, maybe around 1943. It was called Simms Day Nursery. I kept babies and I kept children up to the age

Mrs. Nell Simms

of eight. I was licensed for seventy-five children when I was out on Bolton road. I had five ladies working with me. I had two drivers and five ladies. All of the children were Black. I got twelve dollars a week for babies and eight dollars for the children. Babies are harder because they need more maintenance. Twelve dollars is what I charged and look at what families pay now. Next door to me was a projects apartment complex. I had some children from over there. I had children from all over the city in this area, and I loved all of them. All of them! I guess if my husband had lived, I probably wouldn't have given up. I don't know what it is but as long as there's a man around, you don't have any problems with your help. I guess when I got married I thought my husband was gonna live forever, you know? I guess he got tired of me and just died, you know! That's what I tell folks, he just got tired of me and died! When he passed, I decided I couldn't handle the nursery by myself, so I just decided to sell. He died in 1969. My mother lived here with me until she died. She lived to be ninety-nine. My father was eighty-four when he died. I'll be ninety-four next Wednesday.

I don't know how it is I've lived this long, but I think it's because I love people. My mama and daddy were liked that. I think it's also because I don't frown. I smile a lot and I like to dance! I went dancing just last week and people say, "Nell, how come you can't do the Electric Slide?" Now, that is one dance I just can't do. I tell them, "When you're coming back, I'm just going." I don't know why I can't get that dance.

How you ever been to a nursing home? It just breaks my heart to see those old people there not being cared for and not being loved. I go to visit and sometimes a woman will say to me, "If you see my daughter, tell her to come visit me." Now, that's so sad. It just breaks my heart. I think you can't give up when you get older. That's what I think. You just keep going. There are some things I can't do now. Like I have some plants I want to repot. But I just keep going. I'm not a quitter. I have a friend—you saw her when you came the last time—and she can be so sad. The other day, I asked her, "What's wrong with you?" And she said, "I'm just old." And I said, "You're not as old as me." I try to keep her from giving up, you know, because we grew up together. That's what happens to old people. They give up and one of the reasons they give up is that they think people don't want them around anymore. If I had a million dollars, you know what I would do? I would buy me some acres, about fifty or seventy, and build me a big house and I would have friends of mine who live alone come to live in the house. They could have their chickens and their gardens. They could be together, and they could be happy.

What makes me sad? When I see people hungry. That's what makes me sad, and somebody must have told how I don't like to see people hungry. And to see children hungry! How could we let that happen? It's real sad. When I read about the young lady dropping three children in the water, it just bothered me. How could anyone hurt a child? You know, children, you are supposed to care for them and love them. That's what I think, and I love children. I have loved children all of my life. I like little boys but I like little girls better because you can always dress them. I guess I thought of them as dolls or something, you know? I think I'd live a hundred more years if I had a group of children around me.

God has been good to me, and I don't feel that he's through with me yet because there's a lot of work out there that I can do, you know? Not physical, but something that I can do. And I love children. I would love to have about four running around here now, starting at the age of two. I love animals and flowers and children and old folks. You know, old folks are like children. When they get old they're just like children. I'm not saying that I'm like a child. I can realize that I am getting old, or have gotten old. I don't know. When I was growing up, I didn't ever think I would change so much, you know? But time brings about change. It's getting to me. I can see that I'm getting weaker, you know? I'm not as strong as I used to be. And of course, I guess that's to be expected, you know?

My friends say all the time, "You can write a book, Nell." And you want my story in your book? That's really something.

MISS MARGUERITE SIMON

Memphis, Tennessee

College Professor

We had one dog, and we had several chickens. The chickens came from a rural education class I took at Spelman. One was crippled, and my Spelman classmates named him Byron. I also had a rat, whom they named Schopenhauer after the German philosopher. The rat came from a science class and I kept him in a can in the dorm. One day, by accident, I left the top off the can, and Schopenhauer got out. Of course, I was worried because I knew students would be excited if he started running around. After all, he was a rat. As it turned out, Schopenhauer got out of the can, but, luckily, he didn't get out of my room. I found him in one of the drawers in my dresser. I considered him a pet. Can you imagine that? A pet rat named Schopenhauer? [Laughs]

The full name on my birth certificate is Marguerite Frances Simon, but my family called me Marg. M-A-R-G. I was born in Memphis, Tennessee on October 30, 1912, and I was born at home. There was one Black doctor in Memphis and he would come to your house to care for you. Your generation wouldn't know anything about doctors making house calls, but that was very much the standard when I was born. People were accustomed to seeing the doctor come into the neighborhood carrying a black satchel, and that's probably why my brothers thought I came in the satchel. I had three brothers, all of whom are deceased now. Their names were Edward Lloyd Simon, John Love Simon, and Robert Lewis Simon. My brother John died when he was nine years old.

My mother's name was Laura Dickerson Simon, and she was born in Memphis, Tennessee on February 9, 1875. My father's name was Edward Lee Simon, and he was born in Atlanta, Georgia, on March 4, 1877. He and my mother met in Memphis, and that's where we lived until we moved to Atlanta. My father was a cabinetmaker, and he taught woodwork in a public school in Memphis. He was a cabinetmaker, but his first job was as a printer.

The community in which I grew up in Memphis was a very close-knit community and by close-knit I mean that neighbors knew neighbors. We knew the people who went to our church and who went to our school. We lived close to LeMoyne Normal, which had a connection to the Congregational Church. It was renamed LeMoyne College and some years ago LeMoyne-Owen, but when I was in Memphis it was LeMoyne Normal. . That's where I attended grade school. Of course there were public schools in Memphis, but my parents sent me to the auxiliary school at LeMoyne Normal. The school went from elementary grades to high school, and it was located close enough to where we lived, on Austin Avenue, that I could walk from home to school. All of the students at LeMoyne Normal were Black, but most of the teachers were Whites and most of them came primarily from the North for the express purpose of educating the children of former slaves. You know this history because it is similar to the history of Spelman, Fisk, Talladega, and other the American Missionary Association founded for Blacks after emancipation. I remember that the teachers at LeMoyne Normal lived in little

Miss Marquerite Simon

cottages located near the campus, similar to the cottages we once had at Atlanta University, but some of them might have found harmonious citizens in the city who took them in as boarders. The fact that they were White and living in a Black community and teaching Black children meant that they were practicing integration long before the sixties. That took courage, a great deal of courage, because the law forbade Blacks and Whites from living in the same community, and you know from your studies here at Spelman, and before you came to Spelman, that breaking segregation laws in the South carried strong consequences. You were actually risking your life. That is why I say that the White teachers at LeMoyne Normal were courageous.

You asked me about segregation in Memphis. Of course there was segregation, and I remember some things we simply couldn't do because of segregation. For example, when we went down to the river –you know, Memphis is located on a bluff overlooking the Mississippi River -- we couldn't sit in the Confederate Park. The park had benches and sidewalks, but for White people only. We couldn't walk to the Mississippi River because it was too far from where we lived, so we would ride the streetcar. My family didn't have a car. We didn't have a wagon. We didn't have a buggy. We didn't have a mule. We used public transportation and, of course, it was segregated. We would take the streetcar from our house to the river and as soon as we would go past the post office, the river would come into view. It was a beautiful sight to see. Sometimes the river would be high and would overflow. I think the river deserves its name: the Mighty Mississippi. It is large and wide and, of course, very historic. Memphis is on one side of the river, and Arkansas is on the other side.

My parents had a number of challenges when we were living in Memphis. We moved into a house that had not been fumigated, and my brothers got typhoid fever. My father had no way of knowing that the man who had rented the house to him had not done what was legally required—that is, fumigate the house before new tenants take up residence—nor had he known that someone with typhoid fever had died in the house. The man actually declared the house well. Johnny and Edward were young children at the time, and they developed typhoid. Those were tough times because my parents had the care of sick children. My parents had another challenge with a house. This happened when the stove overheated. You see, we had a cook stove, and my father had a desire to see a bristling fire. This particular day, he built a big fire in the stove and it was so large the pipe got hot. You see, there was wood paneling above the stove and when the pipe got hot, the ceiling caught on fire. Isn't that something? My parents were quite extraordinary people.

We left Memphis in 1923 because my father was offered a job with a construction company in Atlanta, and it just so happened that the job offer came about the same time that my grandfather, my father's father, died. So it was expedient for my father to come to Atlanta to occupy his father's house. If we had stayed in Memphis until it was time for me to go to college, I have no doubt that I would have attended LeMoyne Normal. That's where my mother went to school. My father went to Atlanta University and, of course, that's where he wanted my brothers and me to attend. The job my father was offered here in Atlanta was with a Black company that was building houses for Black people on the West Side of Atlanta. I don't know the name of the company, but I do know that it was a company of Negro men. Your generation might not be aware that back then, in the twenties and thirties and forties, Black men were carpenters and bricklayers and electricians. They were skilled artisans. We need to know this. The company that hired my father was able to find Negro men with the talents and skills needed to build houses in the new area. I say "new" because it was not in the area generally occupied by Negroes--areas like Summer Hill, the Fourth War, Plunkett Town, and so on. Instead, the houses were being built on Collier Road, which was not in Southeast Atlanta, but rather in Northwest Atlanta. You know where Douglass High School is located ? The main street is called H. E. Holmes. However, at the time my father began working for the company, the street was Hightower. It was named H. E. Holmes several years ago in memory of Dr. Hamilton Holmes, who integrated the University of Georgia. Unfortunately, the company disbanded because of some irregularity in the handling of money. My father began teaching cabinet making at Washington High School.

Miss Marguerite Simon

When I was growing up in Atlanta, it was not the thriving metropolis it is today. No city was back then. Today, we go to the big super markets to buy groceries, but that was not the case when I was growing up in Atlanta. I remember there was a market man who came into the community. I think he would come from Stockbridge, Georgia. He was an independent business man with regular customers who expected him to have vegetables and butter. My mother bought mustard and kale from him. I don't know why, but we didn't eat collards that often. Another man would come into the community selling brooms. They would have eight straws laced together with a number of cross strings. They were quite sturdy. I don't think you can find brooms like that anymore. We didn't have refrigeration. We had what was called iceboxes, and I remember that a young man who was in high school with me delivered ice to our house. Ice was delivered with a hook or it was placed in a croaker sack so that the carrier wouldn't get wet.

In Memphis, I attended the private school at LeMoyne Normal, but when we moved to Atlanta, I attended South Atlanta, which was a public school. This area is called South Atlanta, and my school was located over a hill. I could walk to school just as I had done in Memphis, but there were differences between the school at LeMoyne and the public school here in Atlanta. For one, at LeMoyne, we ate in a lunchroom and we had hot meals and milk. We had to pay for our meals, or we could take a lunch to school. My mother used to fix lunch for me everyday so I did not buy one of the hot meals at the school. I ate what she had prepared for me, and she took great care in making my lunch. She made little sandwiches that had no crust. She cut them with little cutters, and they looked like cookies. They were small and pretty and delicious. I never ate all of the lunch my mother prepared for me because I was a poor eater. My mother was a very good cook. When she was preparing fish, because of her training in biology, she would point out different parts of the fish and give us the scientific name for each part.

When you ask me about my mother's employment, the best way I can answer that question is to say, "My mother was a mother." I like the sound of that: "My mother was a mother." What I mean when I say that is that she was totally devoted to the family. She didn't work away from home. She was always there for my brothers and me. We never had a key to the house as children have today because she was always home, and when we entered the house, we could smell the aroma of meals she was preparing. She was always there for us, and because she was a caring person, she was there for others as well—for neighbors and for children in the community and in the church. She had a talent for being able to tune in to people. That explains why one lady thought my mother was a fortune teller. In her mind, whatever my mother said was right. Of course, my mother wasn't a fortune teller. As I said, she just had a talent for being able to tune in to people. She also had a talent for sewing. My mother made all of our clothes, and she made them on a pedal sewing machine. There was no need we had as children that she didn't meet. She was a devoted and caring mother.

I was happy in Atlanta, but I was also happy in Memphis. No matter where I would have lived, I would have been happy because I was with my mother and my father and my brothers. I was very close to my brothers, and we had respect for one another. They were very skillful at making wagons out of boxes and roller skate wheels. My brothers had my father's carpentry talents because the wagons worked just fine. On Saturdays, they would ride their wagons to the store and use them to deliver groceries for people. Isn't that something? My brothers delivered groceries in wagons they made at home. They didn't work in anybody's yard. They delivered groceries in wagons they made with their own hands, and that's how they made a little pocket money. I should explain that not many people had cars back then, so there was always someone who needed their groceries delivered, so my brothers always had customers, so to speak. That's how they earned money, and they always shared what they earned with me. In his adult years, my brother Robert used his skill and talent as a carpenter. My brother Edward was the business type and a very good mathematician. He taught math at Clark and worked as assistant coach of the football team. Also, he was a member of the Board of Trustees of Atlanta Life Insurance Company. Both of my brothers are deceased.

Miss Marquerite Simon

As I was saying, when we were children, my brothers made wagons and they used the wagons to deliver groceries. Of course, I didn't make wagons. I made clothes for my paper dolls, and I think I have some of them somewhere here in the house. How would I make them? Well, I would make the patterns from rolls of paper, and then I would cut the dresses out of prints. I would take a little tab and fold it over the shoulder of the doll's little form, and then the little doll was dressed. My brother Robert didn't play with dolls, but I remember that he made clothes for my dolls. He could sew, and when he got to be a young man, he could **really** sew. In fact, he could beat me sewing. We learned to sew by watching our mother sew. Isn't that how children learn most things? They watch whatever it is their parents are doing. We watched a lot of things my mother did. We watched her sew, and we also watched her cook. My mother was an excellent cook! When we came home from school, we could smell the food she had prepared. I don't think this happens to our children today because they eat out of the store too much. They don't smell a good stew or fresh beans that are cooking on top of the stove or sweet potatoes or delicious desserts that are baking in the oven. You know it's different from what it was when I was growing up in the twenties and thirties.

My family didn't own a car or a horse or a buggy, so we always used public transportation. At first, public transportation was the streetcar, which was similar to the train, but different in that the streetcar was smaller. If you were White, you would sit from the front to the middle of the car or beyond the middle, according to how many people were on the streetcar. If you were Black, you would sit from the back. Negroes knew that if they went beyond the middle, they might have to move back and let a White person sit there if the streetcar took on more passengers and the Whites needed a seat. If I sat behind the motorman on the streetcar here in Atlanta, I knew that I would be asked out because it was beyond the area relegated for Negroes. So that was the arrangement, but it didn't change this neighborhood. It didn't change the West Side. We lived with segregation every day of our lives. I'm talking about the twenties, the thirties and up to the fifties, because, before the Civil Rights Movement, everything was segregated. The races were separated, but Blacks in this community, and I am sure in other communities in Atlanta, were so independent of White people that we didn't think about the separation the way you would think we did. We lived and moved within our own neighborhoods, and we didn't feel the stress of race relations there because we had independent communities. We felt the stress of race relations when we used public transportation and when we went outside our communities to hostile areas closed to Blacks. But, by and large, we lived together in our own communities in spirit. We were independent of Whites in a way that is probably hard for people to understand today. We knew one another and we assisted one another. Now let me clear about this: we didn't like what we experienced when we left our communities. We had to sit in the back of the bus, we had to drink from "colored" water fountains, we couldn't try on hats, and we had to go to the back door of eating places. Those were indignities, and we didn't like them, but in our communities, we were at peace with one another? Does that make sense?

I've lived in this community called South Atlanta since my family moved from Memphis to Atlanta in 1923, and I've lived in this very same house all those years. I have never lived anywhere else. The furniture has been here since we moved into the house. The only piece of furniture that was not here is the piano, and I believe my parents bought the piano when I was nine years old. So this is old, old furniture. Ancient. [Laughs] I'm really exaggerating, but it's old. When I was born, the chair you're sitting in was here, and that table was here. I think we got the pedestal after we had moved into the house. My father made it. In fact, he made most of the furniture in the house. Isn't that something? My father was a gifted carpenter. This was my grandparents' house. In other words, this is family property, and property is something we learned to appreciate. Property. Owned property. I think, generally speaking, that Negroes like to have a connection with their relatives and with their family, and we must have those connections or we are lost. You see how they are tearing down houses in Atlanta and putting up new houses? I doubt that those new houses will remain sturdy for a century as this house has. What we should want is property. So, I keep this house because it's my connection to my family.

Miss Marquerite Simon

When we moved to Atlanta, this was a community of families with children, and most of the adults in the community were associated with Gammon Theological Seminary. The man who lived in the two-story house over there fired the furnace that kept all those buildings warm on Gammon's campus. At that time, heat came from furnaces that burned coal. I can remember that the man would leave his house early in the morning and go down a little alleyway that would take him right up to the first building on Gammon's campus. From our house, we could hear the Gammon bell ringing for breakfast and for various activities taking place on the campus. I remember that there were little cottages for families whose husband or wife worked at the college Most of the houses on this street had front porches and swings and rocking chairs and children. I remember that we had a garden and that we had two fig trees and I would pick figs from the trees. My mother was the gardener in the family. She loved to garden, but she also loved to read the newspapers and read about anything historical and geographical. She would clip articles out of the papers and save them, and then she would discuss the articles with us. She was an avid baseball fan. She would write down the scores of game she listened to on the radio—that was before television, you see—and we would sit in the parlor listening to the radio. I remember her talking about Joe DiMaggio and PeeWee Reese and Pepper Martin and others. That was before Jackie Robinson. My mother did the cooking and the sewing and the gardening, and she also took care of our animals. [Laughs] We had one dog, and we had several chickens. The chickens came from a rural education class I took at Spelman. One was crippled, and we called him Byron. My Spelman classmates gave him that name. Chickens were not the only animals I got from Spelman. I also had a rat, whom my classmates named Schopenhauer after the German philosopher by that same name. The rat came from one of the science classes at Spelman. You see, it was permissible at that time for a student to take animals used for research, but only, of course, when the experiments were over. That's how I happened to get Schopenhauer. I kept him in a can because I didn't have a cage, and I kept the can in the dorm. One day, by accident, I left the top off the can, and Schopenhauer got out. Of course, I was worried because I knew students would be excited if he started running around. After all, he was a rat. As it turned out, Schopenhauer got out of the can, but, luckily, he didn't get out of my room. I found him in one of the drawers in my dresser. I considered him a pet. Can you imagine that? A pet rat named Schopenhauer? [Laughs]

I have happy memories of my years at Spelman. Very happy memories. I graduated in the class of 1935, and after graduation I was hired as an assigned supply teacher at a school in the community called Pittsburgh. I was teaching fourth grade, and I wasn't thinking about doing anything other than what I was doing: teaching the fourth grade. This was during the War, and everyone was encouraged, if not required, to support the War in various ways. Teachers were required to distribute canned goods and kerosene. All teachers had to do that. People needed the canned goods because of rations during the War. In February, a lot of women were called into the War, or they volunteered. That is what people were doing. Volunteering to fight in the War, and that's what the woman who taught physical education at Spelman did.

Her name was Edna Callahan, and she signed up to be in the Women's Army Auxiliary Corps. It's pronounced like Wack. W-A-C-K. She gave up her job at Spelman in order to serve in the Corps. Miss Callahan wrote me a letter asking me to come to see her, and, of course, I agreed to meet with her. When I met her, she said, "Let's walk up to Reynold's Cottage." That's where President Read lived. I had no idea what was about to transpire. When we met with President Read, she asked me immediately if I could help in any way with the physical education program at Spelman. I said, "Whew." I said I would, and so I tried. She sent me to Columbia University in New York and to University of Colorado in Boulder. I took courses there that gave me credentials to teach physical education at the College. When I began teaching physical education at Spelman, I found the students to be very cooperative. They fell in line with what we were doing. We knew we were in an age of stress because of the War. We couldn't buy equipment for them, and they had to make their own suits, but we worked together. I began teaching physical education at Spelman on March 24, 1943. I was at the College when Read Hall was dedicated, and I remember the date: December 6, 1951.

Miss Marquerite Simon

I had the privilege of working at Spelman for thirty-seven years, and I loved every one of those thirty-seven years. I never did anything extra. I didn't have any favorites among my students. I believed in being impartial. I was never late to class, and I supported students in their activities. I tried to be a part of the total experience they had at Spelman. Everything I did I was supposed to do. So, when you ask me how I felt when Spelman named the gymnasium after me, I will tell you that I was honored. Of course I was honored, but I never thought I should get special recognition for my work at Spelman. I wasn't working to be honored by the College. I was working to serve the College. I did what I was supposed to do. I loved my work. I loved the students. I love Spelman.

MRS. EMANUELLA JULIEN SPENCER

New Orleans, Louisiana

Archivist at Amistad Research Center

For thirty-two years, I toiled at the Amistad Research Center, processing collections, typing registers, finding ads of famous people, catering to researchers, and being chief cook and bottle washer. And what did I get for all this work? I got thirty-two years of love, respect, appreciation, awards, and honors from Amistad's Director, Dr. Clifton Johnson, my co-workers, and the many visitors who came to do research at the Center. One gentleman from Africa wanted to marry me, and he already had three wives. So what can I say? I say, I loved my work, and I would do it all over again if I could.

Mrs. Emanuella Spencer

The name on my birth certificate is Emanuella Julien. My last name is spelled with an E. J-u-l-i-e-n. I don't think I was named for anybody. My father just loved that name. In fact, he loved Emanuella so much that he named one of my brothers Emanuel. My father claimed that he named my brother after me, but I think he just loved that name probably because it means "peace with God." My father was a very religious man. His name was Angelo Peter Julien. My mother's name was Alonia Ford Julien. They were both born in New Orleans and lived their entire lives in New Orleans. He was the pastor of Morning Star Baptist Church, and my mother sang in the church choir. She did not work away from the home. How could she? There were nine children, and then, too, she was the wife of a pastor. Being a pastor's wife carries with it more responsibilities than many people realize. My father was committed to the church, and my mother supported him fully in his work. My parents had a beautiful relationship, but my mother would get a bit angry when certain sisters of the church stayed around my father too much, calling on him: "Rev. Julien, can you do this? Can you come over this week?" I guess that goes with being the preacher's wife.

As I said, there were nine children in the family: five boys and four girls. I was in the middle. I was born On August 31, 1933 at Charity Hospital – in New Orleans, of course. Some people believe that the middle child has challenges, but that wasn't the case with me because of all the children I was the one closest to my father. I guess you can say that I was a Daddy's girl. I wish I could show you pictures of me with my parents and with my brothers and sisters-- pictures of my years growing up in New Orleans--but Hurricane Betsy, which hit New Orleans in 1965, destroyed them. I hate that I don't have any pictures, but I have lots of memories. Because our father was a minister, the Julien children were expected to set examples for other children. Our peers went to the movies on Sundays. We couldn't go because we were in church all day: Sunday school at nine; morning service at eleven; BTU (Baptist Training Union) at five; and evening service at seven. My parents had a select group of kids they chose as our associates. That's just the way it was with my parents. My father spent more time with us than my mother did because she had her hands full cooking and washing and caring for our various needs. After all, there were nine of us, but we carried our part of the responsibilities. We washed the dishes, we kept our rooms clean, and we helped with the washing on Saturday. That was laundry day in our family. We hung clothes on the line because in those days there were no dryers, and there weren't any dishwashers either, so we washed and dried dishes. Really, the girls did the housework. The boys would help my father keep the yard clean and cut the grass and things like that, but they didn't work inside the house. I guess back then housework was considered woman's work.

I was closer to my father than I was to my mother, but I also close to my mother's mother, my grandmother. Her name was Mary Ford. She was the only grandparent I knew because her husband, my maternal grandfather, and my father's parents died before I was born. I just loved her so very much. I really did. A lot of people said I looked just like her – fat. I'm the only fatty in the family. Grandma was big, that's why everybody said I was just like her. She lived close to where we lived, and I would visit her all the time. I could talk to her about most anything. She was the one who prayed hardest for me to get baptized. You see, people expected children to be baptized by twelve. When the church had the summer revivals, children would go to the mourners' bench and pray to get religion and if you didn't get religion, the church would assign someone to pray with you. Well, my grandmother was assigned to pray with me, and I was happy about that because we were so close. One day, I was outside jumping rope, and lo and behold, she came out the door. I saw her coming down the street, and in her hand she had a brush that we washed bottles with. I just knew I was gonna get it—for playing, you see, when I was supposed to be praying. When she got to where I was jumping rope, she said, "Manuella"—she always dropped the E in my name and just called me Manuella—"Why in the world are you out here jumping rope when you should be inside on your knees?" She took that brush and started hitting me on my legs. That surprised me because my grandma had never hit me. I ran home and went inside and just sat there pouting. She said, "Oh, you pouting? You better fix your face! You better fix your face because if you don't, I'm gonna give you something to pout about!" "Fix your face" meant stop crying and stop pouting. So, I

Mrs. Emanuella Spencer

fixed my face, and she said, "Now, come on in here. Let's get on our knees." We went into the bedroom and closed the door and got on our knees and started praying. I was supposed to be praying that I would see something. That's what the church believed. When you got religion, you saw something. You know, God gave you a sign? And at revival, you had to get up and tell the church what you saw. When I went to revival that summer—after I had been praying with Grandma—and it was my time to get up and tell the church what I had seen, I couldn't lie, so I said, "I haven't seen anything." The pastor said—and that was my father--"Baby, you got to pray some more. You got to pray hard, and the Lord is gonna give you a sign." Let me tell you, Grandma came to our house every day at twelve o'clock for us to pray together so that I would see a sign. She would ask me, "Manuella, you see anything?" When I would tell her no, she would look at me very disappointed and keep praying. On that Friday before baptism, I still didn't see anything, but I did dream something. I dreamed that Christ was on the mountain preaching to the people. He beckoned me to come to Him and he told me, "These people need to be seated, and I want you to seat them." So I said, "Well, where do you want me to seat the people?" And He said, "You see that tent?" It was a big tent. "You see that tent over there? That's where I want you to seat them." It looked like thousands of people were marching towards that tent, and I didn't know where in the world I was gonna seat that many people because the tent really wasn't that big, but I seated every one of them. I told the church about the tent and the thousands of people I had seated. My father said, "Well, the Lord wants you to be an usher. When you get baptized, you will be an usher in the church." He was just praising the Lord that at last I did have something to say. I was baptized when I turned twelve, and the church put me on the Usher Board with all the older people. I was the only little child on the Usher Board, and I worked as an usher for many, many years –many years.

Although I was an usher in church, my dream was to become a famous singer, a gospel singer. When I was five years old my daddy taught me to play the piano, but I played by ear. I didn't know notes. I had a good singing voice, and he would bring me with him to different churches to sing on programs or before he preached. People who had heard I could sing wanted to put me on their program. I was a little bitty girl. My Father would sit me at the piano and I would play and sing, *O' Lord Search My Heart.* I would get a standing ovation, you hear me! I really wanted to be a famous singer. I didn't get to be famous, but I've done my share of singing. I sang in my church choir, a first soprano and a lead soloist. I have sung in churches all over New Orleans, as well as in churches in Texas, Mississippi and Missouri. For more than ten years I was a member of the Gospel Music Workshop of America.

My grandma was the sweetest, most loving woman I had ever known in my life. She grew up on a plantation in St. James Parish, Louisiana where they grew rice. The rice plants grew in water and there were snakes in the water and she remembered when snakes bit several people. They didn't die because people knew how to draw the poison out. My grandmother didn't talk about slavery, but she did talk about working on the plantation. She was very proud, very proud. She did things no other black woman at that time would do, and I'm talking about the early nineteen hundreds. If grandma met White people who were educated, she could hold a conversation with them like she had a doctoral degree, and she only went to the eighth grade. You know, I think about my grandmother more than my mother because I could go to her if I had a problem and discuss it with her more than I could with my own mother. Every month, when she got her check, she would say, "What ya'll want me to fix for you?" She fixed good dinners, good food, anything we wanted to eat. One of my favorites was sweet potato pone, what they called in those days "potato pone."

We lived in a nice community and, of course, it was all Black. . We lived in the Ninth Ward. That's what sections are called in New Orleans, wards. This was in the late thirties and forties when New Orleans was a very segregated city. All the people in my community were Black except for a man named Sam Collata, a White man, and he was there because he owned the grocery store. White police would come periodically because there were some guys who used to play dice on the corner, and that was illegal. I say White police because there were no Black police at that time. There were teachers in the community, and most of them were women. There were ministers in the community, and all of them were men. Most of the men

Mrs. Emanuella Spencer

were manual laborers. They worked in the sugar refinery and the clothing factory and, of course, they worked the riverfront, loading and unloading ships on the docks of the Mississippi River. That's what they called working on the riverfront. Black men weren't allowed to be foremen at their jobs. Very few had their own businesses. In my neighborhood, they were mostly shoemakers and some had shoeshine stands. I don't remember any Black men having high positions. Most of the Black women were either domestic workers or schoolteachers. The schoolteachers were very respected. I didn't know any Black women who had secretarial jobs in offices. We couldn't go to theatres and we couldn't try on clothes in downtown stores. If you wanted to buy something you had to look at it and be sure it fit you because Black people couldn't return anything. Once you left the store, if you were Black, that was it. And of course, we couldn't sit up front on the bus or the streetcar. But I will say this. We had our own theaters, we had our own churches, we had our own schools, and we had our own parks. We didn't really want to be around White people, you know, because we had our own world. That's something your generation does not understand. We were segregated against, for sure, but we had our own world and we were happy living with other Blacks in that world.

I went to Macarty Elementary School and Joseph S. Clark High School and to Southern University in New Orleans. All of them were Black. In elementary school, all of my teachers were women except one. I had very good teachers, but the best of them all was a woman named Altura Ellis. She taught me math and since I was very good in math, we had a close relationship. If I could talk to somebody from my past, I would want that somebody to be Ms. Ellis because she helped me so much. We didn't learn anything about Black people in elementary school. It might have been against the law for teachers to teach us about Black people. Our books didn't have any pictures of Black people and no information about Black people. Really, when I think about it, we weren't taught much about racial pride, not in the way that children are taught today. In fact, we played with white dolls, not Black dolls, and thought nothing about it. I guess you could say that it didn't seem to matter that much to our parents because we did whatever Blacks did at that time. We knew not to cross the line because New Orleans could be a mean city.

I would not have wanted to be born in any city other than N'awlins. That's how we pronounce it: N'awlins. People from outside the city call it New Or-leans, that's how we know who is a tourist and who is a native. There is no city in the South or in the entire nation like New Orleans. It's colorful and musical and historic. That's why so many tourists come to the city throughout the year, and they come from all over the world: The French Quarter, Bourbon Street, the Casinos, the French Market, the Riverwalk, and Mardi Gras - there is a lot in New Orleans to see and to visit. On Mardi Gras Day, we also called it Carnival Day, everybody would put on costumes and masks and go out to see the parades. Every Carnival Day, my parents would put us all in the car and we would go park on Claiborne Avenue. That was the Carnival street for Black people. The Whites would all go on St. Charles Avenue, uptown, you know. We would stay at Carnival all day. There would be lots of food – New Orleans type food like Red Beans & Rice, Gumbo, Hot Dogs, and Roasted Peanuts. And the music! New Orleans is known for its music, so there would be lots of music and people would be dancing everywhere. We would dance the "Second Line," which comes from New Orleans. And you know, the wonderful thing about this dance is that adults and children do it together. You take a white handkerchief and you dance in a big circle to "Second Line" music and some people twirl umbrellas. The "Second Line" is also danced at funerals for celebrities. After the church service—the funeral service inside a church—people would dance the "Second Line" in the street. Sometimes they would dance from the church all the way to the cemetery. Yes, they would do that in a New Orleans funeral, especially for a Black celebrity. In some instances, they would dance "Second Line" to the person's house, take the coffin out of the hearse and hold it up in the air as a tribute to the person. It's something to see. It's really something to see.

Mrs. Emanuella Spencer

I love New Orleans, and I fell in love in New Orleans. That's where I met my husband. He was not from New Orleans. He was from Hazlehurst, Mississippi. He moved to New Orleans in 1945 when he was eighteen, right after he had finished high school. His brother was a member of my father's church, and that's where I met him, in church. The first time I saw him, I thought he was the most handsome boy I had ever seen in my life and he had a mustache. You know? Trying to be a man. [Laughs] Oh, I just fell head over heels in love with him and, believe it or not, I was only fourteen years old. I was sitting on one end of the pew in church, and he was sitting on the other end of the pew. Every once in a while I would look over at him, you know, trying to see him, and once or twice, I caught him doing the same thing, looking directly at me! There were all those older girls sitting near him, and he was looking at me! After church, his brother was introducing him to the older girls, and I heard him ask, "Who is that little girl over there standing on the steps?" His brother said, "Oh, that's Rev. Julien's daughter. Don't mess with her!" He wanted to meet me, in spite of the fact that I was the pastor's daughter and his brother had said, "Don't mess with her." His brother came over and said, "Emanuella, this is my brother Buddy." I said, "Oh, how do you do, Buddy?" He said, "Fine, how are you?" I said, "I'm fine." He said, "Why you didn't come talk to me with the girls?" I said, "I don't have anything to say to you. Why should I talk to you?" He said, "Oh, alright, Miss Lady. You don't have to talk to me, but you're gonna change that someday." We called him Buddy, but his real name was Albert Spencer, 3rd. His father would say to him affectionately, "Hey, Buddy," and that's what other people started calling him. When I met him, that's how he was introduced to me, as Buddy. When I told him my name was Emanuella, he said, "I can't remember that name. It's too hard. From now on, you're gonna be Butch." And from that time until the Lord called him home, he never called me anything but Butch. In 1948, my father was killed in a car accident. He was on his way to Reserve, Louisiana to preach a Mother's Day sermon. A car lost control and ran head-on into the car my father was in. He was killed instantly. That just shattered my life. I was very close to my father, very close. When I was told he had been killed, I passed out. My mother was worried that I would get sick and stay sick because I loved my father so much. When Buddy came to the house with other people, I was sitting on the bed and he came to me. He pulled me off the bed and sat in a chair and then he sat me on his lap. He cradled me in his arms like I was a baby. And I cried! I just cried and cried. Buddy didn't say anything. He just held me. When I finally stopped crying, he went to the kitchen and came back with a glass of water for me. From that day on, I knew he was going to be my husband. He stayed with me during the wake, and he was with me at the funeral. When I cried so hard that I had to be taken out of the church, he was the one who went with me. After that, Buddy felt that he should be my keeper. He started coming to the house to see me, but he couldn't take me out. We did what was called "keeping company," which is somewhat different from dating. When you date, you can go away from the house. When you "keep company," you have to stay in the house. And that's what we did. We kept company with me sitting with Buddy in the living and Mama sitting in the bedroom with the door open. At nine o'clock, he had to leave. That was Mama's rule, and we always obeyed it.

I begged my mother to let me get married when I finished high school, but she said no. She wanted me to go to college and she would tell me, "You know, your father always told you he wanted you to get an education and you should go to school. You should go to college." I kept on begging and begging until she finally gave in, but not before I promised her that I would still go to college. I finished school on June 6, 1950. I married my husband on June 19, 1950. Oh, I wish I had the pictures of our wedding to show you, but like the pictures of my parents, our wedding pictures were destroyed in the Hurricane, too.

I had been in quite a few hurricanes throughout my lifetime, but Betsy was one of the worst and did the most damage to New Orleans. When the hurricane hit the city, the levees in St. Bernard Parish, near where we lived, gave way and all the water came in on us in our neighborhood. We just did get out in time. My husband and our four children and my niece Marcelle started out in the car, but the water overtook the car, so we had to abandon the car and walk. The current was so strong that it took the shoes off my feet. It was also dangerous

Mrs. Emanuella Spencer

because the wind had blown down electric wires and we could have been electrocuted. We made it safely to my mother's house, then to a friend who lived a couple of blocks away in a two-story house. There were some people who were on top of their houses screaming. Oh, it was horrible. The army ducks had to come to get the people out of their houses. Those are boats the army uses that can travel in water and on land. That's why they are called ducks. A man had his wife and three children and two dogs in a small boat. They were okay until the helicopter frightened the dogs and the dogs did something that turned the boat over. All three of the children drowned, and we saw them. They drowned in front of our eyes. Oh it was horrible. It was tragic. I remember Hurricane Betsy as if it happened yesterday.

I was only seventeen when I got married; Buddy was twenty-two. I kept my promise to my mother and continued my education. I attended Southern University for two years. I loved being married and I loved being a mother. We had four children: Rodney, Royzell, Taronda, and Russell. My husband and I raised our children in church. My oldest son, Rodney, is a schoolteacher in Los Angeles. My second son, Roy, is retired after twenty years in the Air Force. He still works on the base in San Antonio. My youngest son, Russell is a policeman in Tampa. Taronda is the only daughter we had. Of course, you know her because she is the archivist at Spelman. My son Russell was in Iraq, and I thank God he came back safe. Now there is a possibility that the army will send him back. It breaks my heart. It goes all through me. I don't want any more people to be killed. War is a horrible thing.

I became an archivist quite by accident. A Dillard University student who was working at the YWCA, where I was working at the time, told me about an opening in the Accounting Department at Dillard. Well, when I got there, the job he mentioned was already filled, but the lady I talked with told me about a job at the Amistad Research Center that had just recently moved to Dillard's campus. Dr. Clifton Johnson, the Director of the Center, interviewed me. He liked me right off and, after he got good references for me, he hired me. I didn't have any experience doing archival work, but he started me right away on the biggest collection at

Amistad: the Race Relations Collection. Mrs. Florence Borders, the archivist at the Center, helped me learn how to process a collection. Well, it took me three years to do that collection. When I finished, Dr. Johnson said, "This is the best work I've ever seen." I'm so proud of that. I'm really proud of that. Of course, over the years I processed many, many more collections. I was put in charge of processing collections. I was at Amistad for thirty-two years, and I loved my work. The Center is now located at Tulane University. It outgrew the facilities at Dillard and had to find a larger space. I really wanted Amistad to stay on a Black campus, but Tulane University offered so much, money and a building, that I knew the move would be best for Amistad. I loved my work at Amistad. I am proud that I had a hand in building up the Amistad collection. You know, today Amistad is the largest independent archives specializing in the history of African Americans and other ethnic groups in the country. For thirty-two years, I toiled at the Amistad Research Center, processing collections, typing registers, finding ads of famous people, catering to researchers, and being chief cook and bottle washer. And what did I get for all this work? I got thirty-two years of love, respect, appreciation, awards, and honors from Amistad's Director, Dr. Clifton Johnson, my co-workers, and the many visitors who came to do research at the Center. One gentleman from African wanted to marry me, and he already had three wives. So what can I say? I say I loved my work, and I would do it all over again if I could.

MRS. ERNESTINE VICK

Tinus, Louisiana

Housewife

L. S. Steptoe was my real boyfriend, but I didn't like him any more after he told me he was gonna marry a widow woman so he could get her money. . . . Johnny Vick came by the house one day when nobody was home except me. He came to the steps and shouted, "You mighty happy." I was inside sweeping and singing. I gave him some water. He drank the water and then we started talking. That was the beginning. He never stopped coming to see me. We married in Mississippi. That was on December 21, 1041. I was twenty-nine, and Johnny was about the same age.

My name is Ernestine Vick, but it was Ernestine Gilbert before I married Johnny Vick. They called me Tena when I was growing up and then my great grandson Darius started calling me Sugar. Now they call me both Tena and Sugar. My great-grandson died before he was four and so I asked the other grandchildren to call me Sugar in memory of him. He was such a smart and sweet little boy that I called him Sugar Pie, and he called me Sugar. My husband's family called me "Doll Baby".

I was born in Tinus, Louisiana. That's spelled: T-I-N-U-S. But it's not Tinus any more. It's Greensburg. I was born February 22, 1913. A midwife delivered me, but I don't know who she was. When I got older and my mother was still having babies, she would send all the children away from the house when the midwife came. My grandmother delivered my younger sisters and brothers, and we thought she brought the babies to the house. She always carried a huge bag with her and we thought the baby was in the bag.

My mother's name was Phoeby McClendon Gilbert, and she was born in Louisiana, but I don't know where in Louisiana. She was born in 1881 and she died in 1968. Leon Gilbert was my father, and he was from Louisiana, but I don't know where. He was born in 1882. He died in 1959. That was before my mother died. My parents they were farmers and they raised corn and cotton and they grew vegetables. We had pigs, cows, horses, chickens, cats and dogs. I think that is all we had. We had to feed the animals and milk the cows. My mother was sick a lot. She suffered from kidney stones and couldn't do much, but she liked going fishing.

Yes, I remember my grandparents. My grandfather was Joe McClendon. He was my mother's father. He was quite a rascal. He married my grandmother, Hester, and they had ten children. That was in Tinus. She died, and then he married Lubertha, and they had ten or eleven more children. He also had children by two of Lubertha's sisters. He was quite a rascal. They all lived in the same community. Grand Pa Joe –that's what we called him – had a T model Ford and one of his son's did the driving, and he would tell us that his son drove the car so fast it looked like the road was getting narrow. [Laughs]

My father's mother was Ellen and she married Walker Smalls. We called him Uncle

Mrs. Ernestine Vick

Walker. He was my Grandmother Ellen's husband, but not my father's daddy. My father's daddy was a White man by the name of Johnny Cathy or Johnny Gilbert. I'm not sure which one it was, but I know Papa was his only child. They said my father's daddy was supposed to be somebody important. My daddy used to tell us about slavery, but I don't remember it now. I do remember him saying Black people worked themselves to death and received no pay. The only way they could get away was to slip away at night.

Where we lived in Tinus, some White people lived up the street from our house. My daddy would go up to their house, sit on the steps, and talk with them. They would give him coffee to drink. One year he had these Whites to bundle a bale of cotton for him. I don't know if he was paying them for something or what they were doing. My daddy got along fine with those old White folks and we got along fine with White people. I guess it was because my daddy's father was a White man. I don't remember ever seeing him, but I know he was my grandfather on my father's side. My father had a White relative who had a store in Tinus and when my nieces and nephews would go to the store, they would get free candy, so the White people knew we were related and people in the community knew who my grandfather was.

My parents had eleven children—six girls and five boys—Josephine Hester, Carrie Aleen, Otis, Lovie Dee, Willie, Me, Izola, Henry, and Joseph. I was close to Izola. We were like two peas in a pod. We would sew together and wash dishes together, but we couldn't cook together because I thought I should be the boss because I was the oldest and she thought she knew more about cooking than me. So that's why we didn't cook together. I learned to sew and I did the sewing for the family and I did some sewing for people outside the family. My other sisters did the cooking and washing. My momma was always sick, but she wasn't laid up in bed. She couldn't do much, so we children did most of the work. My brothers worked in the fields, and the girls did, too. We did picking and hoeing, and we gathered corn, cotton, green beans, sweet potatoes, strawberries and the like. They hunted, fished, fixed fences, cut wood and a lot of little odd jobs. The boys didn't cook and make up beds. The girls had to beat the shucks inside the mattress until it was smooth. We all had to sweep the yard and keep it as clean as the inside of your hands. The girls pieced scraps of cloth together for quilts and my brothers hunted. I don't ever remember us not having food to eat, but all we got for Christmas was a couple pieces of fruit and candy for Christmas. Life was hard, but we made it. The Depression was real hard. People couldn't even get grease to cook chickens with.

My sister Hester was the first one to get married. She married a man named Robert Hampton, and then they moved to Fernwood, Mississippi, but she died a year after they got married. She got sick when she was pregnant. The doctor said when she was carrying the baby, her blood all went to her head. He said that if they took the baby, she might live. They didn't take the baby, and it died when she died. I don't know why they didn't take the baby. I don't know. My mother and father both took it real hard, but there was nothing they could do.

We moved to Chipola, Louisiana and I was six or seven when we moved. Chipola was about sixty miles from Baton Rouge. That is where I started going to school. We all went to school. My very first teacher was a woman named Lela Irving, and the school was called Jones School. That's where I learned the alphabet and how to count to one hundred. It was a one-room school and we all had the same teacher. We went to school for three or four months out of the year. That's all they gave you. Three or four months until the next year. I remember being in school when it was very hot and when it was very cold. We had a dirt chimney and when it was cold we would all stand around it to keep warm. The school was close to our house. Less than a half mile away. We had to hoe in the garden and milk the cows before we went to school. That's why we would get up at six thirty in the morning. We would do our work and then we would walk to school. We took our lunch to school. I wanted to carry a bucket of food because I saw other chaps with one. Most of the time, I had rice, gravy and biscuit in my bucket.

Mama's sister Idella had a baby and I went to stay with her. I went there to work. I washed clothes and cooked. I was about thirteen then. The tickle part was Aunt Idella wanted me to kill a chicken. I grabbed the chicken by the neck and turned it around, but when I turned it loose, the chicken run off. I couldn't do nothing with that chicken. My aunt had a daughter

Mrs. Ernestine Vick

younger than me who wanted to be grown, so she tried to kill the chicken, but it ran away from her too. My aunt killed the chicken and I cooked it.

I don't remember us going to the doctor much. I think we must have used some kind of home remedies, but I don't remember what we used. But the reason I am deaf today is because of a toothache. They would sometimes give you some calumet powder out of an envelope when you had a toothache. I think you would get about five doses out of the envelope. They used a lot of castor oil, but nobody had to take all of that mess but me. If you had a cut on your leg or arm, they would wrap it up in some kind of grease. My daddy died when he was in his seventies. My mother was in her seventies, too, but she lived nine years longer than him. I never thought she would out live him. He had indigestion and arthritis in his knees, but he hopped around and made a crop that last year. He had corn and cotton. My sister Lovie and baby brother Freddie gathered the crop. They told him not to try to make another crop because he was not able. He was down for about a year, but not in bed. My poor mother was in bed for months at the time. She would get up and stir around a little and then be back in bed again. The doctor said one kidney was completely gone and the other nearly gone. She died because of the kidney problem. I don't know what my father died from. We had moved to Greensburg, Louisiana when they died.

I was sixteen or seventeen when I met Herbert Hall. He was the first boy to come to my house to see me. I started dating with Herbert Hall. We would just sit around and talk. He wanted to get married, but I didn't want him because I heard that he would steal. People used to say he had a lantern and he would go by where White folks lived and steal their bridles and saddles. I heard about this from other people. I knew I didn't want to marry somebody who stole. My next boyfriend was L.S. Steptoe. He was my real boyfriend. One time we were talking and he told me he was going to marry, but he was going to marry widow woman so he could get her money. I told him to "kick his number" if that's what he wanted, and I told him I was going to do the same thing. I think I would have married him if he hadn't said that to me, but maybe not because I didn't like his size. He was a small man and I am a small woman and I was worried he might be too little to get a job and take care of me. I didn't like him anymore after he told me he was going to marry somebody for money. Another boyfriend was Johnny Hampton. He came to New Orleans to work and he was wanting to marry at Christmas, but I wanted to marry before then. I didn't want to marry Johnny Hampton because he was just too jealous. His daddy was crazy about me, but his mother put on she wanted him to court my sister Izola. She said Izola was prettier, but Johnny Hampton said his mother could not pick for him, and I agreed. She pretended like she liked me, but I could tell she didn't care nothing about me. I told Johnny Hampton I was getting married before Christmas and I didn't want to tell a lie. I told him if things changed, I would let him know. Then I started seeing Johnny. Johnny Vick. He was from Mississippi, but he was in Louisiana working on a sawmill not far from our house. I decided I liked him better than I liked Johnny Hampton. He came by the house one day when nobody was home except me. I didn't know it then, but he told me later how he had planned to come to see me. He waited until my parents left and then came asking for some water. He came to the steps and he shouted out at me, "You mighty happy." I was inside sweeping and singing. I gave him some water. He drank the water and then we started talking. That was the beginning. He never stopped coming to see me. He was a cook at the sawmill and he impressed my daddy by making him coffee and serving it to him. After a while, my father told me I needed to marry someone who lived in town because I was too small to work in the fields. I thought I could work as much as anybody else, but I was not as fast as my sisters and brothers.

My father knew Johnny had asked me to marry him and that's why he said I needed to marry Johnny. I told Johnny no because I was always sick. I told him to marry someone else who was not sick. He then said, "What if I marry someone else who is sick and she didn't tell me? I said, "Well, I don't know, but I am telling you I am sick." He then decided to ask my parents, but he wanted to talk to them when there was nobody at home. In other words, he didn't want my brothers and sisters home when he asked for me. I told him, "I don't know when you will get that chance." One day he was at the house and some of our friends came to visit and my sisters and brothers went part of the way home with them. I didn't want to go because I was having cramps. He stopped talking to me and then went see my parents. When he returned, I asked him what did they say? He said they told him "Yes," but they wanted him to know I was sick. I told him, "I told you the same thing twice." He kept coming. We had been seeing each other for about a year then. We married in Mississippi. Rev. S.J. Dickey from McComb performed the marriage. My parents were living in Greensburg and they came to the marriage. That was in December 21, 1941. I was twenty-nine and Johnny was about the same age. I hadn't been married before, but Johnny had had a wife before. His wife died. They didn't have any children and they had been separated for three years before she died. He told me about her and then he wanted to know if that was going to break us up. Him having been married and all. I said since it went on so long ago we might as well carry it on out now. So, we got married. Three months passed and he got drafted into the Army. I was three months pregnant by then and so I went back home to my parents. That's where I stayed while he was gone.

I thought since I was twenty-nine, I couldn't have any chaps, but I got pregnant right away. Lord, Jesus did I get big! In the evenings, I would eat at home and then go across the road to my sister Izola's house, eat and talk with her, and come home and eat again. My mother warned me about eating so much because she thought the baby would be too big for me to deliver. I told her I didn't want a small baby, but before I had him I wished that I had listened to her. Johnny Junior was my first child and he was born at my mother's house on September 26, 1942. When Johnny came home on furlough, the child was one-month old. He was crazy about the baby. I wanted to name the baby after his daddy and have something with Lee in it, so I named him Johnny Lee. I made him a junior, but I didn't know until many years up the road my husband wasn't a Johnny Lee and so my son couldn't be Johnny Lee Junior. But that's his name. Johnny Lee Vick Junior. My husband stayed in the Army for two years and when he got out, the baby did not want to come home with us because he was scared of Johnny. My husband said, "Let him stay." That was, stay with my mother and father. The next time we went home, Johnny Junior went with us.   He came on then.

　　After I had Johnny Junior, I wanted more children. I didn't care if I had a girl or a boy. I wanted another child because one child is so pitiful by itself. I wanted at least two children. At least two. I had my second baby three years after Johnny Junior and it was born in New Orleans at Charity hospital. You see, I had such a hard time with the first one, I thought I needed to go to the hospital for the second one. And it was better. I didn't have that hard a time like with the first child. The baby was a boy and I named him Clovis after one of the doctors. My sister Izola wanted him named after a doctor. I don't think it was because he was going to be a doctor because everybody thought he was going to be a preacher because he had a preacher's head. Round. Long. That's what people called a preacher's head. Round. Long. We had two doctors in St. Helena Parish over in Greensburg, Mississippi. One's name was Emmett Toler and the other one was Clovis Toler. That's the one I named my son after, the one who was son to Emmett Toler.

　　I ate a lot with the first child, but I couldn't eat a lot of greasy food with the second child because I had jaundice. It turned my skin yellow and my "pee" yellow, too. The day before I went to New Orleans to have the baby, I went to my doctor in Greensburg and he told me to take the yellow of an egg or something. I asked him to give me a strip to Charity hospital in New Orleans, and he did. A strip is what they called a letter of transfer. So, I asked for a strip to Charity and that's where Clovis was born. He had jaundice, too, and they kept him a few days. After Clovis, I didn't mind having another baby. I wanted me a girl, and I had one three years after Clovis. She was born at Charity and she was six pounds. I don't remember the ounces. I named her Dorothy Jean. Johnny Junior gave me the name. He said if it is a girl, name her Dorothy Jean or Gloria Dean and, if it is a boy, name him Clifton.

　　After Dorothy Jean, I was not particular about having any more children, but I didn't know anything about birth control, so I got pregnant again. That time, I lost out. I was somewhere between six and twelve weeks and I had a miscarriage. I was close to forty or a little older. I had problems with all of my children, but Johnny Junior was the hardest. I had a midwife with him, but the doctor had to come because the midwife couldn't do a thing. I tried so long to deliver and then my mother said she was going to call the doctor and the midwife said, "We don't need no doctor. She just need to bear the pain." My mother said, "No. Something's wrong." So, my mother called the doctor and the doctor came and ended up having to cut me before the baby could come out. Ella Turner was the midwife's name. She had had a stroke and could hardly get around. The doctor said, "Take her home and let her stay there."

Johnny was the hardest child to deliver because he was so big. Clovis was smaller, but I had yellow jaundice with him. He had it again after he got to be a big size. Then Johnny Junior took it and he had a hard time. We took him to the hospital because he could not eat. I was worried about him, but my husband Johnny wasn't all that worried. I told him that Junior was too sick to stay at home another night. I wanted him to go to the hospital. Johnny then went and got somebody to take us to the hospital. We took him to the hospital in McComb and they put fluid in his arm. I asked Johnny, "Didn't he holler?" He said, "No." I told him, "You see how sick he is." I don't remember how many days he stayed in the hospital, but at least a week. Then he got better. Johnny Junior fought in the Korean War or maybe it was in Vietnam. He stayed in the Army for two years. He got wounded in the head and they flew him somewhere where they doctored on him. My brothers fought in World War II and my husband Johnny fought in World War II. I don't like war.

We lived in Mississippi, in McComb, in a little house on Summit Street. Two families lived there. We stayed on one side and Sister Aleen Goff stayed on the other side. Then we left Summit Street and moved to Lynn Avenue. Sister Goff's husband later built a house behind ours. We remained friends and neighbors until both of them died. Our house had two rooms. One bedroom and a kitchen. The toilet was outside. We already had some furniture before Johnny went into the Army. We paid ten dollars a month rent. We stayed there one year and then we moved up the street to a bigger house. It had three rooms I think: a living room, kitchen and bedroom. Maybe two bedrooms and a kitchen. There was no living room. Bertha Magee lived next door on the other side. We paid twenty dollars a month rent.

C

I did not have any special jobs. I did house work. All of that goes together. I had to wash on my hands. I used a washing board. I would put the clothes in the pot and make a fire. I let them cook for a while and then I would take them out and rinse them off. I then hung them on the clothesline. We finally got a washing machine, but I did not have a dryer, so I still had to take them out and hang them on the line. The first time I had a dryer was when I came to live with Dorothy here in New Orleans, and that was in 1998. I still do the washing here.

I did a lot of sewing when the children were growing up. I made clothes and quilts and things like that. I sewed for people, but very seldom did I make children's clothes. I mostly made grown up clothes. The people would pay me five dollars and sometimes a little bit more. I made short coats for my neighbor Fannie Belle and I charged her five dollars. I would get about eight dollars for a dress. I didn't make ladies suits. Mostly I made pants for ladies. And the pants cost two dollars. It took me two hours to make a pair of pants. I didn't buy patterns. I would look in a book and see something I wanted to make and then I'd cut my own pattern.

White people were bad in Mississippi and in Louisiana. They wanted all Black folks to call them Mr. and Mrs. They even wanted you to call the young ones Mr. or Mrs. and they would call us aunt and uncle. But Whites treated my father pretty good because he was half White. No, we couldn't vote until after the Civil Rights Movement. I remember my oldest sister going to vote and I went with her. She lived in Amite County, Mississippi, and people got money to vote. I think it was about twenty dollars. Some got fifteen dollars and some got twenty. The first time I went to vote was after the Civil Rights people came to Mississippi. I remember when they came to McComb. There were a lot of them, Blacks and Whites. My daughter Dorothy went to a freedom school they had for the children in McComb. She asked me if she could go and I told her, "Ask your daddy." She asked him and he told her, "If you wanna go, go." So, she went to the freedom school. I remember all those people coming to McComb. It was something. It was really something. One of the guys married and he still lives in McComb. I thought the Civil Rights Movement was bad because I thought people might get killed.

Mrs. Ernestine Vick

I liked being a mother a whole lot. I think we were stronger mothers than the ones today because we didn't have all these things to be involved in back then. We went to church. We went to see our friends and then we came on back home. We took good care of our children. I don't think women should get rid of babies. If they get them, they ought to have them.

MRS. ELLA MAE YATES

Atlanta, Georgia

Librarian and Director of Libraries

My mother would read anything, even the back of a matchbook. I owe my interest in books to her influence. She taught me to read before I could go to school. In fact, before I started school, she had taught me to read in Old English. I could read Chaucer's <u>Canterbury Tales</u>. I didn't know what I was reading, but I could read the words. On Fridays when Daddy got off from work, he always brought three things home. He got paid on Fridays. He'd bring my mother a bag of hot peanuts. . There was a big Planter's Peanuts store where he changed buses downtown. He would bring me a bag of caramel candy and a book.

Mrs. Ella Mae Yates

I was born here in Atlanta. I'm a fourth generation Atlantan. My mother's name was Laura Rebecca Moore Gaines, and my father's name was Fred Gaines. My mother was born in Atlanta, and my father was born in Crawfordsville, Georgia, which is about an hour's drive from Atlanta, but they met here in Atlanta. Actually, Kemper Harold at Spelman College introduced them. When I was born, Blacks only had really one hospital, and it was owned by Dr. Georgia Dwelle and located on Boulevard in the Fourth Ward. My mother and father were at choir practice at Friendship Baptist Church when she went into labor, and it was all they could do to get her home. Fortunately, we lived on Vine Street right across from the Morris Brown Stadium, which was within walking distance of the church. People at the church took my Mother home and they put her on the dining room table. That was the best place, and that's where the physician, Dr. Powell, delivered me. His wife Sadie assisted him. She was a practicing nurse and a member of the Board of Trustees at Spelman. The name on my birth certificate is Ella Mae Gaines. After I married, I dropped the "Mae." I find myself getting a little annoyed with my friends who knew me all my life as Ella Mae and now just call me Ella. I don't like that. I like to be called Ella Mae. If I'm out somewhere and somebody says, "Ella Mae," I know that somebody has known me for a long time. I don't know why all of a sudden a lot of my friends that I grew up with her in Atlanta have dropped the Mae and just call me Ella. But I'm Ella Mae. I was named for a woman who used to work over at Spelman, and her daughter worked over at Spelman for a while. Her name was Ella Mae Coles. That was her maiden name. My brother adored her. He thought she could walk on water, and he wanted me named after Ella Mae Coles, and that's how I got my name.

My brother was born five years before me, and he was named Fred Gaines, Jr. after my father. My mother told me that I started talking before I had a tooth in my head, and that was my brother's salvation because I talked for him. He stopped walking and he stopped talking for about a year following a fall. When he started talking again, he had a speech impediment. So, although he was five years older than I was, I did all his talking. He was held back in elementary school and I was moved ahead. He didn't go to high school until I went so that I could talk for him. One teacher ridiculed him so because of his stutter that my mother allowed him to stay out of school. She just got tired of the ridicule. My brother made it to the twelfth grade, but he did not graduate. You know, we would be out in public and this teacher would see us and she would say, "Oh, this is my special child," referring to my brother. I was always very cool and reserved in my relationship with her because I knew that cruel side of her, that mean side, and how it had affected my brother. He died six years ago from a number of things related to diabetes. He was my biological brother, and he and I are children from my father's third marriage. We had the same mother and same father. I have a half-brother and a half-sister. I say half-brother and half-sister because we have the same father but not the same mother. I didn't get to know them until we were adults because they lived out in California. Money was very tight then, so we didn't have any money to travel to California. Their mother kept in touch with my mother through letters. The first time I met her was when I graduated from Library School at Atlanta University in 1951. We've stayed in very close contact until their deaths.

My mother was a social worker, but after she had my brother and me, she stopped work and stayed home to care for us. She didn't think anybody was good enough to raise her children. My mother was in the **first** graduating class of the Atlanta University School of Social Work. She was the literary one in the family. She was not much for card playing, and social clubs, and things like that. She belonged to a few clubs around the church, but they were basically service clubs for the church. My mother would read anything, even the back of a matchbook. I owe my interest in books to her influence. She taught me to read before I could go to school. In fact, before I started school, she had taught me to read in Old English. I could read Chaucer's Canterbury Tales. I didn't know what I was reading, but I could read the words. On Fridays when Daddy got off from work he always brought three things home. He got paid on Fridays. He'd bring my mother a bag of hot peanuts. . There was a big *Planter's Peanuts* store where he changed buses downtown. He would bring me a bag of caramel candy and a book. I developed a love for books because of my mother and an appreciation for art because of my father.

Mrs. Ella Mae Yates

My mother was formally educated. My father was self-educated, but as a mathematician you couldn't run circles around him at all. He had artistic abilities and very, very strong math skills. He was a picture framer and a mat decorator, and he taught himself. He was really quite gifted with his hands. I was quite proud of my father. To be able to do picture framing and mat decorating, in the twenties and thirties at that, was quite an achievement for a Black man. We didn't have Wal-Mart and Kmart and stores like that where you can just go in and buy beautiful frames already together. We didn't have that. If we wanted something framed, we took them to one or two outstanding picture framing stores in the city. My father worked for a firm called Binders, and that's where wealthy people took their pictures to be framed. Daddy was the head framer. One summer, when he was working in a shop owned by a woman named Mary Mobley, I worked with Daddy. He was teaching me to frame. He gave me a picture and told me what to do with it. He stood back and observed. When I finished the job and Daddy told me that the work I had framed was going to the Museum of Modern Art in New York, I was frightened out of my skin. After that experience, I didn't touch another painting. I was too frightened. Some of the pictures my father framed are hanging in the State Capitol. That is an indication of the caliber of his work. He was quite a firebrand, my father. He worked for Whites, but he never allowed them to treat him as less than a man. On one job, the boss rubbed him the wrong way. I was in high school, or maybe junior high, when this happened. Daddy dropped the man's pants and spanked him as if he were a baby. He put on his coat (Daddy never went anywhere without his coat), he came home, loaded his guns, and put them behind the door because he expected retribution, but retribution never came. The next day, the man he had whipped came to the house and apologized and asked him to come back. Daddy worked for that man until he died.

Of course, Atlanta was a very segregated city and, yes, I heard my parents talk about lynchings. Walter White, who was head of the NAACP, was a native Atlantan. He was so white that Whites didn't know he was Black and, as a result, he would go to lynchings and come back and report on what happened. You know about the terrible riot that took place in

Atlanta? I'm sure you've studied it in your classes at Spelman. My father was involved in a melee during the time of the riots. Thirty years after the incident, my father was passing a barbershop and a man called out to him and said, "I've never seen anybody fight with their fists like you did." Daddy lost a tie clip during the fight, and the man had kept that tie clip on him all those years. He gave it back to my father, and I still have it. So, yes, we knew what was going on. We had our Black newspapers. We had *The Atlanta Daily World*, which came out every day, and *The Pittsburgh Courier*. Those papers rapidly reported whatever was going on and wherever it was going on in the country.

A lot of the lynchings took place here in the South. We talked about these things in our civics classes at school, so no one was whispering to keep us from knowing. We were definitely told, and that was a part of our protective system. When we went places out of our local neighborhoods and out of the predominantly Black neighborhoods, we always went in twos and threes and groups. White men of means with chauffeur-driven cars would come into our neighborhoods looking for Black girls. And so, our parents made sure we always had some protective. But, you know, our parents didn't tell me anything about being Black. I knew I was Black, but one thing they did strongly impress upon us, and so did my friends' parents, that we were very, very worthwhile. And you might find this hard to believe, but my mother was not interested in integration of schools when my brother and I were small because she didn't want us to go to school with the poor White trash that lived in our general vicinity and would be assigned to the same school. We were better. That was pumped home in all sorts of ways. "You're better. You're not trash. I don't care what they have. I don't care what the color of their skin is. You are better. You are more intelligent. You have better breeding and you have more exposure to culture. You're better read, so that makes you superior." We kind of grew up with that attitude of superiority. We were poor, but we didn't know we were poor. The kids whose families had money and those whose families didn't have money ran around in the same crowds.

Mrs. Ella Mae Yates

It isn't every day that any of us get a chance to talk about our lineage, and certainly not outside the family circle, so I am very pleased that you are asking me about my grandparents and my great grandparents. Were any of them in slavery? I can tell you that my father's parents were slaves, but my father never talked about it. We knew only because my brother would say that my aunt Elizabeth, the oldest of the thirteen children, was born in slavery. My father said that he left home, left Crawfordsville, because he could no longer stand to see his parents living on the plantation with his mother's White father in the house. In other words, my paternal grandmother's father, my maternal great-grandfather, was a White man. Her name was Cordelia Harden. I don't know how she met my grandfather, whose name was Leroy Gaines. I know that they lived in Crawfordsville. I know that they had thirteen children and that my father was one of the older children. He was named for Frederick Douglass. I also know that my paternal grandfather farmed on the compound and he was also an itinerant minister. He never had any money, but his brother, who rode with the carpetbaggers, was very, very wealthy. During Reconstruction, when carpetbaggers made money, he made money. Land, land, land. He bought land. My father's mother was fair from her White lineage. The children were dark, but none of them were as dark as their father. Of all of my his thirteen children and their descendants, not one named their child after my paternal grandfather, but all of them who had sons named at least one son after my father and named some of their daughters Freddie after my father and some children were named Cordelia after my father's mother. I haven't the faintest idea of the time frame.

My maternal grandmother was Mary Benjamin Moore and her father was Jewish. He brought her to Atlanta from Baltimore and later took her to Germany. She was reared there, but she left Germany when she was an adult and came back to Atlanta with a Jewish family. She remained in Atlanta, and she lived as a Black woman. My mother's father was more White than he was Black. He was a judge here in Atlanta and his Black housekeeper bore him a girl and a boy. He decided the girl was too White to grow up to be Black, so he sent her out to Buckhead to live with his wealthy White family, and they raised her. I will not call her name because she my most shocking experience. I look back in retrospect and I think our parents must have kept us pretty sheltered, as to where we went and what we did, so that we wouldn't meet that kind of White nastiness. When we went downtown on the bus and when we came back home, only Black folks were riding the bus, so we sat anywhere we wanted to sit. So, we didn't run into that mess with, "Get on the back of the bus." I didn't travel in areas where that many Whites rode so I didn't have to run into the nasty, nasty kind of segregation. You know, we stayed basically in our own community rather than go into areas where we would be slapped back. Now, this was just my experience. The parents of some of my acquaintances from school worked in service, and they had to go into White areas in order to work. My mother stayed home and took care of us. Most of my friends' mothers either stayed home or they taught or they did something within the Black community, in our Black school system or in the university school system. So, we didn't encounter racial indignities as did somebody who worked in a subservient capacity. We were protected from those kinds of experiences. Our parents pulled this off with such aplomb without our realizing what they were doing.

I attended E. A. Ware Elementary which was located across the street from Morris Brown College. It's now Jordan Hall. From there I went to Washington High in the seventh grade because we didn't have a middle school on this side of town. Our classrooms were housed in prefab trailer units. It was just a given that I would go to Spelman. The class I should have been in was the Class of 1948, but I stayed out my senior year and worked in the library and so I graduated in the Class of 1949. I went to the Library School at Atlanta University and finished there in 1951. I have lived and worked in different places: Orange, New Jersey; Seattle, Washington; Richmond, Virginia; and, of course, Atlanta. I am now living in Atlanta, and it is such delight that my daughter, Jerri, lives with me. Such delight and such joy.

My work in libraries would fill volumes and, really, I don't know where to begin or where to place by focus. Let me say up front that I love working in libraries and the love probably started when my mother introduced me to books when I was very young. With my skills and my abilities and all the years that I've spent in a library going to school, I was always

Mrs. Ella Mae Yates

picked to head something in a library that had been historically White male. I was breaking down doors here and breaking down doors there and meeting a great deal of resentment. I generally had support from the wealthy corporate White male community, but there was always a White woman or two who tried to make my life very, very difficult. I was out of my place. I was supposed to be subservient to them, and in my position here I am an equal. I was appointed State Librarian for the Commonwealth of Virginia in 1986, number six in its history. I was the first woman, the first non-Virginian, and of course, the first with a permanent suntan. During my watch it was discovered that the building was badly in need of repair, of renovation. The electrical system was shot to pot in my office and on the mezzanine on the second floor. There was so much soot and dust and asbestos in the building that I requisitioned for a study to be done for a new library and archives building. That was done. There was a White woman on the Board who did not want me involved in it at all. She worked around me, over me, under me, and otherwise to make sure I didn't have anything to do with it. But I was the one who initiated the new building. I left before it got up, so my name isn't on the plaque there. What a heady experience seeing, handling, and being responsible for materials and archives that dated back to the sixteen hundreds.

I was appointed director of the Atlanta Public Library System in 1973, and, again, I was a "first." No Black person had ever held that position. A bill had been passed allocating money to put the Central Library downtown, and it fell under my jurisdiction to get the building up. I had one woman on my library Board who would rather have seen the money blown just to say that a nigger couldn't handle the job. I was determined that I would do it, and I did it. If you check at the Atlanta Historical Society, you will find that a director who came after me was given credit for finishing the building construction. That was not the case. You see, there were people on the Library Board who did not want my name on the plaque inside the building. It was very, very ugly. I wrote them and I said, "It doesn't make any difference to me. You don't have to put my name on the building."

Dr. Mays, who was President at Morehouse at the time, told me, "Oh yes, they have to put your name on that building. You did the work." So, he got involved and so did Venable Lawson, who was Dean of the Library School at Emory University. When we had the dedication of the new building, the ribbon cutting, the Friends of the Library decided to have a big extravaganza on the Friday before the Saturday ribbon cutting. They paid the way for the former Director and his wife and daughter to come back to the extravaganza and had them stand in the receiving line. I came home to change clothes because it was a formal affair. At that point, the building had not been turned over to the city. The construction company and the architects had only turned the building over to me personally for them to use that night. I had to open and close the doors. I came home to change clothes and when I went back, the men who were at the door didn't want to let me into the building. I said, "Well, that's fine with me because I'm tired. So, if you don't let me in, then I will cut off the lights and empty the building, and lock it up." One of them jumped up in my face and said, "What do you mean?" I said, "I mean exactly what I said." I had the key on a big block like this. I pulled out the key. I said, "This is what has let you in this building, and this is the one key that will lock you out!" The Black community has never, ever recognized me for what I did. I was the first and only woman in the library profession in the United States who put up a building from scratch. The only one to date! It was a rough row to hoe, but I was successful in bringing in the new downtown Central Library building in 1981 at cost and on time. I recall your asking me, "Why did you stay?" If I had gone somewhere else, it would have been the same thing all over again. I don't know. There's something about me that seems to threaten people, particularly in the library world, in academia, in White settings. All of my jobs have been highly political, highly political. I've always said that libraries are laundry rooms for all the money that comes through scams, graft, everything else. Put it through the library and then take the money out. At all the places I worked, I never allowed any political entity to siphon money from the library.

It's interesting that you should ask me what it means to be a southern woman—of course a Black southern woman. I say it's interesting because although I am a fourth generation

Mrs. Ella Mae Yates

Atlantan, I really don't view myself as a Black woman of the South. I think of myself as a woman, but not necessarily in the context of how southern women are viewed. I'm a hell of a woman, and always have been, but whatever I am, whatever I have become, whatever I have accomplished, I could have done it whether I was from another region of the country. My life has been a never-ending roller coaster ride, but never boring, uneventful, unfulfilling, or unchallenging. In health matters, it has been a daring succession of events that have challenged me to live. My strong belief in God and a dogged determination to survive have kept me here some fifty years beyond predictions. Not one day has been dull or uneventful. I keep the faith and periods of quiet solitude and meditation as my formula for survival. In my professional career, I look back in retrospect and often wonder how did I survive because my positions have always been in areas that have historically been encumbered by White males. I've been likened to a cat with nine lives, always landing on my feet with much to be proud of.

PART TWO:
Tributes and Gratitude

Chanel Cunningham . Kerstin Roper . Ayo Cummings .
Qrescent Mason . Danielle Phillips . Qrescent Mason .
Alexa Harris . Jody Washington . Crystal Bennett .
Noni Bourne . Kyja Wilborn . Cindye Evans .
Kerstin Roper . Niah Shearer . Ebony Carter .
Katherine Strunk-Fobbs . Danielle Phillips . Kira Lynch .
Siobhan Robinson . Jody Washington

A TRIBUTE TO MRS. ANN COOPER

THE WISEST OF THE WISE

Gloria Wade Gayles

The thought that she is a legend surprises her, but legend she is. Who does not know Mrs. Ann Cooper? She has been a presence and a voice in Atlanta since her arrival here in 1922 by train from Nashville, Tennessee. Amazingly, she remembers the weather on that day, the outfit she was wearing, and the pacing of her husband, Dr. Albert Cooper, at the depot. In fact, there are few things Mrs. Cooper does not remember. That she shares her memories with sweet generosity is one of the reasons I could not let go of her. Mrs. Cooper is the longest serving of the Women of Wisdom honored in this book. The richness of her stories and the generosity of her spirit kept me returning to her, for four academic semesters, with individual students and with groups of students. Her laughter always greeted us, and her amazing memory always astonished us. "Now who do we have today?" she would ask me. Always she smiled. Often she laughed. "Have a seat, and tell me who you are," she said to a group of students she welcomed into her home during the fall of 2005-2006. The students spoke in soft voices they thought appropriate for a sacred place. Mrs. Cooper was patient with them as they struggled to find their voice and understanding when a cell phone rang in the middle of the interview. She paused, smiled, waited for the student to turn off the ring, and continued with her remembering. In other interviews, students keep their SIS journals open in order to record details of the aural landscape. No journal was open in this session, so mesmerized the students were by the clarity of Mrs. Cooper's voice and the sharpness of her memory. They were moved by a special grace Mrs. Cooper has that keeps her embracing and joyous in the presence of major losses. You see, the students were aware that she had buried a second child months before our visit. "What keeps you so happy?" one of the students asked. Mrs. Cooper, wrapping her words in laughter, answered, "I think it's about love, you see. I've had a whole lot of love in my life." The students love Mrs. Cooper. I love Mrs. Cooper. And you will love Mrs. Cooper. Her voice strikes the most melodious of chores. Her memories paint the sharpest pictures of family, community, service, and, of course, love. Perhaps, like Bernice Appiah Pinkrah, who had the privilege of interviewing Mrs. Cooper in several sessions, you will write in your journal: "I found myself hanging on to her every word, barely feeling worthy. I stand before her, wanting improvement."

TRIBUTES

A TRIBUTE TO MRS. GEORGIA W. ALLEN
by Chanel Cunningham

"Hold your stomach in. Articulate. Execute." Remembered lines from an unforgettable drama teacher, Mrs. Georgia Allen, a legend in the City of Atlanta and my mentor in SIS. She is a tall woman in every sense of the word and what she inspires you to do, whenever you talk with her, is to see yourself as TALL, reaching toward your dreams. She inspired her students to believe that they could accomplish anything as long as they believed in themselves AND as long as they worked hard and practiced, worked hard and practiced, stretching themselves and reaching high. Mrs. Allen defines the art of execution of high goals. Turning on the tape and recording her wisdom was a pleasure, but finding words that capture the influence she had on me is a major challenge. When you hear her voice in this volume, you will love and respect her as much as I do when you read her words in the volume. This quote comes to mind when I think about Mrs. Allen: *Young beautiful people are acts of nature, but beautiful older people are works of art.* Mrs. Allen is a work of art. I thank you, Mrs. Allen, for inspiring me to stand tall and execute.

A TRIBUTE TO MRS. CORNELIA BAILEY
by Kerstin Roper

We asked, "What did you miss out on as a child, Mrs. Bailey?" Mrs. Cornelia Bailey answered, "How can you miss something you never had?" Mrs. Bailey spoke with a deliberateness and a sharpness that impressed me. I was one of fifteen students in SIS who had the privilege of spending three days on Sapelo Island, birthplace and home to Mrs. Cornelia Bailey: griot, cultural historian, writer, and activist. Literally, we sat at her feet on a cool Saturday night, talking past the time she had given us. We turned to pages in Mrs. Bailey's book, God, Mr. Buzzard and the Bolito Man we had marked with post-its of different colors. What a rare privilege to sit in the parlor with the author of a text we had read for class and to experience very setting about which she wrote! Sapelo is the last sea island in Georgia that has stood up to development. Please take note. I said that Sapelo is standing, but it is quivering from the relentless pressure of investors, tourists, developers and realtor institutions. Mrs. Bailey is committed to saving Sapelo and, in saving Sapelo, to preserve the culture and the history that made her who she is: a powerful, take-charge woman.

A TRIBUTE TO MRS. LEILA BARFIELD
by Ayo Cummings

This first day I went to meet with Mrs. Barfield I was extremely late. Dr Gayles thinks I was half an hour late, but I was much later than that. You see, I had forgotten to call Mrs. Barfield the day before the interview, something Dr. Gayles insists that we do. Fifteen minutes before I was to arrive at her house, I was able to reach Mrs. Barfield by phone. I told her that I was running late, but that I would be there shortly. I hung up the phone and literally ran to my car. Suddenly, I realized I had left my SIS notebook at home, which, in five o-clock traffice, would be an hour's drive. I was at the risk of breaking two rules Dr. Gayles gives us: *Arrive on time* and *Do not cancel appointments at the last minute*. Mrs. Barfield rescued me. When I called her back her, she told me she would see whenever I arrived. Even before meeting her, I liked her and I knew each visit with her would be memorable. Each time I walked in to her home, she embraced me with warmth, and I always left with lessons on character and achievement. The thing that really impressed me was how humble Mrs. Barfield is about her many successes. She was the first Black woman to serve on the City Council in Lawton, Oklahoma and the first Black woman to serve as vice mayor of the city, but she never bragged about these accomplishments. She is a humble and gracious lady who considers love of family to be her blessing. I thank you, Mrs. Barfield, for teaching me what to value and how to achieve.

A TRIBUTE TO MRS. JULIA BOND
by Qrescent Mason

No one ever pays attention to the set of orange brick apartments that sits right in front of what we now call the Spelman College "Front Gate." We speed by in new cars never giving thought to the fact that someone might live in those apartments. Someone does. An extraordinary someone. Mrs. Julia Bond, to be exact. Her ninety-five-year old eyes have seen the community grow from a muddy plain to a developed parking lot. I had the privilege of interview Mrs. Bond for the SIS Oral History Project. Once, when I asked her if there were something she had not yet done in life that she wanted to do, she answered. "I don't know. You know. I'd like to have left some mark. I'd like to have written something or done something that would be permanent, that people would remember." All I could think was, this woman who has done so much and seen so much and been the strength to so many people in the African American community thinks she has no permanent mark on the world? How odd. Weeks later a quote from my Zen Page-a-Day Calendar gave me an answer to the questions that Mrs. Bond had left in my mind: "It's the opposite of what everyone thinks. They assume that when they hang on to the things that matter in this world, they are something. But ask yourself: how could anyone who might not wake up the next morning be important? If, on the other hand, because of your fusion with the Creator you think of yourself as nothing, then you are very great indeed." Mrs. Bond does not know it, but she is very great indeed. I am proud to know her and privileged to play a part in sharing her story with the world.

TRIBUTES

A TRIBUTE TO MRS. FAYE BUSH
by Danielle Phillips

Can you imagine a Black working class woman standing toe to toe with White male government officials, elite members of multinational corporations, and the Ku Klux Klan? I did not have to imagine such a woman because I interviewed her. Her name is Mrs. Faye Bush, and she is the Executive Director of the Newtown Florist Club, a predominately women's organization committed to fighting environmental racism in Newtown, Georgia. Our first interview was scheduled for December 9, 2003. I was nervous. I wanted to make sure I asked her questions that would capture the tremendous accomplishments she has made while fighting for her life and the lives of people in her community. What amazed me about Mrs. Bush was how calmly she talked about her many losses and her many battles. Newtown is located on top of a landfill, within a stone's throw of a metal scrap yard and within constant earshot of noise pollution from freight trains. How could she be so calm and so embracing? Her calm is a testament to her enormous strength, and that strength is what keeps her fighting for change. As an aspiring scholar-activist, I could not have found a better role model than Mrs. Faye Bush. In every sense of the word, she is an activist and a change agent.

A TRIBUTE TO DR. JUNE DOBBS BUTTS
by Qrescent Mason

There are certain people who come into our lives to teach us lessons that we would not otherwise learn. Sometimes they enter our lives when we least expect them, yet their presence is jarring. Dr. June Dobbs-Butts was one such person for me. She was the gift SIS gave me during the first semester of my senior year at Spelman College. More than stories about growing up in Atlanta, her legendary family, and her past alcoholism, she gave me advice on how to live life. "Slow down," she told me. "You must enjoy your time. Realize that the things you think are earth-shaking now will all smooth out in the end." Dr. Butts could not have known in the first interview that I was applying for graduate schools and fellowships, mourning my last days at Spelman, and worrying about my sister who was dealing with a life-threatening illness at the time. I was encouraged by Dr. Butts' words not to lose hope. Rather than rush to complete things, I would look around and be thankful for any circumstances in which I found myself. Rather than mourn, I would learn to celebrate. Rather than worry, I would have faith. My first meeting with Dr. Butts was life-altering, subsequent ones equally so. She taught me lessons I would not otherwise have learned.

A TRIBUTE TO MRS. MARY ELOISE STEPHENS DANSBY
by Alexa A. Harris

I knew I could not be late for an interview with my mentor, so I arrived fifteen minutes early. I sat in my car across the street from her house in an area I thought be out of view should she peak out the window or open the door. To my surprise, I was very much in view. Mrs. Dansby was waiting for me. I remember how cute she was in a beautiful light blue short-sleeved denim dress. She welcomed me into her home and directed me to the den. "Here is where we can work," she said. Mrs. Dansby had prepared for the interview as evidenced by a notepad with words written in cursive with a pencil. "I just want to make sure all my answers are just right." In those initial moments, I knew we would get along just fine. Mrs. Dansby exudes an infectious joy, and she has a youthfulness about her that wins your heart. When she speaks, her eyes light up, and this reminds me of the beauty of life and the privilege of age. She is very spiritual. In fact, she helped me understand the difference between being "religious" and being "spiritual". She taught me more about what family and community meant during the Jim Crow era than I can share in this brief tribute. In spite of segregation, she was taught to love herself and to believe that she was destined to achieve. Bonding with Mrs. Mary Dansby was the highlight of my sophomore year at Spelman College. It is a bonding I will share with my children and, who knows, with a student enrolled in SIS many years from now.

A TRIBUTE TO MRS. EMMA DEGRAFFENREID
by Jody Washington

"I'm five minutes late" is all I kept saying to myself while I was speeding down I-20 to meet my mentor for the first time. The date was April 3, 2004. I was running late because I stopped at the store to buy a gift for my mentor. I exited the expressway and found the neighborhood in which my mentor lives. I rang the doorbell at her house, and Mrs. Emma DeGraffenreid, my mentor, opened the door. After receiving the gifts, my mentor embraced me with a kiss on my cheek, enveloped me with a warm hug, and reassured me with these words: "You're on the ball." After that, I knew Mrs. DeGraffenreid and I would hit it off. In each interview, she made me feel welcomed and valued. I noticed that she didn't look at me often when she responded to questions I would ask her, but in those times when she would look directly at me, I saw her spiritual depth. Her eyes were large and they had an innocence about them. They reflected courage, strength and, of course, the wisdom I was seeking for the SIS project. Whenever Mrs. DeGraffenreid mentioned an experience that truly bothered her or about which she had very strong feelings, she and I would have intense eye contact for a few seconds as if she wanted to let me know how important it was for her to share that memory. Mrs. DeGraffenreid is a very religious and spiritual woman and a humorous woman as well. In every interview there was something she said that made me laugh, and there was always something that made me think, really think. I love Mrs. DeGraffenreid.

TRIBUTES

A TRIBUTE TO MRS. JENNIE DRAKE
by Crystal Bennett

I left campus for my first interview with my mentor, Mrs. Jennie Drake. I turned down _____ Drive. I went up a hill and then down a hill until I reached the number I had been given. I rang the doorbell, but no one answered. I waited. I rang again. I waited. No one answered. I left flowers and a note on the porch and walked disappointedly down the hill. I would learn later that I had been given her daughter's address. Mrs. Jennie Drake was at home waiting for me. We both had been looking forward to the interview and we both had been disappointed. So when we finally met, we had already been through an experience together. We had already created a bond without even meeting each other. I'm grateful for the bond. Mrs. Drake taught me things about life and about Atlanta that I had not learned from anyone else. She always spoke in a sharp, clear, octave reception that was punctuated with wisdom. "There is nothing wrong with thinking for yourself. There is nothing wrong with wearing turquoise earrings, no matter what authority figure tells you otherwise. Live life with so many good times that you can't single one out. Be involved in your community. Go party and dance your heart out. Bread and butter are not important, if you have nylons. Be smart, but do not feel that you have to prove it to anyone. And most importantly, love yourself the most." There is nothing ordinary about Mrs. Jennie Drake. She's free-speaking, authentic and powerful. Mrs. Drake, I miss our time together.

A TRIBUTE TO MRS. ANNA ENGLISH

by Noni Bourne

Perched on the edge of an armchair, my tape-recorder between us and my pen hovering over my SIS journal, I took in Mrs. English's every word. As I think back on the time I spent in her room, wall-papered pretty, and the conversations that took place there, I am filled with questions, mostly to myself: "What color was the couch?" "Why didn't you ask her to tell you about her first day at work, her last day at work, her favorite food?" As I lament all the stories I missed, I realize that I did ask questions. In fact, I asked a lot of questions and I received a lot of answers, but there is no way, no possible way that one life, one incredibly long yet still short, superhuman and somehow natural life, could be captured in so many interviews. Somehow I could never think of the right thing to say after receiving the gift of her stories. My mind raced with questions, but I didn't want to badger, pester, attack, or dig uncomfortably deep. So I held back. But somehow, even with my conspicuous lack of interviewing skills, a story came forth. A story of a "wild little barefooted girl" who admired her father's gentleness when he removed splinters and who hid in trees to read books. A girl who grew into a woman who, as teacher and as principal, cultivated young minds and loved to watch the "aha!" moment of a student who suddenly understands is very important to me; a woman who has raised one daughter and loved many nephews and realized in the process that boys are different from girls; a woman who still pauses when she remembers her husband; a woman who fed me the best pound cake I've ever eaten. Her stories gave me a glimpse at an incredible life. Thank you, Mrs. English, for answering my questions, even those I never asked.

A TRIBUTE TO MRS. ELIZABETH GROSS

by Kiya Wilborn

Mrs. Gross has lived so many lives, collecting the wisdom of many years and maintaining the idealism of youth. For me, she is an example of a life influenced by love for the earth and love for humanity. Mrs. Gross welcomed me into her busy schedule of maintaining her expansive garden, spending time with her family, and giving time to others. She welcomed me so well that when she would describe her family and her ancestors, I would be so thankful that I had such a great family and ancestors, until I realized that I'm not really related to Mrs. Gross—except by fate. In the aftermath of the Presidential election, Mrs. Gross reassured me that voting Green wasn't the worst choice I could have made. When I started attending a new church, of which she is a member, she made me feel a part of the community. And after being attacked in a class for being naïve and unrealistic in my optimistic understanding of the world, Mrs. Gross had only to give me a word from her wisdom to remind me that faith in the goodness of the world is not ridiculous. Just as I stopped believing that a life dedicated to positive change is not worthwhile, Mrs. Gross welcomed me into her garden.

A TRIBUTE TO MRS. LILLIE HARRIS

by Cindye Evans

Let me tell you about the first time I talked to my mentor. "May I speak to Mrs. Lillie Harris, please?" I asked.   "This is she," a soft voice said. I asked her when was she available for the first interview. She asked me, "When are **YOU** available?" I had made contact with Mrs. Lillie Harris, and I was very blessed. Mrs. Harris is petite, but strong and very sharp. She worked for many years as a resident director at Spelman College, and I know she was a confidant for students, an inspiration for students, and a role model for students because she has been all that for me. I learned from her what dignity means and what devotion to family means. I learned what it was like to ride a Jim Crow train. Mrs. Harris said, and I quote, "I not only remember segregation, I lived it." So many of her stories have stayed with me, but there is one in particular I will never forget: the story of her father's death. He worked on the Southern Railway as a dining car waiter, and on this particular day, her brother was a passenger on the very train her father was working in. He was sitting in a different car and he was sitting in that car only because his father had told him to sit there. In the train collision that took place, everyone in the car the father was in was killed. Mrs. Harris has experienced major losses, but she has a large and loving family, which is why her home is filled with pictures of her four children, fourteen grandchildren, twenty-three great grandchildren, and three great-great grandchildren. I think her gallery is missing a picture because her family now includes a new member, a SIS mentee named Cindy Evans. Mrs. Harris, I thank you.

TRIBUTES

A TRIBUTE TO DR. CARRIE JOHNSON
by Kerstin Roper

"You know, Miss Roper, you are capable of practically anything." What began as SIS interviews with one of Atlanta's treasures, Dr. Carrie Johnson, developed into a rich bonding and learning experience for me. In every interview, Dr. Johnson gazed out of her dining room window and traveled back through years of memories with me and my tape recorder tagging along. When I had to turn the tape over, Dr. Johnson would pause, sit back, watch for the cue, and resume as if she had paused only to inhale. I left each interview inspired by her many accomplishments. For example, she was honored as one of Atlanta's Most Influential Women this year. Hours and hours of conversations on and off the recorder fill the halls of my memory, discourse so varied that full documentation would create a volume in itself. The needs of young Black women, the decrease in respect and honor given to elders, images of Black women in the media are among the topics that ricocheted off the walls around the two of us. The bonding between us was rich and genuine. I am inspired by all of her accomplishments, but inspired most of all by her belief in the Black women's leadership. If I should ever doubt myself, I will turn on the tape of my memories of hours with Dr. Johnson and hear her say, "You know, Miss Roper, you are capable of practically anything."

A TRIBUTE TO MISS ANNIE JEWELL MOORE
by Niah Shearer

Miss Moore's appearance, demeanor, home, and life stories were the epitome of elegance, grace and strength. In the very first interview, I became an instant fan. I was glad that we have so much in common. I am an economics major: Miss Moore graduated from Spelman as an economics major. I jokingly refer to myself as a "fashionista" because of my love for fashion, but Miss Moore is a true "fashionista." In fact, as I learned from attending a program at Clark Atlanta held in her honor and as I learned in subsequent interviews, to say that Miss Moore is a fashion designer is an understatement. She is a Black woman pioneer in the field! I sat on the edge of my seat when she told me about the shop she established in Detroit—Ann Moore Couturiere-and the prominent people who sought her out as their designer. And of course they did because her designs were so incredible; one of them appeared in Vogue Magazine in 1953. She maintained her shop for twenty years, but she never got the credit she deserved because she is a single Black woman. There is sadness in her stories, and yet there is the joy of accomplishment. Miss Moore inspired me to have a dream and to do everything I can to achieve it. I will always be her fan, and I will always be grateful to her for the ways she has inspired me.

A TRIBUTE TO DR. ZELMA PAYNE
by Ebony Carter

The first time I spoke to my mentor by phone, she suddenly cut me off. I said to myself, "Did she just give me the brush off." In the first interview, I was sweating buckets and dropping everything on the floor. I was so nervous and she would give me long lectures on what a successful woman needs to know. But the one experience that stays in my memory was when I saw the car she drives. It is a green Toyota Avalon. I had envisioned the kind of car she drives. She told me she started driving at thirteen and that her father taught her. I remember laughing so hard. She said, "Why are you laughing?" I said, "I always saw you as the type of person who had someone chauffeuring you around town. That with the snap of your fingers, you had a Dr. Payne personal driver. " I never thought she would be driving a 2003 Toyota Avalon because she is very dignified, you know, like Miss Daisy, who is taken care of. I started humming the tune from the movie. I gave her the nickname of Miss Daisy, but I want you to understand that only I can call her Miss Daisy. Of course, Dr. Payne is nothing like Miss Daisy. She is an African American woman of fierce independence. She has taken herself to many achievements, and she is still behind the wheel. She is a serious, classy and sophisticated woman with a sense of humor and a generous spirit. I know because since the very beginning of our relationship, I have received her generosity and I have received her love. Dr. Payne believes in me, and she has helped me believe in myself. I have no doubt that I will achieve my goals, because I will have Dr. Payne telling me, "Now, Ebony, watch this curve. Stay on course." Thank you, Dr. Payne.

A TRIBUTE TO MRS. LAURA LYNEM RATES
by Katherine Strunk-Fobbs

I rang the doorbell. Mrs. Laura Rates greeted me with a warm smile and invited me to have a seat in the dining room. I felt such peace and contentment and genuineness. There was no pretense about Mrs. Rates. No pretense at all. She was naturally—and for real--gracious and sincere and gentle and loving and kind and humble. That is what I felt about her in those first seconds of meeting her, and that is what I experienced in my relationship with Mrs. Laura Rates. Her dining room became our safe space, our special room, for bonding. It was there that she shared stories about growing up in Kentucky during the Jim Crow era and about life during World War II. As senior class president, she directed her classmates "to keep smiling no matter what." She served Spelman College for more than thirty years—in the registrar's office and in the office of the College minister. As she talked about those thirty years of service and about her life before Spelman, I learned what dignity means and what devotion requires and what joy both of them bring. You will read Mrs. Rates' stories in the second SIS volume, but I took much more than those stories from our interviews because sometimes we sat in her dining room with the tape off. What I learned in those non-SIS bonding experience is my special and personal gift. Mrs. Rates, I thank you for teaching me the importance of eternal growth and exploration. I will always keep smiling.

TRIBUTES

A TRIBUTE TO MRS. RUTH SCOTT SIMMONS

by Gloria Wade Gayles

"Mrs. Simmons is a study in Southern grace and elegance." That is how Ann Lister described her after accompanying me to a two-hour clarifying session with Mrs. Simmons. Ann was right. Mrs. Simmons exemplifies what we mean, in the positive sense of the phrase, when we say of someone, "She is a lady," more precisely a "southern lady." Equal emphasis, please, on **lady** and **southern**. She enjoys telling the story of how her paternal grandfather, a slave, was able to send his son to Hiram College in Ohio, where he would meet her maternal grandmother, offspring, too, of former slaves. It is an incredible story, deserving more space than we are able to give in this small volume. So much there is in Mrs. Simmons' memories to read again and again about the making of a strong family, but it is the story of Mrs. Simmons' love for her older sister Esther that will win your heart. It is quite simply priceless, as is Mrs. Simmons in her grace, elegance, and little-girl sweetness.

A TRIBUTE TO MISS MARGUERITE F. SIMON
by Danielle Phillips

On October 30,2003 at 12:10 p.m., I called Miss Simon to schedule our first interview. Before I could ask to speak to her, she quickly said, "Yes, this is Miss Simon." Her promptness let me know that she was sharp as a whip and that my interviews with her would be an unforgettable experience. She agreed to begin our first interview the following Monday. On Monday, November 3, 2003 at 12:00p.m. clear skies and a bright sun guided me to Miss Simon's house. She greeted me with her characteristic Miss Simon strong handshake and warm hug. When I entered her home, I saw household appliances I had never seen before except in museums. Stories about attending LeMoyne Normal, The University of Colorado, and Columbia University were only some of the memories that intrigued me during our conversations. What surprised me the most during our interviews was the story of how she came to teach physical education at Spelman. Miss Simon wanted to be a biologist! She sacrificed this dream to serve Spelman during World War II. I was very excited when President Tatum announced in convocation that the gymnasium in Read Hall would be named in honor of Miss Simon. What a dedication ceremony that will be: The Marguerite F. Simon Gymnasium. Miss Simon deserves that honor! She also deserves my eternal gratitude for the gift of her stories and the power of her presence in my life. Miss Simon, your memories are treasures I will always hold. Thank you.

A TRIBUTE TO MRS. NELL SIMMS
by Kira Lynch

I want to paint a picture of Mrs. Nell Sims because she is beautiful in a regal way. When I met her, I couldn't help thinking about the photograph of Septima Clark that graces the cover of a book that greets us from the coffee table of thousands of homes and leans for our choosing from shelves in bookstores across the nation. Septima Clark, one of the fighters of the sixties, is a symbol of resistance and strength. In the photograph, she is looking into the future, not into the past, as if there is something she has already seen. Something she already knows. Each time I have seen that picture, I have had a hundred questions to ask Septima Clark about growing older and remaining strong. What was she thinking when the photographer took her picture? What did she remember about the past? What does she see for the future? What advice does she have for the present? I was privileged to ask those questions of my mentor, Mrs. Nell Sims. Her sharp mind taught me more than I could have ever learned about the wisdom that comes with the addition of years to one's life. As her photo in this volume shows, she is a study in beauty and grace. Mrs. Sims is ninety-five years of age. Ninety-five! , Before retirement, she was director of a successful day care center. In fact, Mrs. Simms was the first Black woman in Atlanta to found and operate such a center. When we talked, she remembered Jim Crow and racial violence and struggles, but in one of her rememberings did she speak of defeat. Her theme is victory. Her theme is achievement. Her theme is strength. I think the photograph of Mrs. Nell Simms should be framed and hung in galleries that we would know the beauty and wisdom of women on whose shoulders we stand. Mrs. Sims, we value and honor you.

A TRIBUTE TO MRS. EMANUELLA SPENCER
by Siobhan Robinson

Mrs. Emanuella Julian Spencer is quite a remarkable woman, full of profound wisdom and infectious joy. She always made certain that I ate lunch before returning to campus. On this particular day, she served me a turkey sandwich with lettuce, tomato, and mayonnaise on wheat toasted bread; a huge icy glass of coke; and cookies and candy. That wasn't all. She surprised me with a cake that was quite simply delicious. When I asked her the name of the cake, Mrs. Spencer slowly turned toward me and said, slightly smirking, "Better than sex!" Mrs. Spencer swears to this day that is the name of the cake: "Better than sex." She shared many stories with me, but the one I will always cherish is the story of Buddy and Butch. She is Buddy, and her husband is "Butch." After the death of her father, when Mrs. Spencer was fourteen, she was immobilized by grief. Buddy came to visit her, and he rocked her back and forth as if she were a baby. Something in her broke and for the first time since her father's death, she cried. Buddy did not interrupt her. After she had cried for about half an hour, he sat her on the bed and asked, "Are you okay now? Do you feel better?" She answered, "Yes. I feel better." At that moment, Mrs. Spencer knew that Buddy would one day be her husband. And he was, for thirty plus wonderful years. At a time when I had almost begun to believe that love between Black men and Black women does not exist, I heard about Butch and Buddy. All of Mrs. Spencer's stories touched me in special ways because she paints them with details. I thank you, Mrs. Spencer, for the snacks, the cakes, the wisdom, and the stories about love, courage, faith, and persistence. You have had a tremendous on my life.

TRIBUTES

A TRIBUTE TO MRS. ERNESTINE VICK

by Gloria Wade Gayles

Mrs. Vick is a woman of few words, but many stories. To many of the questions you ask her, she gives one-sentence answers. She pauses and waits for the next question. Oddly enough, Mrs. Vick is a gifted storyteller or, as people might say in the Louisiana of her birth and in the Mississippi of her youth, a "natural-born" storyteller. That is how Barbara Thompson, who assisted with the interviews, describes Mrs. Vick. "You have to wait for the stories, but they are sure to come." Mrs. Vick slips in humor when you least expect it, not intentionally, but naturally. The recalling of small details and what Gwendolyn Brooks calls the "ordinariness" of life make her stories a special gift to this volume.. You see the porch on which she stands when Johnny Vick comes asking for water and the dipper she hands him. You hear her asking for a transfer to Charity Hospital in New Orleans, where she can have her third child without the pain she heard when she birthed the first two children. And you hear her pride at being a woman in her nineties who has chores: "I still do the laundry." Mrs. Vick lives in a professor's apartment on the campus of Dillard University with her daughter Dorothy, a professor of history. Often she sits in a rocking chair that stays still as she reads newspapers from different cities in the nation, papers Dorothy's friends have sent her, but when she speaks, as she does in this volume, you say to yourself, "Zora would have loved to talk to Mrs. Vick." Her chapter is the stuff of which novels are made and cultural songs are written.

A TRIBUTE TO MRS. ELLA MAE YATES

by Jody Washington

Even before I met my mentor, Mrs. Ella Mae Yates, I knew that she is a woman about the business of getting things done. She called me to schedule our first interview. That made me very special and very valued. When I went to her house for the interview, she was waiting for me. She opened the door and gave me a hug. A small dog was near her, just barking. Mrs. Yates told me the dog is a member of the family. I did say she is about the business of getting things done, didn't I? She had prepared a meal for us. She assumed that since I was a student, I would be hungry. Mrs. Yates is a very attractive woman with a presence. I have no doubt that when she enters a room, people know right away that she has arrived. She has very intense eyes, and she speaks with emphasis. Mrs. Yates has many achievements. She was the first Black and the first woman to head a library in the State of Virginia. That's impressive! And she was director of libraries here in Atlanta when the central building was constructed downtown. Mrs. Yates has not received recognition for her accomplishments, but she keeps going. That is what I admire about her. She is a fighter. You can be sure that if it's right, Mrs. Yates is not going to give up the fight. She believes in Black women, and that is a gift she has given me. I like Mrs. Yates and I respect Mrs. Yates. I thank her for all the lessons about endurance and excellence she taught me.